An Articulate
Country

Kay Ferres, MA PhD, is a Senior Lecturer in Applied Ethics and Gender Studies at Griffith University. She has had extensive experience as a university teacher, at the Townsville and Cairns campuses of James Cook University and, since 1988, at Griffith University. Her most recent book, co-authored with Jane Crisp and Gillian Swanson, is *Deciphering Culture: Ordinary Curiosities and Subjective Narratives* (Routledge). Her current research includes projects on publicity and public opinion, and youth, community and citizenship.

Denise Meredyth, PhD Dip.Ed., is a Senior Research Fellow in Cultural Studies at the University of the West of England, Bristol. She completed this book while working as a Research Fellow at the Institute for Social Research, Swinburne University. Previously, she was an Australian Research Council Postdoctoral Fellow at Griffith University and, some time before, a secondary English, History and Social Studies teacher. She has published widely on citizenship, education and public policy and is a co-author of *Real Time: Computers, Change and Schooling* (Meredyth et al, DETYA 1999) and co-editor of *Citizenship and Cultural Policy Statecraft, Markets and Community* (Meredyth and Minson, Sage 2001).

An Articulate Country

Re-inventing Citizenship in Australia

Kay Ferres and Denise Meredyth

University of Queensland Press

First published 2001 by University of Queensland Press
Box 6042, St Lucia, Queensland 4067 Australia

www.uqp.uq.edu.au

Printed in Australia by McPherson's Printing Group

Distributed in the USA and Canada by
International Specialized Book Services, Inc.,
5824 N.E. Hassalo Street, Portland, Oregon 97213–3640

Cataloguing in Publication Data
National Library of Australia

Ferres, Kay, 1951–   .
   An articulate country: Re-inventing citizenship in Australia

   Bibliography
   Includes index

   1. Civics, Australian — Study and teaching. 2. Educational
   sociology — Australia. 3. Citizenship — Study and teaching.
   I. Meredyth, Denise. II. Title.

370.115

ISBN 0 7022 3118 5

Contents

Preface

Since the Berlin wall came down, an old order has given way in Eastern Europe to new more democratic regimes. Last week, the last of the dictators yielded to the people's will. Slobodan Milosevic had been defeated in an election, but relinquished power only when protesters in the streets stormed the parliament in support of Vojuslav Kostunica and the Democratic Opposition of Serbia. Closer to home, the people voted for independence in East Timor. But who can forget the picture of the man standing resolutely before the procession of tanks in Tiananmen Square or the images of mass murder in Cambodia? In the new world of mass communication, we cannot turn our faces from the horror stories in Kosovo, in the West Bank, in Ireland or East Timor.

From Berlin to Belgrade, the end of old regimes has posed new questions for democracy: these are questions about justice and about the role of government in protecting and preserving democratic values of freedom and equality. Australia has had to consider its obligations to uphold those values in the international community as well as in the national interest. It has made controversial decisions. It has sent forces to the Gulf war, and has contributed to peacekeeping in Kosovo and East Timor. The current debate about the treatment of refugees and illegal immigrants demonstrates the need for a judicious balance of conflicting interests and principles.

Australia has always been aware of its position in an international community. But since the 1980s, the phenomenon of "globalisation" has produced a borderless world. Even as ethnic conflict about national borders has escalated, populations are increasingly mobile. Australia has reflected this increasing multi-ethnicity, as have other immigrant societies like Canada and the US. The influence of IT on mass communication has also compressed time and collapsed jurisdictional boundaries. The increasing influence of international agencies and multi-national corporations poses questions about the extent of national sovereignty and the limits of governance.

In this context, the language of "citizenship" has a new currency. In Eastern Europe, the transition to democracy has revealed how a vital civil society supports and enhances democratic processes. In the US, the problems of urban decay and the disenchantment of voters are attributed by many commentators to the decline in associational life. Responding to problems of this kind, both national governments and international agencies have given priority to educational initiatives. In Australia, after a series of reports from Senate committees and the Civics Expert Group, the commonwealth has sponsored *Discovering Democracy,* a program of civics and citizenship education aimed at schools, tertiary institutions and adult and community education.

This book is designed for teachers charged with implementing the Curriculum Corporation's *Discovering Democracy* curriculum in primary and secondary schools. The Corporation's materials provide rich and detailed resources for classroom teachers, who can adapt and develop the materials to their local school community. This book aims to stimulate thinking about the rationales of the program and to raise questions about the role of the school in education for citizenship. A larger question underlies our approach: it is a question about the ways government protects individual freedoms and promotes equality among its citizens. How can the school develop students' understanding and practice of the democratic values of freedom and equality? In 1912, the early Australian civics educator, Walter Murdoch, thought that the answer was to show how government was liberty's best friend. In a recent book about the ways to resolve the tensions between "equality" and the recognition of "cultural difference" in multi-ethnic societies, the French sociologist Alain Touraine argues that educational policy is critical. In a nation where public schooling is determinedly secular, he makes a case for a new acceptance of diversity and inter-cultural understanding. In pluralist societies, he claims, school governance must enhance students' freedoms: schools must democratise and communicate.

What does good citizenship require? How should students be educated for citizenship? Does the school have a primary obligation to produce "citizens", and how does this obligation sit alongside other obligations to prepare students for employment, or even for "lifelong learning"? Part 1 of this book, "The Citizenship Solution", surveys educational debates about civics education. Do we want to promote patriotism and "sentimental" citizenship? Does the demand for self-governing citizens, capable of "critical reason" ask too much of citizens and teachers? How does *Discovering Democracy* change the paradigm of citizenship education: does it diminish an emphasis on "participation" and "social justice"? The international and historical contexts surveyed in Part 1 offer some useful comparisons, particularly in the light of the real problems and competing claims faced by government in pluralist, multi-ethnic societies.

In Part 2, "Reimagining Australian Democracy", we set a dual agenda in place. On the one hand, we explore various dimensions of the Australian democratic tradition: liberal constitutionalism, federalism and the expansion of rights. Where Part 1 takes a philosophical approach to the question of the citizen's capacities for critical reason, Part 2 emphasises the practical wisdom entailed in "civic virtue". The second objective of Part 2 is to consider the ways education for citizenship can extend across the curriculum. Legal studies, politics and government, history, English and cultural studies all provide case studies in "articulate citizenship".

The photograph on the cover of this book offers a finely nuanced comment on Australian citizenship and democratic traditions. The artist, Chris Barry, is the Australian-born daughter of Polish immigrants who came to Australia in 1950. The image is about the ways identity and belonging are reinvented by this new generation of Australians. Memories and artefacts of ethnic identity are central, but those images and their vividness belong to another generation. Australia, and national identity, is a watery outline. The confident young woman is at the beach, a location which represents egalitarianism and pleasure — even hedonism. Her history and her future are works in progress. This image reminds us of the concern expressed by Alexis de Tocqueville — that the increasing intensity of the pleasures of private life would diminish the public spiritedness which guarantees that democratic government works. This optimistic image suggests otherwise.

Chapter 1

Democratic Sentiments

Imaginary town meetings

In a famous episode of *The Simpsons*, the American animated television series screening in a global loop, Springfield is celebrating its bicentenary and the legacy of its founder. The precocious Lisa Simpson is doing a school project on the life of Jebediah Obediah Zacharia Jebediah Springfield, the town founder and hero, who is credited with uttering the town motto "A noble spirit embiggens the smallest man". Finding a secret confession by Jebediah, Lisa discovers that he was a pirate, Hans Sprungfeld, the most evil man of the 1780s, who tried to kill George Washington, and whose oratorical "silver tongue" was a prosthetic device, acquired when his tongue was bitten off by a Turk in a groghouse fight. Setting out to expose Jebediah Springfield to the town, Lisa battles against small-town loyalty to the myth, up to the moment where she confronts the crowd at the town festival, stepping up to the microphone to report on her school project. But faced with the whole town, joined in fellow feeling and local identity, she backs down and just stammers out that what she'd discovered was that Jebediah was "great...he was great".

What is this — an American civics class, broadcast into Australia? Or a spoof on civics? *The Simpsons* is at its best as satire when it plays with popular cultural genres and conventions — including the convention of the happy ending. The episode plays off others in the series. In one, Lisa features in an episode parodying the famous Frank Capra film *Mr Smith Goes to Washington* (1939). In another, Bart discovers that Springfield's Whacking Day, in which snakes are ritually thumped by the townsfolk, was not established by Jebediah Springfield in the eighteenth century, but started some eighty years later, as an excuse to beat up the Irish. The episode is cynical about history, national myths and small-town parochialism. There's a joke on pious educationists keen on civics, virtuous patriots and enlarging community sentiment. But there's also a joke on those who earnestly reveal hidden historical truths: it's there in the very excessiveness of the revelation that Jebediah the orator has a "silver tongue" prosthesis. So what to make of the moment where Lisa falters in the face of genuine community feeling? The lesson seems to be that the truth of history doesn't matter. What matters is how the stories that people tell bind communities together.

The episode is taking the mickey out of Americans, but it's also funny outside the United States. This is so partly because the image of American civic patriotism, frontier sentiment and small town virtue is so familiar, not only to the generations who grew up with American television, but also to those weaned on Westerns. But another reason why the episode works is because it plays off some more general themes in popular culture, a theme about community, belonging and the limits of cynicism. To risk a generalisation, the key theme of the 1990s was the importance of maintaining communities, family connections and a sense of place and locality, in the midst of change. Think of globally marketed shows such as the Canadian *Northern Exposure*, the Irish *Ballykissangel* and the Scottish *Hamish Macbeth*, not to mention the Australian *SeaChange*. In each case, an outsider explores a community, full of quirky local customs and irrational practices, usually with an eclectic ethnic mix. The real joke is on the would-be cynic, though, since we find out that even if the local institutions — the courts, the doctor's surgery, the church, the police station — don't work as they're supposed to, the locals have cobbled together a modus vivendi. The town manages to be tolerant and peaceful, without taking itself too seriously. The city cynic is "embiggened" by the experience.

It's interesting to think about this episode from *The Simpsons* from Australia, because it seems to capture two key elements of our own understanding of citizenship, nation and community. On the one hand, Australians tend to enjoy send-ups of American civic ceremonies, because we are used to poking fun at how seriously Americans take themselves. By contrast (we tell ourselves) Australians have a healthy scepticism about patriotism and civic ceremonies. We cheerfully forget our national founders and our parliamentary leaders. We prefer larrikins and rebels like the jolly swagman and Ned Kelly. We are bored by debates on national identity.

On the other hand, there is also a strong element of nostalgia in Australian popular culture, especially about the bush and about the small country town and its community values. Part of the reason why shows such as *SeaChange* are so popular is because they celebrate character types who are part of our national mythology; quirky small town people with odd bush knowledge and stories to tell. Many of the episodes are about the local history, about memory and what can and can't be forgotten. Think for instance of the *SeaChange* episode where the community has to confront the secrets of the past. The locals stole the wood from which the town was built and find that the wood is rotten and riddled with borers. The question is whether they should tell the truth, apologise and make reparation. As it turns out, there's no moment of public revelation, because a bigger secret is revealed. But reparation is made nonetheless. There's a clear link to Reconciliation and the question of whether an apology should be made to the stolen generation. Like *The Simpsons*, this episode explores the idea that communities bind themselves together — for good or ill — through the way they tell and retell stories of the past, remaking their own values.

In the tradition of political satire, these comedies touch on some of the most contentious issues in current political debate. How are political communities "held together"? In our two examples, the question is how much people need to know about their political community and its history. Can they cope with the realisation that their political community is imperfect, even corrupt, or do they have a legitimate need to believe in the stories the community tells itself? Should individuals take it upon themselves to expose myths, cover-up and sentimentality, or is community feeling too valuable to be destroyed by cynicism? It is not hard to debunk ideas about the nation or national heritage; historical study can rapidly disillusion students about those whom they were reared to regard as heroic, pure and innocent. It is harder to equip people with a positive understanding of politics and governance, one that could enable them to have a critical understanding, without just displaying cynicism.

Good citizens

The education philosopher Eamonn Callan discusses some of these issues in relation to civic education, primarily in the United States. As a civic educator, Callan is concerned about the "sentimental" aspects of the ways in which people identify with their nations and communities. He is stern about "feel good" patriotism, of the kind that allows people to identify with national heroes and founding fathers, as if they were "morally invulnerable". Sentimentality, he argues (citing Oscar Wilde) is "emotion one has not paid for", an unearned insight or feeling that takes no critical effort. The cost of encouraging citizens to be sentimental, Callan argues, is that it restricts people's historical imagination, reducing their ability to deal with ambiguities and moral complexity. If people are allowed to believe in the purity of national heroes, then they are likely to demonise the causes they oppose. Citizens become less able to consider the possibility that events may have taken a different course or to understand how present problems might be analysed in the light of the past.

Civics experts and ardent citizens fear that if public emotions "atrophy", and if politics becomes merely cynical, then the polity "cannot evoke in its citizens a loyalty more substantial than the calculating view that the political order is worth supporting to advance private interests". Society suffers if people withdraw from the public sphere, choosing to live "beyond the reach of public emotions". On the other hand, public emotion should not be founded on stereotypes and misrepresentation, or on fictions of morally pure heroes and heroines. Liberal democratic traditions need to be preserved and enriched by informed, tough-minded critical reason, not by mindless loyalty. They depend on electors making wise decisions and using judgement when they give their loyalty to leaders. For that reason, he argues, the school systems should aim for a wide distribution of the "virtues of critical reason".[1]

Callan's discussion works through some old problems: he assumes that the peace, justice and virtue of the political community depends on the critical capacities of its citizens — on their ability to freely choose the good, through the use of critical reason. His take on these questions draws on traditions of liberal education philosophy, especially on the traditions of thought associated with the moral philosopher Immanuel Kant and his modern reinterpreters.

Kant, to give a simple account, was centrally concerned with means of achieving a morally enlightened understanding of universal principles such as justice. For him, an enlightened understanding of "the good" was the highest end of human existence: appreciation of absolute moral truths. However, individuals could not learn such truths by being informed of them, through religious doctrine for instance. Kantian moral philosophy prescribed a much more demanding way of reaching enlightenment, through self-examination and critical reason. Individuals could only come to know the good if they were prepared to put aside the moral rules they had been taught and to contemplate moral principles for their own sake, as absolutes and universals. This involved asking themselves whether they were universal principles, in the sense that any rational individual would recognise them and agree to obey them as a moral law. Rational choice was critical; once a moral principle had been recognised as universally true, on the basis of reason, then the individual would be obliged to obey it, respect it and commit to it, thus becoming virtuous by rational insight and free choice. For Kant, these were not just abstruse spiritual exercises; they were a recipe for forming citizens and just political states. If all citizens were virtuous — capable of choosing the good through critical reason — then political communities could also become just and enlightened. Citizens would freely choose to conduct their lives according to the principles of justice and civic virtue; thus the state would become just.[2] In turn, the just state could then become an environment in which citizens would be able to feel the force of moral principles, through critical reason.

These understandings of justice, moral universals and critical reason have been deeply influential, not just for philosophy but for moral, political and educational thought more generally. As we shall see in the following chapters, much of contemporary debate on citizenship, civic formation and education borrows from Kantian thinking, especially in its faith in critical reason and moral reflection as the basis for civic virtue and justice. But at the same time, it has also wrestled with the problem of whether or not all citizens are capable of reaching the levels of enlightenment prescribed for the virtuous citizen and the rational individual.[3]

Callan troubles over the gap between his ideal of the community of citizens, who have thought hard about what commits them to liberal democratic ideals, and the messy reality of apathetic populations moved only by facile patriotic myths, which allow them to believe in the innocence and purity of national heroes and false histories. He notes that a number of his fellow philosophers hold out little hope that citizens are capable of comprehending more than this. William Galston, for instance, argues that it is dangerous to expect too much of ordinary citizens, and especially of their capacity for critical reason.[4] Only a minority of citizens are capable of understanding the abstruse reasons why political institutions operate as they do, and why they differ from the ideals expressed in liberal democratic doctrines. Most people are able to do their civic duty — to vote, to abide by the law — with a minimal understanding of the political system and with a largely sentimental and unreflective attachment to the idea of the nation. What matters is that citizens do identify with the national community, and that social and political cohesion is maintained.

For Callan, however, accepting that citizens link themselves to their communities through moral fictions is a prescription for "rather grievous political vice". He is unprepared to give up the idea that civic education should involve training in critical reason. Citizens need to have an emotional attachment to ideals of justice, he argues, but they also need a capacity for social criticism. Civic education should involve more than just debunking sentimental national myths, since this will only encourage nihilism and civic apathy. Instead, students, as citizens, should be challenged by more generous and historically sensitive accounts of the past, and encouraged to understand the best of its traditions. Literature and historical narrative can be used to awaken both the historical imagination and critical acuity; students can gain "a generous susceptibility to those public emotions that bind us to the body politic".[5]

As an answer to the problem faced by Lisa Simpson — and critical intellectuals or teachers who charge themselves with the task of enlightening public opinion — this is a relentless position. Educators cannot give up on building civic virtues by inculcating the capacity for critical reason. Despite the extent of civic apathy, indifference, ignorance and bigotry, human beings and human communities have the potential to live according to the absolute moral principles of justice, liberty, equality and the rule of law. This potential cannot be imposed, but individuals can be encouraged to recognise it for themselves. The rational individual can choose the good, once he or she has done the hard ethical work of moral and critical reflection. In the process, the political community will itself become just; for Callan, this means that it will be tolerant and pluralistic, overcoming racism and bigotry and recognising liberal democratic reasons to live with cultural difference, within a common political culture.

Callan acknowledges a second and related problem. However committed enlightened educators might be to the ideals of achieving pluralism through a common civic formation oriented to critical reason, it is very likely that this will be seen as excluding groups and individuals who maintain their right to separate cultural identities, or indeed to a rival basis in core values. In the American context, African American citizens might well feel that they have little reason to be grateful to the liberal democratic political ideal, given that their peoples have "endured much of the worst and enjoyed little of the best" of the tradition. True to his Kantian orientation, Callan concedes that citizens cannot be brought to believe in civic and moral principles by direct moral teaching; this will not prompt their free choice to commit to the principles of liberal democracy. The issue is how to bring them to feel the moral force of democratic principle, through reason. Civic educators must therefore engage in a process of persuasion, in which cultural groups are invited to see liberal democratic values and traditions as a common inheritance, seeing their people's struggle for freedom, equality and self-determination as part of this legacy.[6]

The move from popular television to post-Kantian moral philosophy might seem like a big leap. The point though is that the issue of civic virtue and civic education is one that spans popular and academic discussion. Politicians and governments consistently appeal to the ideals of citizenship, of civil society, civic virtue and community. As subsequent chapters will show, this is not just talk; we are living within a "neo-liberal" period of public policy; in the Western developed nations, citizens' relationships to social welfare states have been comprehensively reorganised. "Mutual responsibility" is the catch-cry of these reforms, designed to reduce the onus on government and make individuals and communities more responsible for themselves. Citizens are expected to be self-governing agents, accountable for their choices and responsible to the community, involving themselves voluntarily in a thick network of civic associations. The tasks of government — schooling, social welfare and health — are being devolved to local communities. Civil society is the new hope for government. But even though it is said that we are seeing the end of "big government", community regeneration takes extensive governmental planning. In part, this is because it is not clear that citizens and communities have the capacity to make sound choices about their own health, schooling and financial options. Establishing civil society and social capital may take some time. This is one reason why education is high on the political agenda for the governments of North America and Western Europe. Not only do workers in the new global economy need new skills, but so too do citizens living in rapidly changing societies and political and commercial environments.

Intellectuals are still assessing the implications of this political rhetoric, but many are convinced that there is a need for intervention, since the advanced liberal democracies are facing a crisis of citizenship.[7] At the very same time that democratic rule has been embraced by ex-communist nations and those emerging from dictatorship, it is said, the advanced Western democracies are suffering from a deep disenchantment with democracy, reflected in low voter turn-outs, indifference to pressing injustice and the decline in community involvement.[8]

This is part of a broader trend. A 1999 issue of *The Economist,* for instance, cited statistics indicating that in the United States, Western Europe, Japan, North America and Australia, there had been a steady decline in people's opinion of the honesty of their leaders and the caring capacities of politicians. Since the mid 1970s, citizens in these countries have become more ready to distrust politicians, the judiciary, the armed services, the public service and the police.[9] At the same time, they are passively dependent on authority and unwilling to take responsibility as citizens; they do not see themselves as responsible for following political debate and monitoring the actions of government. Nevertheless, *The Economist* goes on to say, respondents do seem to be willing to act as responsible agents within their own families, communities and neighbourhoods, despite their declining confidence in their political leaders and institutions. There still seems to be scope for a renewal of political participation and civic feeling, especially at the local level of community decision-making. The hope here is that citizens will find ways to be public-spirited and public-minded, motivated by a common interest. The crisis may resolve itself in a radical reinvention of civic participation.

According to Etzioni, schools must step in to restore the moral infrastructure of communities, in the face of the failure of family, neighbourhoods and religious institutions. Citizens are apathetic, concerned only with their private affairs. Voting rates are falling, citizens are locked into ghettoes marked out by race, class and income, many of the most disadvantaged refusing to vote. Consumerism and commerce have overtaken public life: candidates are buying their way into power and private corporations are overtaking the public airways. Etzioni urges the importance of rebuilding the social virtues and reestablishing settled values: "character", hard work, self-discipline, respect for others. His strong focus on the need for community involvement in the life of the family takes him a long way from liberal conceptions of freedom, privacy and autonomy. Many of his proposals for the way in which the community should support civic values seem normative and indeed intrusive. For instance, he advocates the establishment of stricter marital law, the tactical use of schools as a way to restore "moral infrastructure" in communities, in the face of the failure of family, neighbourhoods and religious institutions.[10]

Even the most enthusiastic proponents of civic renewal tend to be uncomfortable about such proposals. It seems paradoxical to argue, on the one hand, that the remedy for civic apathy is to free individuals, civil society and civic association from the heavy hand of the state, while at the same time using state authority to impose mutual responsibility as a compulsory moral code[11]. Governments seem to be expanding their scope, even as they maintain that the impetus for change is coming from within communities. The result, it is argued, is intrusion into the previously protected domains of private life.

Making it national

Opinion polls in Australia certainly demonstrate a decline in the reputation of politicians for ethics and honesty, a growth in electoral cynicism around the credibility of election promises and a weakening of party identification. Over the last twenty years, the Australian public's estimation of politicians' ethics and honesty has declined by nearly half. People are now more likely to say that politicians lie, especially in election promises. This is not to say that Australians' level of trust in politicians has ever been high. Australians, over the last two decades, have been unlikely to agree that "people in government" will do the right thing, and more likely to say that they are "too interested in looking after themselves". Disenchantment with democratic politics seems to be linked to a lack of trust in government more generally. Cyclic disillusionment with federal governments appears to be accompanied by reduced confidence in "the legal system, the public service, the armed forces, the church, the police, trade unions and the press".[12]

The recent debate raised by One Nation candidates may have articulated a longer-standing distrust of politicians and government. Many who strongly opposed Pauline Hanson's views on race and immigration saw her as voicing a strong majority opinion highly critical of "economic rationalist" trends in Australian political, social and economic life and of the explanations offered by elite opinion. Election results between 1996 and 1999 seemed to reflect the argument that people did not see themselves as "represented" by politicians. Government and social policy, it was said, was in the hands of an elite faction of politicians, journalists, academics and other professionals, not in the hands of the people[13].

For John Hirst, an eminent Australian historian, political debate in this country has already faced a test of citizens' political competence. Writing candidly as a supporter of a move to an Australian republic, he reflects on his own disappointment at the level of public debate before the 1999 referendum, especially debate on the rival options of appointing or electing an Australian head of state. In submissions to the Republican Advisory Committee, supporters of the direct election model argued that politicians could not be trusted to refrain from appointing a head of state from amongst themselves. For Hirst, this reflected a "contempt for politics and politicians ... so strong that people simply do not trust any part of the present political structure to produce a satisfactory president. To get the president they want, the people think they will have to take charge of the procedure themselves".[14] As an avowed republican, he despaired of persuading his opponents. As an educator and reformer, however, he took a longer view, hoping that civic education might be able to generate a debate in which all sides were able to be persuasive, because they were informed as well as being passionate.

The debate goes directly to the question Callan raises, about the role of myth-making in forging national identity, and about the extent to which citizens, of themselves, are capable of reaching sophisticated understandings of the political communities in which they live. Perhaps the most difficult issue here is the extent to which citizens understand the relationship between the people and institutions of government — parliamentary liberal democracy, in the Australian case. To pick up Callan's term again, the issue is the extent to which debates on the proper balance between "the people" and government have become sentimental, to the point of losing touch with the ways in which political life is actually organised; with the imperfect, improvised mechanisms of democracy that we happen to have.

The argument was made, some time ago, that nations, or the sense of a common past and common culture shared by a people, are "imagined" communities.[15] Nations and national communities are modern constructs; each national territory and national culture has a history of having been invented and imagined into being. But they are not just imagined by the people spontaneously. Modern nations have been constructed through military and administrative fiat: sovereignty and subjecthood are established through annexations, treaty, legal decision and institutional jurisdiction. This is reinforced by the cultural processes of nation-building and mythmaking. Through stories, symbols, ceremonies, maps and charts, histories and literature, something substantial is "imagined" into being, something capable of generating loyalty and allegiance.

The process of building national identity and allegiance to national cultures is constant and intentional on the part of nation states. States depend on building, in those who live within their territories, a sense of allegiance to that nation. This includes obedience to the rule of law and willingness to take on the rights and responsibility of residents, citizens, taxpayers, householders and community members. Now and in the past, states discuss this process explicitly, not only in the context of decisions about immigration, but also in decisions on the design of school systems, national ceremonies, public architecture, heritage and cultural policy.

The process of constructing national identity is a fragile, partial and contested one. We live with the powerful and persuasive myth that individuals have a primary identification with their nation. But since the relatively recent emergence of nations, over the last two centuries, individuals have always had many forms of identification, with their family, region, ethnicity, faith, associations and so on; they have held dual citizenships and sustained multiple allegiances. Historians of modern nations can tell the story of vigorous internal dispute and resistance to the imposition of national identity, not least from those who resisted in the name of religion, but also from ethnic or racial groups who regard themselves as separate peoples, unassimilated to the nation.

The past three decades have generated various intellectual and political movements critical of national "ideology". Historians and cultural critics have exposed the means by which women, minorities, recent immigrants and indigenous peoples have been excluded and suppressed by national myth-making. They have also explored the historical and contemporary variety of identity, allegiance and belonging, emphasising the active processes of cultural negotiation and subjectivity. Australian Studies has been centrally concerned, in recent years, with exploring the implications of unwritten, ignored or misinterpreted elements of national mythologies. Understandings of Australian history have been reshaped by revisionist work on the roles of women, in public life and in private domains, on the history of indigenous peoples and on diasporic immigrant cultures, stories that are often told through social history, oral history and "history from below".

These are not just academic debates. In print, radio and television journalism, in films, in schools, on talkback radio and in community events and ceremonies, there has been substantial discussion of national history, memory and commemoration. Such issues — as played out in positions on republicanism or Reconciliation — mark some of the most visible differences between the major political parties. The Keating Labor government promoted a "big picture" approach to Australian links with Britain, America and the Asia-Pacific region and to relationships between indigenous and non-indigenous Australians. The subsequent government argued that this republicanist and regionalist emphasis was a distraction from the issues of economic and social stability and community values. The national debate on how to approach the past continues, especially in response to debates on the stolen generation. There is considerable support for an official apology from the state, but a large majority appears to feel that there has been enough discussion of the issue. Many sympathetic to Reconciliation also argue that it is best to move on, rather than dwelling on the past; stories of victimisation will not help communities to be robust and independent. The best prospect for Reconciliation, it is said, lies in individuals taking personal responsibility for themselves as citizens and community members.

Putting the positive case for "compassionate conservatism", the current government has emphasised the need for Australians to consolidate a sense of identity, keeping our historical and cultural ties to Britain and avoiding the excesses of "black armband" history, or history that emphasises only the negative aspects of Australia's colonisation, growth and democratic system. The argument, to give it its due, is about balance; in the interest of correcting the historical account and of reforming public language, rules and customs, it is argued, we are in danger of promoting a corrosive sense of cynicism, especially in the young. There is too much emphasis on debunking ideas such as national identity, the family and the community. Schools are overemphasising the teaching of critique and scepticism; the result is that people are increasingly apathetic, uninterested in political life and the affairs of the nation or their community, and unwilling to involve themselves as citizens. This is part of the diagnosis of what plagues the society in general; apathy and cynicism is linked to dependence on welfare, reluctance to seek work and the abandonment of duty and community ties. What we need to do, it is said, is build more sense of mutual obligation, linking people to family and community and to a sense of the greater good. We need to be positive about our common historical legacy, relearning what the city cynics have forgotten.

The theme was picked up in the television advertisements promoting the 2001 celebrations of the Centenary of Federation. The father who can't answer his son's question about the first Prime Minister of Australia is just a bit embarrassed, as are the nice people in the city street, though the older folk in the bush are proud to remember Edmund Barton. The kid with his civics assignment is nudging the nation's memory, kept in the trust of older Australians close to the land. "What kind of nation is it?" the advertisement asked, "that doesn't know its first Prime Minister, but has no trouble remembering the name of the first President of the United States?" Maybe, it goes on to say, it's because Australia wasn't founded in war, or by a revolution. It was based on agreements made at the time of Federation, agreements largely forgotten now, despite the achievements of a peaceful, happy multicultural society. We might like ourselves for being so lackadaisical, but isn't it time we took some pride in the nation's achievements?

Above and beneath the nation

The Centenary of Federation seems like an opportunity to join Australians in an uncontentious national celebration of independence and national consolidation. Unlike the 1988 Bicentenary of Australian settlement, it does not raise the spectre of racial violence. Unlike the 1999 referendum, it does not threaten radical constitutional change. The problem, though, is that the process of Federation has little popular appeal. The events are little known. It is hard to find an inspiring national narrative like those told in French patriotic ceremonies. Australian democracy was not fired by a single republican moment or by a popular mobilisation to win democratic self-governance.[16] This is not a nation founded on democratic doctrines enshrined in sacred documents. There is no single document that could be said to sum up a national ethos or an abstract ideal of Australian democracy. The Australian constitution itself is "not much more than an uninspiring division of powers between federal and state governments"[17]. Unlike the Americans, we do not study our constitution or cite it whenever our rights are threatened, and nor are we comfortable with displays of patriotic fervour. Despite the legacy of early experimentation in political systems and government, we tend to place a much higher value on free and easy social relations, egalitarianism and anti-authoritarianism.[18]

For Mary Kalantzis, there is something to be celebrated in these national characteristics, since they save us from "atavistic nationalism". But at the same time, she argues, the lack of a civic tradition leaves Australians unable to articulate what is distinctive about Australian democracy, separating it from "a world of civic horror stories", many of which immigrants to this country know all too well. She argues that, if we want to celebrate the achievements of Australian democracy, there is little point looking at the printed pages of the Constitution and the speeches of political leaders. We need to find ways to articulate what it is that is worth celebrating in the "unobtrusive hard work" that went into creating social consensus and settlement. One of our virtues, for Kalantzis, is that "we have got so much done, and done in a peace that is all too rare in the world"[19]. Immigrant communities had a vital impact on these social achievements. We should recognise this, celebrating the contribution made by immigrant communities, who worked hard to forge new communities, new social contracts and a vibrant civil society, in part through their involvements with government.

This is a persuasive piece of advocacy. The difficulty appears when Kalantzis urges that the national and government-organised Centenary of Federation celebrations could be an opportunity to articulate a "postnationalistic sense of common purpose". That is, there should be a national event that could celebrate the transcendence of loyalty to the nation state. Such an event, she argues, should be inclusive and popular, but it should not assume that every citizen and resident has a single, assimilated allegiance to one culture or to the one nation state. Rather than emphasising loyalty to a nation state, we should see Australians as those who share a geographical space, while keeping other links and loyalties. If the Centenary takes on such a brief, it could be a "stabilising way to defuse past animosities" as we "negotiate and live with difference within the body politic."[20]

The comment raises some interesting issues about how pluralistic the emphasis on community really is. One of the dangers of the current enthusiasm for the revival of civil society and the vitality of civic associations is that it is too easy to forget precisely how hard it can be to sustain civil peace, negotiate settlements and co-exist within multiethnic populations. As Kalantzis points out, the historical means for achieving such settlements, in Australia, have been between state authorities and communities. The Centenary of Federation is an official event, part of the public ceremony surrounding national sovereignty. This makes it difficult to expect that its official events and rhetoric will be "postnational". To expect this is to ask for the ceremony to express a single moral vision, based on a metaphysical conception of multiethnic pluralism. Far from settling animosities and establishing social accords, this would be more likely to provoke animosity and ethnic sectarianism, if not handled very carefully.

Those responsible for planning the Centenary have to enable communities to articulate their self-images, in all their diversity. But at the same time they have to play the role of educators, shaping those self-images, eliciting involvement and enthusiasm and combating cynicism and apathy. There will be intense pressure to make the planning process accountable for the use of public monies, and part of this will involve argument about the extent to which the planned events fully represent the Australian nation as it is understood by articulate interest groups and by that mysterious factor, public opinion. It is government, not civil society, or community, that will be held responsible for the eventual outcomes. The Commonwealth government has its own interests in such an event, distinct from those brought to the planning table by lobby groups, associations, local governments and the states. These interests are those of a state seeking to enhance both its national stability and its international prestige, not least by establishing a sophisticated representation of national histories and cultures, through the display of a distinctive heritage and a vibrant public culture, represented by the high arts, exhibitions, publications and public events. Political parties will be judged on the extent to which they deliver on this obligation of government; at the same time, they will be expected to ensure that the event is also conspicuously democratic, participatory and representative, involving local communities of all sorts and giving each state its fair share of the funding and the limelight. Even the celebrated Sydney 2000 Olympics were preceded by public wrangling and concern about official corruption.

A national civics lesson

The events planned for the 2001 celebrations of the Centenary of Federation are already controversial. Commentators have already questioned the decision to open the events with Australia Week, held in London in July 2000, a sensitive decision given that the referendum on the republic is still recent. The event was a ceremonial acknowledgement of Australia's colonial allegiance to Britain and of Australian sovereignty; it was a coming of age and filial farewell to the mother country, with a staged parliamentary debate, a royal dinner and displays by intellectuals, artists and expatriates. The dignity of the event was slightly compromised by the reaction of the Australian press, who pointed out that the exercise was scheduled for the very day when the Goods and Services Tax came into effect, meaning that the Prime Minister was absent. This was an effective piece of political theatre; the event stressed historical continuity, tradition and heritage. This will be echoed in the opening of the 2001 celebrations, which will start with an English-style ringing of bells around the country and with an "Uluru sunrise" event with indigenous ceremonies.

The organising committees have sought to play out the theme of Federal co-ordination; while there are some national events, much of the focus is on state and local activities. There will be commemorative parliamentary sessions, televised debates between former prime ministers, air shows and military displays. There will also be new public buildings and displays: a national arts and culture festival, an academic conference, science demonstrations and the opening of the National Archives Federation Gallery and the National Museum of Australia. But these will be balanced by celebrations of clubs and associations: a parade of rural bush fire services, centenary cricket and football matches, car club meetings and surf life-saving. Municipal parks, playgrounds, school ovals and private gardens are to be filled with Federation Arches modelled on those of 1901, to be designed and donated by local councils and by industry and community groups. The *People's Voices* initiative invites ordinary people in "every town, suburb and city in Australia" to contribute the historical story of their community to a website. Along the same theme, the *Peoplescape* scheme will invite communities to fill the slopes of Parliament House with thousands of "person-shaped canvas figures" representing ordinary people's "personal hero". Symbolically, the famously inaccessible Parliamentary Hill will be filled by the people and their ideals.

Lest we should think this is not popular enough (even to the point of sentimentality, recalling Callan), the Centenary will also leave a legacy in community-based research and public education. The *History and Education Program* has provided competitive funding for projects on historical change. The Council for Aboriginal Reconciliation has offered a "Sharing Local History" project, working with communities to develop social histories inclusive of indigenous peoples. Other groups will tell stories ranging from the role of sport in the Australian way of life to the history of the Australian Chinese community and of industrial relations. The product will include school-based competitions, CD-ROMs and study kits, academic histories, biographies, diaries, exhibitions, websites, forums, documentaries, radio series, reference works, coffee-table books, travel guides, photography, exhibitions, walking trails, plays, operas, art works, on-line electronic records, digitalised archives, comics and posters.

Neither the young nor the old will be forgotten, we are reassured. Commemorative medallions will be struck as a "keepsake" for all children of primary school age. Meanwhile, the Youth Envoys scheme will select a hundred young Australians to attend key national events and to record their impressions for peers and for posterity; they are to be a living link between the young people involved in Federation activities in the 1890s and the sesquicentenary of Federation planned for 2051. Meanwhile, radio programs will air an oral history archive of Australians a hundred years old or over.[21]

These resources will be dedicated to the new national effort in civic and citizenship education. By 2001, it is hoped, Australian school students will have a clearer understanding of the meaning of Federation than most of us. Through the *Discovering Democracy* program, young people will have been enabled to "engage in civic communities and take their part in the Australian 'social coalition'", celebrating their liberal democratic political heritage.[22] Teachers are encouraged to use the Centenary of Federation Web site with their students, keeping tabs on planned local and national events and using the archival and research material to build a link between the 2001 celebrations and those of 1901. Classes are also invited to discuss ways in which ordinary people might have celebrated in 1901, putting their investigations to work in planning a Centenary celebration for the school or the town.

Through activities such as this, it is hoped, citizenship education will spread beyond the classroom. Students will be encouraged to involve themselves in student councils, school boards, community decision-making and "service-based projects", working with groups ranging from Meals on Wheels to conservation, heritage, cultural, and sports associations.[23] At the same time, through commonwealth-funded initiatives in adult and community education, community-based reading and discussion groups will be planted in the community. These Learning Circles involve local group-based discussion of materials on civic issues, facilitated by a community volunteer and working to seed a "grassroots" interest in democratic life. This is all part of the greater civics lesson; that involvement in civil society and its associational life can help to create the bonds of trust, the skills of cooperation and the values that bind communities together.[24]

True to its emphasis on community history, the commonwealth is returning here to the community-building tactics of the 1940s and 1950s; to tried and true methods of combating civic apathy, poor morale and "maladjusted" youth. The remedy for these problems was to encourage young people to involve themselves in civic associations: public works, sporting groups, charities and churches.[25] During the 1950s, voluntary "character education" and civics initiatives surrounded the school: from youth clubs to the Boy Scouts, the Surf Life Saving Association, the YWCA, the Young Christian Workers, or the St John's Ambulance Brigade.[26] Then, as now, informal civic education extended to technical schooling and adult education, which generated learning circles outside the school. In other respects, the Centenary celebrations recall the earlier forms of "empire civics" that, early in the twentieth century, made young Australians dedicate themselves, through patriotic drill, to a nation with a British imperial heritage.

The Centenary is a national civics lesson, designed to make apathetic citizens active and interested by getting them to talk about their own experiences. It represents a move away from the "big picture" visions of government and towards a strategy of devolving responsibility to local governments, communities and civic associations. The outcome could be regarded as socially conservative, especially in comparison with hopes of achieving a cosmopolitan event that could transcend the nation; what we have instead might look like nostalgia and tokenism.

It is easy to be cynical about these civic commemorations and projects. On the face of it, it does seem as though people are being invited to enjoy ideas about the purity and innocence not just of national heroes, but of the community as hero. Following Kalantzis, we could ask whether the busy multiculturalism of the planners hides the white-bread homogeneity of the stories being told about the state, the towns and suburbs. On the other hand, we should be careful about the romantic attitudes that often go with cultivated cynicism. It is not as though the Centenary could have sprung spontaneously from the community, rather than being planned within a political process. This is an official public festival organised by a combination of appointees, delegates, advocates and public servants, overseen by the government of the day who are responsible to the voters. No doubt the decisions made were political, in the sense that they were made in the context of party-political battles, state-commonwealth relations and the process of lobbying and advocacy (by ethnic communities and indigenous groups as well as by the Returned Services League, the churches and sporting associations). We should not underestimate how contentious the politics of community and civil society can be, especially when it comes to articulations of identity and tradition. The Centenary celebrations are one attempt to manage this, in part by deferring the work and the choices to the local level. The problem, for civic idealists, is that the community is not as pretty as its publicity shots.

The question that will surely be put is whether the event is truly democratic. But what does this mean; that it should be "representative" of the nation, of states and local districts, of citizens, of communities? Or that is should be fully participative, allowing each and all to have their say? It is likely to fail either test. But how perfectionist can we afford to be about Australian democracy, if the main thing we want to celebrate about it is the still unfinished process of settlement and negotiation? We may have to come to terms with the gap between the moral and metaphysical ideal of what the democratic community could be and the patchy and imperfect process through which nations, communities and citizens are formed. We will find similar lessons in debates about the governmental programme of reviving civics and citizenship education in Australian schools.

Chapter 2
Citizens and Experts

It may be something of a fiction to say that national communities share an historical legacy, which gives citizens common forms of identity and mutual democratic values. The fiction is a deliberate artefact, built through the hard work of committees and planners, local and national, co-ordinated by government. The broader process of national celebration, commemoration and community regeneration involves persuading citizens and communities that they have ownership of the process, that they can participate as active citizens, belonging to a common space and culture. It involves a complex process of negotiation, generating sometimes creative solutions to sectional tensions and competing interests. This process is not natural or organic; it is political. Schools play an extremely important part in this political process. Now and in the past, governments have looked to the school system to build not only national sentiment, but also the sense of a common national heritage and culture, sufficient to bind a diverse citizenry to the nation. In Australia, we are seeing an instance of this in the national program to reinvent civics and citizenship education.

The *Discovering Democracy* programme is an ambitious Commonwealth initiative in curriculum reform, co-ordinating the reintroduction of civics and citizenship education into all Australian schools, with links to adult, community, vocational and higher education. Launched in May 1997 by David Kemp, Minister for Schools, Vocational Education and Training, it developed into a four-year process of curriculum design, resource development and professional development, overseen by the Curriculum Corporation and guided by the Civics Education Group, led by its Chair John Hirst.

Launching the programme, Minister Kemp welcomed the opportunity to give all Australian young people greater understanding of both "the history and operations of Australia's system of government and institutions" and "the principles that support Australian democracy".[1] Across the States and Territories, within their distinct curriculum frameworks, schools will be able to introduce students to a combination of contemporary and historical study, covering key moments in the definition of the Australian version of democracy, as well as the broader history of democratic ideas and institutions. The aim, put simply, is to enable students "to understand the way we govern ourselves and to think of themselves as active citizens".[2] To do so, they need to understand how Australian political and legal institutions operate, now and in the past. They also need to recognise the principles that underpin Australian democracy: the rule of law, freedom of speech, religion and association and the right to participate in forms of governance and to choose that governance. Australian national identity is linked to key democratic achievements: the development of the secret ballot, the comparatively early achievement of votes for women and the "successful melding of immigrants" into a tolerant democratic nation. While we may not be proud of some elements of our nation history, such as the dispossession of indigenous peoples and the White Australia policy, our concern about this should be balanced by an appreciation of the democratic vision that "motivated" Australian political, social and cultural life.

Discovering Democracy

From November 1997, *Discovering Democracy* materials designed for student and teacher use were sent to all Australian schools in four stages. These teaching and learning kits included *Discovering Democracy* units, supplemented by books, videos, posters, Websites and CD-ROMs (*Stories of Democracy* and *Parliament at Work*). The Curriculum Corporation published John Hirst's primer, *Discovering Democracy: A guide to government and law in Australia*. From late 1999, a series of Readers offered extracts from Australian art and literature, accompanied by teachers' notes. In July 2000, all schools were sent books of structured assessment activities linked to the units, adapted to age and learning stage. Consultation and review processes have continued throughout.

The *Discovering Democracy* initiative builds on at least two decades of concern about the extent to which Australia schooling gives citizens an understanding of political, electoral and constitutional processes and of the ethos of "active citizenship". During the 1990s, social studies and Australian Studies lobbied for a revival of political studies.[3] In 1994, the government-appointed Civics Experts Group released a substantial report entitled *Whereas the People...* which identified significant gaps in young Australians' political, constitutional and historical understanding.[4] By 1997, after a change of government and extensive debate, the Howard government appointed a reconstituted Civics Education Group and committed considerable public resources to the production of *Discovering Democracy* units, resources and professional development. The materials, developed for years 4-10, are designed to be adapted by education authorities, schools and teachers, and to be used in teaching SOSE, history and English; they also encourage the use of multimedia. By 1998, the draft material had been trialled in schools across the country. As teachers adapted the units of work, State and Territory education authorities were able to collect models of innovative projects and lesson plans, often made available in on-line form.

Launching *Discovering Democracy* in schools in March 1998, Minister Kemp remarked that the core problem in educating citizens is to balance two elements: commitment to "promoting the freedom of the individual, which entails respect for diversity", and establishing "some degree of consensus and congruence" among citizens. In the interests of their own stability, strength and survival, democracies need to make sure that each new generation is inducted into knowledge of democratic principles and into informed participation: this is the basis of unity, as distinct from uniformity. Young people should be encouraged to see themselves both as inheritors of democratic traditions and as custodians, responsible for developing their own knowledges, skills and understandings, including being "able to ask the hard questions" about how government works, why it works as it does and how it could be improved. The historical dimension to this understanding is indispensable.

While the Minister stressed that "no single vision of the past possesses the truth", he emphasised the importance of a civic debate on the past, one that generates "civil, courteous and continuing dialogue". Historical study, within the *Discovering Democracy* units, will enable students to "develop critical abilities, including the ability to assess evidence, weigh up conflicting points of view, analyse problems and present the results in a clear, meaningful way". Far from simply inculcating a set of facts, historically-oriented civic and citizenship education should challenge students to be active and critical. As they use and adapt the unit outlines and support materials, teachers should be encouraging classes to investigate, evaluate, research and argue, reaching "informed conclusions" about important matters of Australian civic debate now and in the past.[5]

This emphasis is integrated in the design of both the primary and secondary school materials developed by the Curriculum Corporation and now adapted to curriculum frameworks at a state and local level. The units address four themes: "Who Rules?"; "Law and Rights"; "The Australian Nation"; and "Citizens and Public Life". Units linked to these themes are designed for modular use from middle primary to middle secondary levels. The units are designed to build increasingly sophisticated political and historical understanding. The middle primary unit "Stories of the people and rulers", for instance, invites students to reflect on how "rule" worked in Ancient Egypt and Greece. The upper primary unit "Parliament versus monarch" draws on the story of the English Civil War to explore the historical achievement of parliamentary democracy. As the "Who Rules" theme extends in the lower secondary school, students investigate Athenian and Spartan political systems and compare them with Australia's systems of representative democracy. In the same year, they are likely to be doing biographical study of Australian parliamentarians and activists, in the "Men and women in political life" unit. By the middle secondary years, the "Who Rules" theme extends to a study of political party: the "Parties control Parliament" unit focuses on pre-Federation party politics and on case studies from the 1949 and 1972 federal elections. In the same year, students might study a local political campaign, or do a project on the Franklin River Dam dispute, within the "Citizens and Public Life" theme. With another teacher, perhaps, they will investigate the fragility of democratic systems, studying the rise of the Nazi party in Germany. Their growing conceptual grasp of political and historical complexity should feed, in turn, into critical reflection on local, practical projects, such as running a campaign or working with community groups, in units such as "Getting things done". Much depends, however, on decisions at state, school and classroom level.

Ardent citizens and experts

The success of *Discovering Democracy* rests, in large part, with teachers and teacher educators. Adapting the units and resources to classroom use involves significant challenges.[6] Professional development programs have been developed, and the Commonwealth has pledged further resources, prompted by studies indicating that teachers still have concerns about the extent to which they themselves have sufficient historical, legal and constitutional knowledge to teach the new units.[7] Teachers are, however, imaginatively adapting the units to their schools and to students' interests. Instances are offered as a resource on the Curriculum Corporation's Website. Many build directly on social studies traditions: students identify an important local issue and investigate its civic, political, legal and administrative dimensions. Together, they define the issue, develop hypotheses, research the background, analyse information and test their conclusions, participating in the political process while studying it. Others use engaging historical narratives, awaking students' imagination about the present by stories of the past, encouraging students to identify with past achievements, political struggles and peaceful settlements.

No doubt the units are ambitious, calling for good general knowledge and dexterity in dealing with complex issues. The middle secondary unit "Human rights", for instance, pursues the focus question "How universal are human rights?" Teachers are given examples of court cases, in different jurisdictions, that hinged on how international human rights treaties and provisions were interpreted by Australian courts. The teachers' notes supply the "answers" to the legal questions posed, but the idea is to ask the class to debate how the legal judgements worked in each case. Students, it is suggested, could debate options for change, from a shift in legal interpretation to the drafting of revised legislation or the mounting of political campaigns.

What is involved in running this unit of work in the middle secondary school classroom? To understand the cases, both teachers and students need some comprehension of common law, of the relationship between legislation and judge-made law, of the differences between international law and domestic law and of the respective jurisdictions of the State and the Commonwealth. Students also need to be able to discuss why these legal decisions may not correspond to their own principles of justice. Teachers can be guided by the Hirst primer's account of Magna Carta, the Bill of Rights, the French Declaration of Rights of Man and Citizen and the People's Charter to draw out the historical character of our understandings of rights and of the way they have been institutionalised. The primer's discussion of "Law and Rights" could inform a robust debate about whether Australia needs a Bill of Rights. Students' instinctive understandings of "natural" rights provide a point of departure for discussions of the sources of moral and political authority, the tensions between individual liberty and government and the emergence of secular society. Making an effective case involves being able to articulate and distinguish between moral and political principles and defend them, while also showing some understanding of the character of common law thinking and the distinction between legal and moral reasoning. The challenge, for the teacher, is to build students' interest in the issue and relate it to their experience and immediate environment. At the same time, they have to enable students to develop a more complex understanding of the historical context of current problems and of how arguments for change may be made within existing political, legal and institutional contexts.

Clearly, there has been no lack of thought or resources given to the problems that we explored in our previous chapter. Put simply, this is the question of how to get young people to be interested in the pressing issues of democratic political life, in a way that combines critical understanding with a commitment to democratic values and a willingness to get involved. These are exercises designed to fire the political and historical imagination, opening up "democratic play" in the classroom, to use Callan's term, and setting students both intellectual and ethical challenges.

As we might have come to expect, though, there is a gap between ideal expectation and the working reality of the *Discovering Democracy* project as it has been implemented. A 1999 national review of the civics and citizenship education initiative in schools found that, at its most successful, it had fostered creative ways of involving students within and beyond the school, in class meetings, student councils, school rallies, mock referenda within the school and formal debates on issues such as Aboriginal reconciliation, the republic referendum, foreign affairs and immigration.[8] Schools at the cutting edge had also encouraged students to be active citizens in the community: organising forums, workshops and interviews, debating local issues, working with local radio stations, presenting community petitions to local, state or federal authorities or organising community activities such as "cleaning up a creek, developing a garden, or visiting the sick or elderly".[9] Students have also been encouraged to involve themselves in youth forums, including the national School Constitutional Conventions and the National Youth Roundtable, where young people discussed social and political issues, and prepared their representatives to report their views in "direct dialogue" with policy-makers.

Despite these successes, though, classroom use of the *Discovering Democracy* frameworks and materials had been patchy. Many of the kits and resources had sat unused in school libraries,[10] or their use had been limited, especially at the secondary level, to a single unit of work within subject areas such as history, geography or commerce.[11] Alternatively, where they had been used in the classroom, and had not been adapted, the outcome was "death by worksheet", as pre-prepared material produced "passive regurgitation" of facts and information. Where there was someone in the school to champion the new curriculum units, they had been adopted across the curriculum, often in highly innovative ways. However, teachers tended to say that, given the competing demands on their time and the pressures of an already overcrowded curriculum, they did not have the time to come to grips with a demanding new area.[12] Many reported that they found the materials difficult; they tended not to be confident about discussing technically complex issues such as constitutional provisions, jurisdictional questions or the relationships between the courts and parliament. They felt even less equipped to discuss these issues in historical terms; some found the focus on history inappropriate and irrelevant to students.

In summary, the review found that "[w]hat separates the exceptional teaching of *Discovering Democracy* from the ordinary is the extent to which the content and accompanying activities are made to live for students. The best teaching saw the social/historical material contained in the kits firmly anchored to students' current real world experiences".[13] This meant teachers working out a balance between content and process, clarifying their aims in using these materials and the learning outcomes associated with them. The problem, for those implementing the civic and citizenship education program, is to find forms of professional development that will allay teachers' doubts, especially about the historical scope of the frameworks. The worry is that, if neither teachers nor students have enough historical context to make sense of the materials, then *Discovering Democracy* may tend only to sentimentalise the past and confuse students about the present.

Civics and its critics

Many of these concerns about the academic difficulty of the *Discovering Democracy* material were raised when the programme was first proposed. At that point, various commentators saw the revival of civics as an academic and bureaucratic incursion into the schools, one with a narrow and outdated focus. Why, they asked, should the knowledge of experts be elevated above the know-how of classroom teachers?[14] Experienced teachers of social education, it was argued, were well aware of the need to equip students for active, critical and effective citizenship; they already worked to involve students in participatory decision-making in the school and community.[15] Social education was already about social issues, such as indigenous politics and global environmentalist movements. Given the current success of social and environmental education, and given that young people have a strong interest in these issues, why force them to learn about formal politics and government? At the grassroots of politics, it was argued, people were much more concerned with their identity, their local community and the ways they contributed to it.[16] In any case, young people already had plenty of access to information about politics; they were saturated with media coverage of a parliamentary process that was petty, adversarial and unlovely. Social education should not be about politics in this limited sense; it should be a catalyst for social change and struggles for social justice. By contrast with this ideal, the new civics education seemed to offer a much more limited prospect of building simple-minded patriotism, imposing conformity and maintaining the status quo.

There were some commentators who did advocate civics and citizenship education as a means to build social cohesion; for some educational traditionalists, *Discovering Democracy* was a welcome move away from the relativism associated with social studies and "values clarification".[17] Instead of just expressing their own opinions about social issues, on the understanding that nothing was true and everything was relative, students should be given a more confident induction into liberal democratic values such as civility, tolerance, reasonableness and fairness.[18] Such firmness was justified, it was argued, because the state had a legitimate authority to prescribe core skills, knowledges and attitudes for citizens, as well as a duty to give all citizens access to a common national culture. Cultural relativism and "political correctness" should not get in the way of this; while schools should acknowledge the different ethnic or religious traditions that students bring with them, they should focus on these cultures' contribution to Australian heritage, not on divisive differences.[19]

As Stuart Macintyre noted, one of the problems in enlisting support for *Discovering Democracy* has been that its impetus came, not from teachers, but from the enthusiasm of experts and ardent citizens.[20] To some eyes, this makes the civics enterprise look like a paradox: an undemocratic push for education in democracy. In part, this is a political and philosophical argument; schools and classrooms should be democratic, in the sense of being spaces where participatory democracy is practiced. But it is also a pedagogic argument; teaching and learning should be democratic in the sense that the classroom, the school and the school system themselves should be forums for participatory decision-making.

We can see both senses combined in the developing debate on civics and citizenship. Commissioned to comment on the problem of how to teach civic values, the education researcher Laurence Splitter argued against any attempt to impose an identified core of civic values on learners. "To 'teach' someone civic 'knowledge'", as he put it "is to subject them to the all-too-familiar process of absorbing and regurgitating that which has already been deemed to be true and/or important". If what is regarded as important, for instance, is the story of a nation founded on consensus and co-operation, rather than conflict, then students are at risk of having misrepresentations and myths imposed upon them. This is not so much education as "(attempted) indoctrination, which has no place in a syllabus which claims to be educating young people in, and for, a democracy".

Where values are learned, he argued, this is properly the outcome of a "constructive and deliberative process", in which students identify their own values, which emerge as "reflective outcomes on inquiry". Genuine values cannot be handed down in the classroom. Instead, good teaching involves a process where values are "constructed anew", when learners internalise questions and come to their own conclusions. What this needs, to bring it into being, is a "pedagogy of conversation and dialogue".[21]

This argument is representative of many made in the wake of *Discovering Democracy*. Teachers, it is said, must defend real educational principles, resisting the forces of instrumentalism. Their focus should be on making each child and each educational community fully "active", not just as citizens but as human beings, capable of choice, critical reason and self-realisation. Children must be self-motivating in making themselves as fully critical citizens; the democratic ideals and processes studied must be mirrored in the mode of study. Both the classroom and the school itself must become democratic, opening themselves both to the active and critical interrogation of the students and the community; civics must become a "whole school" affair, finding the ethical, moral and political lesson in each institutional interaction, and drawing it into students' self-directed learning.[22]

As it turns out, however, these concerns are also expressed by advocates of civics, many of whom share the conviction that effective education for citizenship involves a process of enabling individuals to become fully critical, rational and self-governing, through "reflective outcomes on inquiry". Stuart Macintyre, for instance, in a published exchange with the education historian Alan Barcan, distances himself from those who see the reintroduction of civics as a chance to rescue the academic disciplines of history and geography. For Barcan, this is an opportunity to undo what he sees as the damage done to educational standards by the radicalism and relativism of the 1960s and 1970s, especially by social studies, with its emphasis on project-based learning and on the discussion of social issues such as multiculturalism and identity politics.[23] Macintyre, by contrast, argues that education for citizenship can and should tackle controversial social issues in the classroom; young Australians need to explore the implications of a world reshaped by internationalisation and by identity politics, amongst other factors.

Nevertheless, he regrets the decline of historical study in the schools. For him, the new civics and citizenship education frameworks should make it possible to reintroduce an historical understanding of change, one that does not retreat from the idea of a "knowable past".[24] While remarking that the rise of social studies since the 1960s has meant a gradual decline in history teaching and historical understanding, he makes it clear that he is not suggesting that history, as taught in universities, should be reimplanted in the schools as an academic discipline. The teaching of history in primary and secondary schools, he urges, should not be abstract and nor should it be preoccupied with critical uncertainties and deconstruction; this will not bring students back to history, and nor will it connect them to political life. Historically oriented teaching should involve imagination, narratives, empathy, investigation and problem-solving.[25] Teachers should be able to draw on history in ways that are "civically engaged and uplifting while remaining genuinely critical".[26] They should not aim to make simple-minded nationalists, but nor should they treat young people as apprentice philosophers or academic historians.

It would be hard to characterise Macintyre's views as educationally "regressive". He is modest about experts' and academics' claims to understand the complexity of the school system and he acknowledges the many competing pressures on school systems and teachers. Nevertheless, he is willing to argue that it is legitimate for government to start policy processes that involve interventions into the school system from outside experts. He is willing to put a view about what citizens should know and be able to do, as an educator undertaking a public duty and accountable to government and the public. He is perhaps most persuasive when he speaks as an advocate of "social partnerships": collaborations between schools and the civic associations that make up civil society, supported in turn by universities, national, state and local government. Speaking in these terms can provide a more positive perspective on civics and citizenship education as a project of government in the broadest sense: specifically, a project of the contemporary forms of neo-liberal governance that enlist citizens in governing themselves, and that persuade communities to participate in their own reshaping according to identified problems and solutions. But to understand how civics and citizenship education works in this way — and to prevent ourselves from reflex rejections of its governmental elements — we need to understand more about the different available interpretations of the relationship between government, citizenship and schooling in modern liberal democracies. We turn then to one version of the history of Australian civics; and thence to some alternative accounts.

History for civics

The revival of Australian civics has renewed interest in the history of education for citizenship. When did young people lose the chance to learn, in school, about key aspects of Australian history, or about the country's political, constitutional and legal traditions? Why did civics teaching disappear? Julian Thomas, a consultant to the 1994 inquiry, suggested that, with the rise of social studies in the mid 1960s, especially with the new focus on project learning and the discussion of social issues, some of the elements of an earlier tradition of civic education had been dissipated.[27] His task involved retrieving some neglected elements of civics, as it was taught in elementary schools of the first three decades of the last century. Despite its reputation for quaintness, dullness and jingoism, civics was diverse. Civics textbooks, such as those by Walter Murdoch (1912)[28] and Alice Hoy (1934)[29], did contain lesson materials covering elements of Australian political and civic life. This was understood broadly, however; while outlining the operations of party politics and the various levels of government, along with the public service, the courts and commercial life, the texts ranged from local government to national citizenship and international obligations. Civic educators took civic life to extend to the workplace, the home, the school, the shops and the community; civic formation of the 1930s also included "everyday ethical lessons"; good citizenship was treated as the effect of habits, attitudes and dispositions built within the "whole school" environment. School civics programs had close links to "character-forming" community activities.[30] Civic education initiatives outside the school included "social service" schemes with voluntary organisations, youth camping associations and hostels, Christian youth schemes and adult education.

No doubt civics in the 1930s, was often dry, dull and didactic; this was certainly Alice Hoy's judgement when she completed her

1934 report on history and civics in Victorian secondary schools. Like other progressive educators of the time, she promoted a model of civics teaching strongly influenced by the "child-centred" models of the New Education movement and by American civics teaching on the Deweyan model of inquiry-based learning. Criticising the reliance on textbooks and drilling in political facts, she urged schools to focus on practical activity and local projects which encouraged students to participate giving them a readiness to play a part in public life, a wide instead of a narrow patriotism and the ability to think for themselves instead of being dominated by party politics. Civic education should give students not only "a good general knowledge of our political institutions" and "an easily roused interest in public affairs", but also "a ready recognition of the fact that since there are two sides to every question it is folly to champion one side without trying to get the point of view and arguments of the other side".[31]

Modern social studies teaching owes many of its pedagogic innovations to civics teaching of the period from the 1930s to the 1950s, which saw enthusiastic experimentation with classroom parliaments, round-table debates and hypotheticals. The idea — still being urged today — was that civics must be taught through the "whole school" environment, involving students in democratic decision-making; it must also extend beyond the school to the library, the records office, museum, local history association and to nature study and the environment. But at the same time, as civics educators promoted classroom-based activity and lively debates on public issues, they also continued to emphasise the importance of interesting students in the way in which government, in the broad sense, worked. Civics materials, as Thomas describes them, addressed Australian political structures, finance and justice and social welfare. The consistent theme was the elements that made Australian citizenship distinctive, including its history of regional, trade and imperial connections

By the mid to late 1960s, however, many of the elements of civics had been disaggregated into different parts of the syllabus. In part, this was due to the increasing influence of inquiry-based and project-based learning, which found a strong base in the new subject "social studies". Compared to earlier civics teaching, with its focus on the mechanisms of politics, law and citizens' relations to government, social studies turned out to have a stronger focus on the students' immediate experience, environment and views on social issues. There was still an emphasis on the need for educate for citizenship, but understood as a process focusing on the adolescent as a whole person, equipped for work, leisure and citizenship by the ability to think critically and to clarify his or her own values. These "general competencies" could be taught in various subjects, within the new comprehensive secondary schools, from English, history and geography to "general studies", "guidance", physical education or human relations. Residual citizenship courses remained, such as those used up to Year 10 in Queensland high schools at least until 1997. Compared with early civics education programs, however, there was little direct attention given to formal politics, to the role of government or to the history of Australian constitutional and legal thinking. Nor was the study of the ethical life of the citizen as clearly linked, in teaching, to integrated discussion of how rights and duties accrued to citizens living within Australian households, neighborhoods, public agencies, businesses, tax systems, legal environments and communities. Gradually, the teaching of politics was also detached from the historical discussion of distinctive Australian circumstances that shaped civic life in these environments.

Old and new civics

Not surprisingly, the story has been told differently. Even advocates of the new civics dismiss its earlier incarnation as irredeemably dull; both dry and dripping with moralism. The "old civics", it is said, was pedantic, imperialistic and drill-based; it combined flag saluting and rote learning with crude moral lessons.[32] In a more intensive reading of early civics teaching manuals, Malcolm Vick aims to expose the ideological dimensions of these texts. The version of citizenship given to teachers (and presumably repeated in the classroom) was based on liberal political assumptions, he argues: although the individual is described as "self-directing", she is also represented as properly obedient to social norms and loyal to the nation state. For Vick, this reinforces the hegemony of the nation, "naturalises" class, cultural and gender hierarchies and justifies "strong government".[33] These texts, he argues, asserted an

Australian "shared culture", in the face of diversity of class and gender.

From the perspective of a modern commitment to critical education and "reflective inquiry", civics of the past looks like a crude version of "values transmission" and direct "socialisation of children".[34] Lindsay Parry describes how educators of the 1930s set out to form "'patriotic' and 'loyal' citizens with the 'right' attitudes and 'appropriate' social behaviour". Even in the late 1950s, Parry argues, civics was still taught in this way. When the American educator R. Freeman Butts came to Australia in 1954, he found the schools to be "uniform, traditional, formal and rigid", drill-based and teacher-centred, lacking the focus on "relevance" of social problems and on student-centred learning more characteristic of the emergent American social studies. But by the mid 1970s, Australian educators had been caught up in an international movement in educational thought.[35] Embracing social studies, they took up a new emphasis on teaching for change and on critical thinking, extending the child-centred teaching of the 1930s into a focus on discovery learning, conceptual development and "process" rather than "content". The real educational promise of social studies was not fully realised however — it tended to degenerate into group work and project-based teaching that often amounted to little more than "a lot of pictures stuck on to bits of paper". It is only now that civics education, as social studies, can realise the historical potential of progressive teaching methods.[36]

Some civics advocates are confident that, unlike 1930s civics, the new civics will be able to take up this challenge, opening contentious political issues to discussion in the classroom.[37] It will not be value neutral; it will transcend nationalism, teaching a global ethic of cultural and ethnic tolerance, social justice, civility between peoples and the "principles of a civil society".[38] It will open children's eyes to liberal myths and promote more active models of civic participation, discovered by the students themselves within a critical process of reflective inquiry, based on "students" self-selection of problems".[39] Others are less optimistic; today's civics is unlikely to be "empowering", Vick argues, in the sense that it will give young citizens the ability to alter economic, civic and cultural life. The models of citizenship in use are too limited, he argues, being mortgaged to the model of allegiance to the nation state, and ignoring broader issues such as economic production and class. Civics might offer "solidarity" within the community, but one of the conditions is the assimilation of difference and the "solidification of inequalities". Civics will fail the test of living up to true democratic principles of freedom, justice and equality.[40]

These accounts take very different approaches to the writing of history; each involves decisions about the extent to which the account should be told looking backwards from the present. That is, some of these writers tend to treat earlier teachers as though they were stuck on the historical path to enlightened political and educational ideas. The danger for the historian is that of treating the past dismissively, as if it were inevitable that we should now value the ideal of reflective inquiry or globalist ethics.[41] Thomas, on the other hand, aims to avoid assuming that there is a natural path of progress, in Australian educational thought, leading from imperialistic jingoism to nationalism and to globalism; nor is there a natural path of enlightenment from liberalism to republican ideals of participatory democracy on a world scale. Early twentieth century discussions of citizenship, he argues, were more complex than this. Certainly educators such as Walter Murdoch exhibited the liberal aspirations of his time, but Murdoch defined Australian citizenship in a variety of ways: as an affiliation to the nation-state; as a distinctive set of democratic principles and as a more mundane and everyday product of the way in which working life, civic life and domestic life was organised by Australian social and political institutions. For Thomas, this is the most interesting element of this liberal reforming vision; its willingness to argue that freedom depends on good government — that, as Murdoch put it, "government is the best friend liberty has".[42]

History from above

There is an interesting overlap here with Alastair Davidson's caustic account of Australian citizenship. For Davidson, turn of the century liberal political thinkers such as Murdoch, Peter Board or indeed Alfred Deakin, were articulate exponents of British liberal constitutionalism, a political tradition traceable to Burke and Locke — but one which was still only shakily established in Australia at the time of Federation. Murdoch and Board emphasise a "social contract" model of liberal democracy: the good citizen of the modern nation-state agrees to obey the law and serve his or her country; in exchange, the responsible government protects individual liberties and provides legal and political equality and a "social safety net".[43] But citizens had to commit themselves to this deal, and civic education played a part. Australian civic educators' emphasis on civics was part of the project of social consolidation, replacing divisions along occupational lines with a form of social unity, and thus building a "common social outlook".[44] Despite the prevailing complacency about Australia as the most democratic of countries, and despite the appeal to comradeship and community, this was a backward-looking and parochial understanding of citizenship. Australian democracy is substantially undemocratic, both in its electoral system — which never realised the principle of one vote of equal value for each citizen — and in the way in which the relationship between citizen and state is conceived.[45]

What Australia took from Great Britain, Davidson argues, was a model of the relationship between nation states and citizens that was directly derived from the political settlements made in the early modern period, when nation states established sovereignty over war-torn regions, language groups and religious faiths. The problem, for states, was how to manage these new national territories in such a way that states could depend on a core allegiance, from populations in those territories, to the centralised state power, both for external wars against other states and as protection against ethnic, confessional and regional groups within the territory.[46] Once the solution had been found, in the political invention of a private domain of financial interest or commitment to kin or community of faith, the problem was how these private citizens could be persuaded to put aside personal interest, giving their allegiance to the state and supporting its judicial authority.

Davidson holds that nation states had alternative ways of achieving such a settlement and of establishing a political community. One way was for the state to create and impose a fictional version of the nation as a community, with collective values and a common history.[47] States did so by suppressing difference and setting up criteria for eligibility to the entitlements of citizens, according to either descent or territory. They also found ways, during the eighteenth and nineteenth centuries, to attach citizens to the state, by granting settlements that recognised political and social rights.[48] During the postwar period, the social welfare state was able to provide what might now be called social solidarity; a sense of a common civilisation, despite disparities of income and inherited privilege. Shifts in law and social administration meant that each citizen now had equal standing in relation to the law, to voting and standing for office, to the school system, to health and to social welfare. Governments took on responsibility for ensuring that, in these arenas, citizens were on more or less equal terms, with more or less equal basic resources. This egalitarian logic put the pressure on government to acknowledge further rights claims, which were gradually adapted into social administration.[49] According to T.H. Marshall's influential formulation, citizenship and the egalitarian logic of social rights acted as a counterweight to capitalism. School systems, for instance, regarded each future citizen as equally entitled to an education, but schools sorted children according to ability and vocational aptitude; what citizens had was the "equal right to be treated unequally" for the purpose of schooling.[50]

For Davidson, this version of "legitimate inequality" is a meagre substitute for citizenship. What it provided, he argues, was a political solution to internal tensions within the nation-state. Governments prevented classes and interests from coming to blows, by ensuring that "heads were counted rather than cut off."[51] This meant that the "political" dimension of the citizen's active fight for rights was replaced by a sociological concern with how social goods were divided up. Citizenship, in Britain and then in Australia, came to be thought of not in terms of what a person *does* but in terms of what they *get*.[52] Even though these liberal democratic settlements were initially about finding ways to defend individual liberties and the right to difference, the political system has become increasingly focused on building conformity and loyalty through common social rights, social welfare systems and schools.

Historically, Davidson argues, these strategies coexisted with a second model, in which states found ways for citizens to maintain their allegiance to the political culture, through active civic participation and self-governance. He associates this second model with a conception of popular sovereignty and active citizenship derived from Kant and to Rousseau. For Kant, the solution to the problem of how to reconcile the interests of private individuals or cultural communities with the "obligation to justice in a wider society of the modern state" lay in creating the ideal of the autonomous reasoning citizen, encouraged to see himself as part of something larger than a community: as a "potentially universal world citizen who would only make and obey law which could be universal".[53] Extending this, Rousseau developed models of new democratic virtue, taken up in the French republican tradition. These models were taken up by continental European states, which extended the limited models of representative democracy developed by the Anglo-Saxon countries, increasing the role of local government and developing a plenary model of participatory decision-making, leading to substantial legal recognition of social and economic rights, increasingly formulated as internationally recognised entitlements of citizenship, that surpass the jurisdiction of nations.[54]

Australia did not take up these options. Arbitrarily, in Davidson's view, it maintained its attachment to British conceptions of citizenship, along with its tradition of common law reasoning, which maintains a distance between the people and the "centralising managerial system of experts", while propounding the myth that the law draws on a collective memory and tradition.[55] The attachment is arbitrary because Australia now has an increasingly diverse citizenry, many of whom have no *reason* to give their allegiance to these models. They can only be persuaded to do so if they are also persuaded to give up the model, which many of them bring with them from their countries of origin, of the critical rational citizen who owes allegiance only to universal principles derived from reason.

For Davidson, then, when liberal-thinking Australian educators in the early twentieth century, such as Walter Murdoch, Peter Board or Alice Hoy, taught young Australians that "government is the best friend that liberty has", they were inducting them into views about citizenship that, measured by the standard of neo-Kantian political theory, do not look democratic.[56] To that extent, his analysis of contemporary civics programs is close to that offered by some of the commentators reviewed above, who assess rationales for reviving civics and citizenship education in terms of an ideal and abstract conception of democracy. The policy process itself is expected to be democratic; sometimes in the sense that it should be transparent, but often in the sense that it should be fully participatory, generated by the will of the students, teachers and school communities. Where curriculum reform does not correspond to this ideal, it is judged to be "undemocratic". Our review of different perspectives on the history of civics and schooling in Australia has already complicated that picture; we will find that international comparisons make it even more difficult to rush to judgement on Australian civic curriculum reforms.

Democratic doctrines and imperfect institutions

Drawing together some threads from this and the previous chapter, we return to a recurrent theme: why should national governments take it upon themselves to ensure that children have the skills, knowledges and values to exercise their rights and duties as citizens?

There is a rationale for governmental concern with citizens' capacity to act as citizens. At one level, as we saw in the recent American Presidential elections, the stability of the government depends, in large part, on government's capacity to claim that it holds power by virtue of a rational and competent choice on the part of the electorate. Once the reliability of the electoral system or the citizens' capacity for choice comes into serious doubt, political life becomes insecure, riven by faction and the potential for violence and tyranny. In their own interests, it is argued, democracies need to lay a secure foundation in civic formation. Citizens and citizenries are made, not born. It is the role of the school to make them, as a means to preserve democracy.

These liberal democratic rationales for common civic education through government-organised campaigns in schooling were clearly articulated in the public statements and speeches that accompanied the launch of *Discovering Democracy*. The "teaching and learning of the history of and the principles that support Australian democracy", Dr Kemp assured teachers, will give future citizens more common points of reference in their discussions. Historical points of reference are important for constructive public debate and dialogue, he remarked, because "common exploration of the past creates bonds between citizens who are otherwise strangers. They provide intellectual terrain in which understandings, views, bias and prejudice can be navigated and explored". But commonality need not mean uniformity, he maintained. On the contrary: civics and citizenship education can also give Australians a common stock of unresolved controversies and conflicting points of view, on which they can draw in vigorous public debate. Informed disagreement on such matters can work to reinforce social bonds.

In this way, Dr Kemp predicts, it will be possible to build a "common sense of purpose" without imposing uniformity through the school system, as long as young Australians also learn to value the "commitment to negotiation and compromise". As long as respect for "the freedom of the individual" is maintained (which also means respecting diversity), then there is no barrier to building a "degree of consensus and congruence amongst citizens", through government-organised school campaigns in civics and citizenship education. Furthermore, it is possible to state confidently that there is "an identifiable Australian culture". It is one based on democratic commitment to "individual freedom, equality before the law, justice for all, tolerance and recognition of merit".[57]

Contrasting this with Alistair Davidson's analysis of the relationship between Australian government and liberal democratic traditions, we can begin to appreciate why it is that the civics and citizenship education reform programme has been contentious. Davidson, remember, questions whether it is indeed legitimate for governments to build conformity and loyalty through school systems. For him, the rationales provided for *Discovering Democracy* might be a good example of a style of Australian governance that he regards as centralised, expert and detached from the popular will of the people.

Certainly, as we have seen, there are some who, like Davidson, would prefer to reinvent Australian citizenship along civic republican lines, rather than maintain a "collective memory" based on colonial adaptations of British traditions. Like Davidson, they regret the lost opportunity to build a political culture based on ideals of active civic participation and on universalist moral principles, drawn from philosophers such as Kant and Rousseau. From such a perspective, education for democracy is only really democratic if it flows from a communal democratic will, the will of the self-governing community, explored and expressed through the great civic classroom of participatory democracy. Citizens should not be made, but should make themselves. They should not be told by government to commit themselves to historically arbitrary political, legal and constitutional traditions, just because "we" happen to have "inherited" them. Instead, it is possible to have a more universalist conception of citizenship and a more international idea of allegiance and belonging.

No doubt these arguments will continue, with participants debating the possibility of finding common ground even as they seek to clarify the basis for disagreement, by reference to traditions of political thought. Most contributors to the continuing debate on civic education would share the expectation that schooling should realise an historical potential for democracy and citizenship. They might see this differently, of course, emphasising either the liberal vision of the autonomous rational individual, freely choosing to exercise civic rights and duties, or the civic republican or communitarian ideal of the self-governing community of active citizens.

These common assumptions provide the basis for most abstract reflections on what is at stake when governments use school systems to make and shape citizenries. Such debates have currency not only in Australia, but across education debates in modern liberal democracies, as we shall see in the case of Britain, Canada and the United States. What we will also see, however, is that there are dangers in treating the school system as though it were a political philosophy brought to life. Hovering above the school system, it may well look as though Australian teachers and educationists straggled off a path they should have taken, one that led to the realisation of democratic political principles and modern educational ideals. But equally, it may be arbitrary to expect school systems to deliver on a philosophical promise that they never made.[58] The historical relationship between political thought and mass schooling is more complex than this – a point to which we will return in the following chapter. So too are the contemporary politics of curriculum reform, which owe as much to the pragmatics of political negotiation as they do to the language of philsophical ideals.

Implementing the *Discovering Democracy* program is a vexed political process; it has involved often difficult negotiations between education authorities, stakeholders, interest groups, advocates and critics.[59] The gap between expectations and outcomes demonstrates the improvised and imperfect character of democratic institutions and political negotiation. Experts do not always hear what teachers have to say; teachers in the audience of the professional development workshop may not really feel much "ownership" of the reform process. They may suspect that this is a "top-down" operation, one that is not democratic because it is not fully participative.[60] Such criticisms, and such demands for consultation and accountability, must be recognised as indispensable elements of vigorous public and professional debate. By the same token, though, teachers and educationists can be expected to concede that those who speak in the name of government (politicians, bureaucrats, experts) have a legitimate concern with whether or not schools are giving future citizens the abilities they need to exercise their rights and duties and to sustain a stable liberal democracy in times of change , mobility and social conflict.

We might not now be as sure as Walter Murdoch was, in 1912, that government is a friend to liberty, but it is hard to see how the liberties of citizens could be enjoyed if government did not take some responsibility for enabling citizens, through the school system and the educative community, to become self-governing. Whether they are self-determining to the extent that citizenship theorists expect is a different question. It is a question that has been made possible, arguably, by the achievements involved in establishing civil peace and social stability through political solutions, including those that entail counting heads rather than cutting them off, to recall Davidson. One of the central elements in these settlements is the establishment, through the school system, of a common environment for civic formation. The question is, how perfectionist we should be in our expectations of what democratic governance can achieve, either in promoting consensus or in enacting the popular will of an active citizenry. It is a question that we will take up in the next chapter, as we continue to investigate the politics of civics, within a broader international context of debate on citizenship, membership, pluralism and common political traditions.

Chapter 3

Cosmopolitan Citizens

We have begun to broaden our sense of the political issues associated with current efforts to reshape Australian citizenship and build a more vital attachment to civic and political life, informed by an historical understanding of the legacies of Australian democracy. We have located a central dynamic. Citizens are seen as agents who make free choices, including the choice to commit themselves to the political community (local, national or global). But in modern liberal democracies, the citizen is also governed, not least by his or herself. We learn to behave appropriately in particular environments — in the school, in the family, in the supermarket, in the workplace, at the doctor's, on the road, on the pavement, in the tax system, in the courts, at the voting booth, watching television, using the Net and email. Each of these environments is a space of "regulated freedom". That is, each places us in a role or status (as student, teacher, child or parent, customer, consumer, taxpayer) and each role requires us to have abilities, including mental and emotional habits that restrain us from behaving in uncivil or irresponsible ways. Each of these roles, in other words, has a civic element. But it is possible to be in these roles — to see a doctor, to drive, to go to school — without being a citizen. In one sense, citizenship is a more limited and formal status, one recognised by a passport or a birth certificate. But because the term "citizen" has so much moral force now, we tend to use it to encompass many of the roles discussed above, treating it as a term that links all the allegiances we might have: to family, workplaces, legal systems, commercial life, social life and, by extension, to a nation and its political, constitutional and legal systems.

Citizenship is a useful term when we are in the business of developing an overarching moral vision that could link our sense of the responsibilities of each and all. But it is easy, when doing this, to lose a sense of the everyday dimensions of life within the complex environments of modern liberal democracies, a life that involves negotiating a number of roles, rights and responsibilities. It is also easy to lose a sense that citizenship, as we know it, is a definite status that is not shared by all those living in these environments. Modern patterns of immigration and internationalisation mean that populations are made up of residents, tourists, itinerant workers and aliens, both legal and illegal. They may not be citizens of the country in which they are living, but they are still within civic environments, negotiating the terrain of housing, health, banking, work, driving, rights and liabilities. They may have strong associational ties: to local communities, to workplaces, to one or more ethnic, religious or language groups or to language groups and to an international diaspora of familial, ethnic or religious affiliations. Many have to negotiate the effects of racism, xenophobia and religious intolerance, not only from members of the majority culture of the country in which they are living, but also from within and between immigrant communities.

These patterns of international movement and migration have presented some common dilemmas to the Western liberal democracies. In Europe and North America, nations are struggling to manage the effects of immigration. The major cities and industrial centres have formed clusters, over some decades, of comparatively impoverished communities of itinerant workers and their families. These are areas riven by long-standing economic, ethnic and religious tensions, but there is just as much potential for civil violence in the majority cultures. This is especially the case where there are strong political factions that reject the call to respect cultural diversity, urging limits to immigration and the enforcement of cultural assimilation. The term "citizenship" is only of limited use in this context. On the one hand, it is possible to put the case that, as citizens, each individual has a right to expect equal protection from the state, including guaranteed recognition of cultural rights, as well as civil, political and social rights. On the other hand, because citizenship is a term that distinguishes between those who are members of the political community and those who are not, the risk is that resident aliens, legal and illegal, will be treated in ways that breach their human rights.[1] The difficulty, both for national governments and for the voters assessing their response to these dilemmas, is that the egalitarian elements of modern conceptions of citizenship only extend so far — to members of the political community and not to those excluded from it.

Some citizenship theorists hold that, as the scope of international law and governance expands, it will be possible to consolidate a more cosmopolitan conception of citizenship, recognising universalistic conceptions of membership within a global political community with a collective political conscience.[2] Globalisation and the international movements of capital, peoples and technology may be creating disparities of wealth and power, especially between developed and developing nations, and they may also mean that the regulatory powers of nation states have been trumped by supranational corporations.[3] On the other hand, the global reach of new communications may also mean that nation states can no longer protect themselves from international inspection of their human rights records, given that activists and minority cultural groups have ready appeal to the forum of international opinion, through international advocacy groups, non-government agencies and voluntary associations.[4] The dialectical tension between sovereign states and mass social movements of citizens will resolve itself in the moment we all participate in global consensus.[5]

It is hard to be too cynical about such expectations in the year of the Sydney 2000 Olympics. Such an event makes it look easy, given enough goodwill, to transcend the bounds of the nation. Surely the Olympic ideal of peace and cosmopolitanism gives some model of how we can keep national loyalty, while making the nation transparent enough to celebrate what unites us all? But we have to remember not only the stirring moment when Cathy Freeman became part of the Olympic flame, but also the "hidden" mechanisms that faltered when raising the cauldron. Faulty as they may be, the mechanisms of civic accord are just as vital as the sentiment that they engender.

This is the theme of this and the following chapters: two comparative studies of European and North American debates on civic formation, national culture and cultural difference, placing these in the context of broader international and regional change. In Britain, the United States and Canada, national education systems have sought, in different ways, to maintain social cohesion and national culture, in the face of social, economic, cultural and technological change, usually through strengthening the schools' role in providing common civic formation. However, each is also seeking to negotiate the issue of how to adapt that common culture to the cultural rights of a multiethnic and multifaith population. The problem, in general terms, is to construct consensus, but to do so in a pluralist manner, which shows conspicuous respect for liberal freedoms, while keeping a lid on potentially explosive cultural, ethnic and religious disputes. First however, a review of the terms in which Australian educators have understood these issues.

Core and common values

Australian debates on civics and citizenship education have tried to find a balance between stressing common traditions and recognising freedom of opinion. Is there indeed a core of values to which all Australian citizens subscribe? Curriculum designers have sought to find a pluralistic approach to this question. This means encouraging the discussion of the issue and prompting critical reflection, as students reach new stages of moral and conceptual development.[6]

This is exemplified in *This Australian Nation – Exploring national identity,* on-line classroom activities distributed by the Curriculum Corporation.[7] The exercises begin, at the primary level, with play (children imagine they are explorers and describe Australian customs, beliefs and values), consolidated in discussion. Pictures of culturally diverse groups are used to stimulate discussion of the "main values most Australians would believe in". A list of "Recommended Core Civic Values" is offered as a resource. These "main values" might include commitment to land, the rule of law, equality under the law, freedom of opinion, principles of tolerance and fairness, acceptance of cultural diversity and to the wellbeing of all Australians, as well as commitment to recognising the unique status of the Aboriginal and Torres Strait Islander peoples.[8] The class can then make a poster that displays these characteristics. Is this indoctrination?

For liberal education philosopher Brian Crittenden, there is little doubt that school systems are justified in prescribing common values, skills, knowledges and attitudes. While it is important to be pluralistic, up to a point, educators need to recognise core and common values: civility, tolerance, reasonableness and fairness. If these values are not recognised, he argues, communities can hardly decide to be tolerant. He adds though that civics experts have failed to tackle the hard question of where pluralism should begin and end. Cultural practices that are not themselves liberal and pluralist should not be tolerated. Nor should beliefs that threaten cohesion. Instead, we should concentrate on the "common distinctive nature of our culture" and on the role that diverse ethnic and other groups can play in shaping it.[9]

The objection to this could be that, in a pluralistic society, it makes little sense to speak of a common political tradition, or one public sphere in which all cultural groups meet. Should all students be asked to *commit themselves* to such values, or is this an intrusion on personal freedoms and privacy? At what point do lessons in civic ethics overlap with morality, partisan politics or religion, and what happens when civics lessons conflict with family values or ethnic tradition?[10]

The 1994 *Whereas the People* report took a clear stance on this issue. It conceded that it may not be possible to assume that, in Australia, there was an already-existing consensus on the "common set of values shared by all". Perhaps it had been possible to assert consensus on the nature of Australian citizenship a century before, but contemporary Australia could not be comfortable with early twentieth century ideals of "a White Australia of British descent and imperial loyalty where men would be breadwinners and women should be dependents". But instead of rejecting the ideal of a community-based consensus on Australian liberal democratic values, the report urged that, in the context of change, it was all the more important to develop a pluralistic consensus on the core "values and attitudes" that are central to the "civil sphere", giving all citizens access to the educational, personal, social, moral and spiritual values to which the majority of citizens subscribe. State-organised school systems cannot and do not pretend to be "value free". In other contexts, the Australian government had legislated to recognise and enforce values perspectives; the report cited anti-discrimination legislation as an instance. Furthermore, the Australian government was also justified in following examples of international best practice, as exemplified in United Nations and UNESCO initiatives, which had already established international codes of core liberal democratic values that Australia had recognised.[11]

Global civic enterprises

Insofar as Australian debates on civics have drawn on international comparisons, this tends to be done either in a way that distances Australian civic traditions from American civic patriotism — or alternatively, that cites American and French civic republican models as a philosophical foundation for new forms of citizenship oriented to participation and active, critical inquiry. Australian citizenship, measured against these civic republican ideals, falls short. The existing commentary tends to assume that Australian education shares much with British traditions, for better or worse, owing little to continental European or North American models of civic formation. At the same time, a number of writers see the reinvention of Australian citizenship as an opportunity to transcend limited national traditions that owe so much to a colonial past, orienting education and civic discussions instead to more global values and imperatives, such as those enshrined in United Nations conceptions of human rights and human potential.

During the 1980s and 1990s, a number of international agencies, including the United Nations, UNESCO and the OECD, embarked on world-wide programs of civic education. These internationalist enterprises in civics education supplement the efforts of various international agencies (including the World Bank and the International Monetary Fund) to maintain sufficient international stability to foster international trade and industrialisation. In the wake of widespread political change, including the breakup of the Eastern European communist bloc, these agencies set out to achieve civic settlement in unstable new democracies — campaigns that have since extended to South-East Asia, Latin America and Africa. The aim is to accelerate modernisation and industrialisation, introducing both market liberalism and liberal democratic values, while at the same time preventing these unstable areas from exploding into civil wars between rival ethnic and religious minorities, no longer restrained by punitive state actions against private civic associations.[12] The preferred recipe for these social settlements is the rebuilding of social trust, transforming sectarian loyalties into a healthy network of private civic association, separate from the public domain of the political.[13] The key to this, according to the UNESCO program "What education for what citizenship?" is "intercultural dialogue". Democratic life depends on "ethical" conditions: bringing citizens to recognise universal liberal democratic principles, including respect for the rule of law and human rights. International agencies can help new democracies to "find their own way" to these universal values, by working with local educators to establish international standards of effective civic education.[14] Through dialogue, citizens can learn to find common ground, appreciating what they share in local traditions, family ties and religious and moral doctrines. Nevertheless, educators have to ensure that what links people together does not make them into a mob.

International agencies rarely over-rule national sovereignty; more often, they achieve stabilisation and change through providing assistance, often in the form of research and development, especially international benchmarking. Comparative research on education and training, for instance, involves expert consultations, conferences, roundtables and structured dialogue. As exercises in international governance, they loosen the cultural ground in which liberal economic and political doctrines can be transplanted.[15] Regions that are unstable, from the point of view of the Western powers, can be brought to see that there is a path of moral maturity that peoples and nations can choose, one as natural as the path that every human being takes, as he or she becomes a moral adult. Just as the child moves "from self-centred values to more sophisticated and inclusive values" so too can nations move to an understanding of universal ethical principles.[16] The problem, however, lies in applying this liberal model of critical reason to citizens who do not subscribe to liberal doctrines. For nations that subscribe to a state religion or doctrine, such as Islamic fundamentalism, these universalistic models of liberal democratic values may well look like cultural imperialism, especially where they have a secular emphasis on the critical appraisal of values.

Similar questions arise within the Western liberal democracies, which now contain multiethnic and multifaith immigrant communities. Article 8 of the Maastricht Treaty introduced the concept of European citizenship; subsequently, the European Commission has urged each European member state to introduce their citizens to this concept, encouraging them to identify with a common core of internationally recognised principles, such as justice, equality and solidarity.[17] Seeking to persuade national governments to induct their citizens into a broader identification with European citizenship, one able to transcend ethnic, regional and religious difference, the Council has sponsored models for multicultural and multilingual citizenship education. These are to be supplemented by youth exchanges, training packs, and various staged "cross-cultural encounters", from anti-racism classes to discussions of multiculturalism and prejudice.[18] The idea is to teach that there is a common European cultural heritage (a history of the "people's Europe"), which is enriched by combining national cultural traditions within an emergent "world order", in which all humankind is progressing towards the realisation of the democratic principles recognised in international treaties such as the United Nations Charter and the Universal Declaration of Human Rights.[19]

Various European nations including Scotland, France, Denmark, Sweden and Germany, have introduced national civics curricula. Germany, for instance, has had to adapt its traditions of civic education (*Politische Bildung*), retaining common national traditions but adapting to changing definitions of citizenship, including the children of those families now eligible for citizenship, who will need to be inducted into new civic identities, rights and responsibilities.[20] France has also begun to adapt its syllabuses to civic formation for a more multicultural population, with a focus on "the child as a member of social groups".[21] This is a key shift, given that traditional French civic republican education has been determinedly indifferent to public debates on cultural diversity and toleration.[22] For Muslim French communities, this has posed severe problems, especially where the schools have aggressively defended public prohibitions on the wearing of the chador or scarf, seen both as a religious symbol banned from public display in the secular state school system, and also as a symbol of female subordination, breaching the civic republican ethos of the equal treatment of all citizens. The resultant public debate on the issue continues, opening internal schisms in liberal, civic republican and feminist positions.[23]

Meanwhile, in the United Kingdom, the 1998 report of the Advisory Group on Citizenship, chaired by Bernard Crick, has made a strong case for change. Not only must British education adapt to European unionisation, it was argued, but it should also address the internal cultural changes resulting from immigration, multiculturalism and the recognition of multiple allegiances within a multi-national state, comprising the English, Welsh, Scots and Irish.[24] The Report puts the case for civics as a means to resolve class, ethnic, national and regional tensions, arguing that majorities "must respect, understand and tolerate minorities and minorities must learn and respect the laws, codes and conventions as much as the majority". British citizens "need to learn more about each other", including becoming more familiar with the civic traditions particular to all four component parts of the United Kingdom. But they also need to know more about "the European, Commonwealth and global dimensions of citizenship, with due regard being given to the homelands of our minority communities and to the main countries of British emigration".[25]

Despite these indications of change, however, it is by no means clear that it will be possible to generate a conception of European citizenship through the means provided by existing national school systems. Education continues to be a highly sensitive area of international negotiations. European member states tend to resist interference in their education systems, partly because such systems are often highly localised and therefore hard to reform at a national or international level. But education is also a politically sensitive domestic issue, because it is so closely connected to the historical settlements made at the point where these nations consolidated themselves, using school systems to establish commonality between ethnic, regional, religious and class factions. Many of these settlements — now seen as national cultural traditions — are now being renegotiated under the pressure of greater cultural diversity and international exchange.

States and citizens

We can recognise here the continuation of a long historical process, one in which, from the sixteenth century onwards, modern Western European nations emerged from the turmoil of religious civil war, securing territories and establishing liberal political settlements.[26] The key to this was the establishment by absolutist states of a form of governance based in the state rather than in religious faith. This process of "deconfessionalisation" is critical to understanding modern forms of government, in which the state regards itself as indifferent to sectional moral passions and as primarily concerned with its own security, with maintaining territory and with securing the peace and prosperity of the population, separating this from religion and from ethnicity.

As Ian Hunter has argued, the development of state-based schooling was critical to this process of liberal settlement. At different periods and in varying circumstances, the European states established state-run school systems.[27] There were models available; as part of the extended battle between Catholic and Protestant confessions, the rival churches had undertaken massive campaigns, throughout Western Europe, to educate lay populations sufficiently to understand the word of God. In Prussia, Pietist pastoral schools provided the reforming state with models of school architecture and discipline, combining instruction in literacy with moral training. Adapting these teaching techniques, but stripping them of their doctrinal religious elements, the Prussian state developed a common school system designed to make the population literate, civil and healthy. The state made the calculation that an educated population was more valuable to the state than an uneducated one, and that an ignorant and illiterate one was positively dangerous to civil peace. As Hunter puts it, "the capacities and conducts of democratic citizenship rightly prized by liberal philosophers—the renunciation of violence, toleration of different opinions, informed discussion of national issues, compromise—were the achievement of that immense labour of government through which administrative states pacified, disciplined, trained and cared for populations".[28]

This process took different forms, depending on national context. In Prussia, state-organised schooling served to modernise the rural peasantry, making them into a resource of the state. In France, the emphasis was more on the consolidation of regions and language groups into a French-speaking nation. Postrevolutionary French governments invented and promoted a secular civic religion of patriotism as a means to break the hold of organised religion and to achieve the linguistic and cultural unification of the regions that made up the nation state.[29] The highly centralised state school system developed in the nineteenth century was designed to promote equality, national unity and cultural conformity, reinforced through formal curricula and examinations. It was also designed to be aggressively secular. As servants of the state, teachers were trained to regard themselves as dedicated, on behalf of the state, to providing equal instruction for all, remaining scrupulously indifferent to students' religious, familial, regional or linguistic backgrounds.[30] As citizens, students were to be treated identically, given equal measures of the core academic knowledges specified in centrally dictated syllabuses and inducted alike into republican ideals and institutions and into general moral principles of the secular French systems of government.

In Britain, popular schooling was taken over by the state as a means to reform the physical and moral condition of the children of the urban poor, rescuing them from the moral influence of crime-riddled streets and vice-addicted families and making them literate and self-governing.[31] The early education bureaucracy, headed by James Kay-Shuttleworth, adapted the pedagogic techniques of Christian educators such as David Stow. Drawing on the experiments of German and other continental European movements in Christian pastoral schooling, Stow developed an experimental environment designed to promote moral improvement: the modern playground, where teachers could observe children, later touching on the moral issues related to their behaviour in classroom question-and-answer sessions.[32] Under the kind but relentlessly questioning gaze of the teacher, each child was prompted to be aware of their own behaviour. The more children were encouraged to express themselves through play and moral experiment, under moral supervision, then the more likely it was that they would bring themselves to be virtuous, polite and civilised. Far more efficient than rote learning and physical punishment, this was an extraordinarily effective mechanism for making citizens moral, one that the reforming state took up with enthusiasm by the 1840s in its campaigns to reform the crowded, unsanitary and crime-ridden industrial cities.[33] In its own interest, the state took on the social training of citizens, adapting Christian spiritual training to the end of enhancing the wealth and stability of the state.

Such an account can help to give an added dimension to the understanding we have begun to build about what is at stake when states take on the project of common civic formation through the school system. We can begin to see that now, as in the past four centuries, states are still negotiating the difficult task of "deconfessionalising" populations — that is, they are still engaged in the task of sustaining civil peace between sectarian religious, ethnic and regional groups. They have done so, in part, by adapting faith-based customs of moral and spiritual formation into the public institutions of the secular state and the public domain. In France's case, this took the form of an invented "civic religion", while in Britain, schools and other institutions adapted the techniques of spiritual training and translated them into moral, literary, sporting and civic lessons embedded in the pedagogy of "personal development". We can see elements of this, adapted to Australian concerns, in the early civic training of the twentieth century, in the notionally "free, compulsory and secular" state school system established to settle an unstable colony, which borrowed the technologies that Western European states had devised to solve the problems of an unstable population, with passionate rival commitments to church, kin, clan, class and country of origin. As it turned out, these forms of moral and "character" education, derived from non-democratic and illiberal regimes, were remarkably adaptable to liberal democratic societies, and became the cornerstone of a civic formation oriented to equality of opportunity, if not to equality in its fullest philosophical sense.[34]

This historical process of state settlement, secularisation and civic education is by no means complete. Released just two years ago, the Crick Report on citizenship education urges the nation's educators to find or restore (it is not clear which) "a sense of common citizenship, including a national identity that is secure enough to find a place for the plurality of nations, cultures, ethnic identities and religions long found in the United Kingdom".[35] This is an emphatic statement of the liberal argument that, while religious toleration and cultural pluralism are important, a common national identity must be *secure* before pluralism can be achieved. It is the job of the school system to achieve this security, through civic commonality.

This review of the circumstances in which the nation state came into being helps to clarify some elements of current discussions of citizenship in Europe. Given this history, in which states improvised common national school systems out of the fragments of pastoral schooling, putting them to work on the security of the state, it is no wonder that nations are now unprepared to set about the rationalisation of their peculiar forms of civic education; it is not as though there was a single rationale or philosophy that underlay these education systems in the first place. This observation makes it less odd that, asked to develop a model of civic education like that of France or Germany, British educators have defended their own traditions fiercely, pointing out that it has not been thought necessary to teach political education directly. Patriotic ceremonies and civic education, it is said, are "distinctively 'un-English' and have the smell of the Continent about them".[36] This may be more than xenophobia, helping to pinpoint instead the difficulty of using philosophical rationales to clarify educational arrangements and commitments that sprang up in a piecemeal and improvised fashion, out of the fragments of church-based forms of schooling, in order to meet the needs of state planning and national consolidation. In part, the resistance to adopting Continental European conceptions of citizenship can be traced to the defence of the English liberal constitutional tradition, which, as we have seen, stemmed from a distinctive blend of political reasoning and common law thinking.

This would not daunt those who argue that citizenship can find new foundations, in a cosmopolitan conception that could allow peoples to transcend nationalism and the old disputes on sovereignty and security between states, recognising more universalistic principles grounded in critical reason. The argument, we will recall, is that immigration and multi-ethnic coexistence have swept away the markers that nation states drew across territory, making it impossible to regulate the new trade in political and moral ideas. Could this be the new ground for a politics of civic education in Britain?

Civic Britain

Civic education will be phased into British schools in stages, between 2000 and 2004, as schools adapt frameworks that include the following: the study of democratic practices and institutions (parties, pressure groups and voluntary bodies); the links between formal political activity and civic society, in the context of the UK, Europe and the wider world; and personal, social and economic skills.[37] No doubt this process of implementation will be just as controversial in Britain as it has been in Australia. It has been just as difficult, in the wake of the Crick Report, to persuade teachers that there is a need for citizenship education in this form. Some are resistant to the idea of American or French-style patriotic ceremony; others fear that civic education will really be a form of moralism, promoting little more than assimilation and social conformity.[38] Perhaps the strongest objections have come from those who see this as yet another centralist initiative that will undermine the autonomy of teachers, schools and education authorities, undoing the important work of those who have genuinely sought to adjust to cultural change in Britain, adapting to the needs of students and communities who are negotiating multiple ethnic, cultural, gender and regional identities.[39] The real politics of civics, it is argued, is a liberal conservatism that is radically out of touch with the needs and interests of young people.

There are clear parallels here with Australian debates, but the differences are just as interesting. The British initiatives have been less prescriptive than their Australian precursors, and more cautious about specifying curriculum content. Civics will not be linked to academic disciplines such as history or social studies. It falls between two curriculum areas: PSHE (Personal, Social and Health Education) and SMSC (Spiritual, Moral, Social and Cultural Development). As in Australia, there is an emphasis on civic participation in community-based projects and in the civic environments of the school and local communities. These activities will not be formal parts of the curriculum. Nor will civics be formally assessed, except in annual reports to parents on learning outcomes. There seems to be little interest in testing or benchmarking outcomes.[40]

These decisions reflect the Blair government's strategy of backing off from central bureaucratic decision-making. While there is a national curriculum framework, it is designed to be reinterpreted in the local areas and debated within the school communities in a way that is responsive to the education market. The strategy builds on the Conservative government's neo-liberal tactics, deregulating and decentralising while maintaining a central emphasis on competition and choice.[41] Parents have been given greater consumer choice, which is supposed to make room for diversity, as school communities identify the values of the local institution.[42] At the same time, under the heading of "mutual obligation", parents are expected to commit themselves to contracts with the school, providing time, support and supervision for homework. The challenge, for commentators, is to come to terms with a striking combination of political rhetoric, which blends a liberal emphasis on market freedom and privatisation with the moralism of a communitarian emphasis on core values, community consultation and dialogue.[43]

This rhetoric of community consensus, critics have argued, drastically underestimates the economic, social, gender and cultural divisions in contemporary Britain.[44] The expectation is that all members of the school community will participate responsibly in identifying "core values". The reality, warns Jack Demaine, will be rule by a moral community, as middle class parents dominate, being better at the forms of "dialogue", in public meetings, that look participatory and responsible.[45] The communitarian versions of participatory democracy, it is argued, sometimes sound as though they are committed to "dialogue" for the sake of it, "whatever discomfort it may bring". The presumption is that dialogue will lead to community consensus. Arguably, though, these models of civic conversation rely on educated, middle-class ideas of what kinds of speaking and listening count as civil communication between citizens, or what models of argument count as dialogical. Such styles tend to be exhibited by those "already transformed by education from being 'ordinary people' into the different beings called 'citizens' ".[46]

Instead of emphasising mutual obligations, coalition and solidarity, critics argue, civics needs to explore political division and resistance of class, gender, ethnicity and region.[47] Those from oppressed and marginal cultural groups need to see the public domain as a place for struggle and contestation, one in which individuals are far from equal, in terms of status, power and resources.[48] They need to be able to think politically as members of cultural groups and classes, while negotiating the roles and allegiances they take up.[49] The obstacle to this, it is argued, is the liberal assumption that it is legitimate for governments to aim to "resolve class, ethnic, national and regional tensions", as the Crick Report puts it, by making each individual responsible for his or her own personal and moral development and own commitment to "common citizenship". To many, it looks as though New Labor's calls for change are yet another version of the liberal democratic settlements that have kept the lid on authentic political contestation, disabling an effective politics of culture, race and region in Britain and reinforcing apathy, cynicism and alienation. In this context —

where government seems to have claimed the moral high ground of both liberalism and communitarianism — critics are left searching for a response that does not look simply nostalgic.

The politics of virtue

In Britain then, as in Australia, it is important to understand what is at stake when governments put the case for using civic education as a tool of settlement, in the face of change. The Crick Report puts the case that it is legitimate for governments to use school systems in order to achieve the security provided by a common sense of citizenship, sufficient to unify to build the pluralistic recognition of difference. This is an emphatic statement of a liberal argument, which we might recognise from Crittenden's stance on Australian civics, that the politics of culture has gone too far. The argument is that, while toleration is important, it requires security; as a political community, we must be sufficiently secure about what binds us before we can decide what it is prepared to include and exclude. It is the job of the school system to achieve this security, by building a common culture that equips us all for public dialogue.

Various educational philosophers, commenting on this approach, have emphasised the importance of following through on liberal positions on citizenship, encouraging teachers to develop students' independence and open-mindedness, self-restraint and respect for the rights of others. The liberal virtues, however, also require developing "a level of intellectual, if not emotional, detachment from their own cultures, group affiliations, and conceptions of the good". This detachment is fundamental to the non-sectarian nature of the liberal state.[50] It should be balanced, though, by the willingness to make informed judgements on public affairs and to engage in debate.[51]

The question that divides liberal philosophers is whether these civic virtues of neutrality, responsibility and toleration are learned through reflection on principles, or through civic participation itself, either in public forums or in more informal associations. Each of these versions has its problems. A conception of justice in the abstract, even if it is shared, doesn't necessarily do the work of building a shared citizenship identity *within* a political community, much less one that will supersede rival ethnically-based identities. Equivalent problems face those who argue that it is participation, rather than universal principles, that will equip people with civic virtues. The problem with this is that emphasising participation "does not yet explain how to ensure that citizens participate *responsibly* — that is, in a public-spirited, rather than self-interested or prejudiced, way". People cannot be coerced into exercising the kind of co-operation and restraint required to place the common good above blood ties or religious loyalty, or private concerns. It is not as though citizens can be *required* to be philosophically rational or altruistic, and nor can this be made a condition for political participation, "any more than those with little or no interest in politics can be stripped of their citizenship status".[52]

In Britain, as in Australia, we can find articulate objections to a "virtue-based politics". The argument is that communities and parents have a right to rear their children outside of the majority culture, giving their allegiances to a region, ethnicity, race or faith.[53] This is in part a right to culture, but it is also grounded in liberal rights to freedom and privacy. The argument is that it is dangerous for the polity itself to insist on "collective virtue or an unflinching uniform will". The question is at what point efforts to link citizens together by building a common history, language or religion become dangerous to freedoms. To insist on common civic values or virtues may "overburden individual conscience, force a character standardization on citizens and deprive society of an extra-political variety of selves".[54]

The response to this argument has been that, while people cannot be forced to be free, they can be required to give their children access, through the schools, to the universal democratic principles enshrined in the Western liberal heritage of Plato, Rousseau and Dewey. As members of a democracy, such cultural enclaves need to see that democracy is more than just a political machinery; the machinery embodies the "values of justice, freedom and personal autonomy". Robust democracies can sustain vigorous debates about these democratic ideals, and they can also cope with distrust and suspicion of the political system, especially since distrust actually works to protect the system and the well-being of citizens. If the free press and the schools are doing their jobs well, then we should expect a vigilant public to insist on transparency and to express judicious criticism of democratic procedures. But there is a key difference between "procedural" distrust and fundamental distrust of democracy. Democracy becomes fragile if there is no shared public morality to animate and support its institutions. Democrats do not simply need appropriate knowledge and skills: "they need to be certain sorts of people". This involves shaping what once was called "character".[55]

From an historical point of view, there is nothing startling about the proposition that states build security by using school systems to establish common cultures. This has been a pragmatic practice of statecraft throughout the modern period, and one that has now extended to the tactics of regional and international governance. Nor is it surprising to see governments use "personal development", moral and spiritual education as an aid to civic formation. Historically, as it happened, state-run schools picked these techniques up from pastoral Christian discipline, as ways of getting children to make themselves into moral beings and model citizens, through play, discussion and self-expression. There is something intriguing, though, from a comparative perspective, about the British government's strong emphasis on religious values as a foundation for civic life. As it seeks to invent a new politics of civic virtue, Britain (like France) faces the problem of how to maintain a secular civic environment, while respecting cultural difference and identities that are strongly tied to faith. While it is possible to establish an official version of public culture and "core values", popularising it through schooling, people cannot be forced to participate in a common culture, giving up their allegiances to other ways of life.[56] This is a problem shared alike by liberal and by civic republican approaches to citizenship. It is a problem we shall explore more fully in the following chapter, where we pick up the trail of these debates in the very different political context of North America.

Chapter 4

American Civics Lessons

There is an extensive North American literature on the theme we have discussed in the Australian and European context: the question of how to find a balance between the need to maintain national cohesion, social accord and a common order and the equally pressing imperative to respect liberal democratic freedoms, accommodating the plurality of beliefs, practices and whole ways of life that make up civil societies. These debates, which fill library shelves and syllabuses in the American and Canadian academies, span philosophy, theology, ethics and American Studies, along with critical sociology, cultural studies, women's studies, Afro-American studies and the analysis of cultural identity, cultural rights and difference.

Around these academic debates is a sprawling mass of material; pamphlets, reports, position papers and on-line discussions generated by advocacy groups, think tanks and associational networks, from parents' organisations and Christian lobby groups to radical organisations dedicated to fostering grassroots anti-school initiatives. Some of this material is localised and isolationist, making a stance against outside interference in the liberties of a self-identified community, especially from the state. At another extreme, some is generated from a crusading internationalism, determined to spread a civic enthusiasm more broadly. In the midst of this, we can locate efforts, on the part of national, state and provincial governments, to forge a direction on national culture and civic formation that will content the various lobby groups and electoral expectations; meet government's interest in securing civil peace and developing the population as a resource; and meet its obligations to rights-bearing citizens and children in need of care and pastoral protection.

In the United States and Canada as in Britain and Australia, there is a strong push, in national education policy, to raise standards in literacy, numeracy, informational skills and civic understanding. In the United States, national civics standards have been in place since 1994, when the *Goals 2000: Educate America Act* introduced new national civics frameworks and assessment standards, soon followed up by national tests, competitions and campaigns to persuade the state education systems to come on board — which many have done with some reluctance.[1] Canada is still developing its civic education initiatives, within a long process of consultation, research and deliberation. A recent report stressed that Canadian citizenship education must aspire to be more than "a lower level task of instructing the young in the factual intricacies of government or of welcoming newcomers". Instead, civics experts aim to develop a more pluralistic model, oriented to multiethnic coexistence and cultural rights, one "which is likely to be able to form a citizenry respectful of multiple identities, sharing a common sense of belonging".[2]

On the face of it, the two national debates appear to be starkly different. We will find, however, that they cast up comparable problems. In both national contexts, the speeches of the major political parties focus on education as a route to national prosperity and competitiveness — especially in the information age — but also as the path out of inter-generational poverty and the ghetto and into the realm of unlimited personal improvement. Civic education, along with literacy, numeracy and information and communications technologies, remains a high priority for government. Less clear, though, is the role of the state in overseeing education planning and resourcing; increasingly, in the US and Canada, as in Britain, neoliberal governments are deferring this role to the choice-making parent, school community and consumer.[3] At the same time, the liberal political thinking that justifies this move — in the name of both market freedoms and personal liberties — has had to come to terms with questions of rights and responsibilities that are not just posed in terms of individual liberties, but in terms of the claims of groups and communities, identified by faith, language group, race, region and ethnicity. As we have seen, these are international issues, but they entail delicate negotiation on the part of national governments that seek to settle civil discord and promote a healthy civil society and associational life, supported by a secure and prosperous state and an educated population. We turn first to the Canadian case.

The Canadian mosaic

Canadian debates on civic education are embedded in complex arguments about multiculturalism and cultural rights. Like Australia, this former colony is coming to terms with a history of settlement, conquest, indigenous dispossession, immigration and official multiculturalism.[4] The latter has generated the image of the Canadian "cultural mosaic", to contrast with American assimilation; it signals the idea that all the assembled cultures, languages and histories are prized and allowed to shine. However, the image has a scratchy reverse face. Domestic tensions include the secessionist battles of the Québécois, the long process of redressing the treatment of First Nations peoples, popular pressure to reduce immigration and racial prejudice towards Asian residents and other cultural minorities.[5]

In this context, Canadian governments have sought to develop cultural policies designed both to highlight the national cultural mix and to secure a confident national culture.[6] They have done so, in part, as a policy of trade protection, in efforts to avoid becoming assimilated to the popular culture of the United States; this includes efforts to restrict the importation of American popular cultural products and sustain national publishing, film and media production.[7] But the debates are also internal. One of the major controversies has concerned the issue of language policies.[8] These are designed to protect cultural minorities based on language groups, by ensuring for instance that schools are inclusive of both Anglophone and Francophone communities. The rationale for this is equal respect and the promotion of self-esteem for members of cultures; these are regarded as recognitions of "group rights" possessed by members of a culture, including the right to have their cultural identity sustained. The liberal polity, it is argued, must recognise that a precondition for individual self-fulfillment is citizens' entitlement to the cultural resources that are a "source of the self".[9] Citizens have a human "right to culture", and states must therefore give full recognition to all the culturally diverse forms of humanity, especially where the cultural survival of minority language groups is in danger.[10] Recognition of cultural right requires nation states to provide the resources that all citizens need in order to protect and express their cultural identities and heritages. This means, in Canada, bilingual and multilingual classrooms. The policy problem is to define the extent of governments' responsibility to provide these resources.[11]

Yvonne Hebert, an educationist closely involved in the formulation of new curriculum guidelines on civics, draws on such rationales when advocating that citizenship education should be centrally concerned with "multiple identities and ways of belonging". Policy on citizenship education, she argues, must begin from the assumption that Canada is not only a polyethnic state, but also a multinational one, containing a number of indigenous peoples who claim sovereignty and self-determination; it should recognise the longstanding existence of common historical and social bonds, such as language, tribal custom and law, which predate colonization or annexation. This should be supplemented by respect for the cultural identity of the "many ethnic, cultural and racial groups [who] entered the country after it was founded, intending to make it their home". People's sense of cultural belonging, for Hebert, cannot be understood in terms of a single link between each individual and the nation state; it comes from a more complex and collective process of identifying and being identified by others. Civic education is primarily about learning to recognise, respect and accept "otherness", while reflecting on one's own sense of belonging.[12]

This approach, with its emphasis on multiple roles and allegiance, seeks to negotiate some thorny issues associated with cultural rights, identity and citizenship, not the least of them being the question of whether such policies should make a distinction between indigenous cultural rights and claims to self-determination and those rights claims made by immigrant cultural minorities. Are both kinds of group entitled to equivalent claims to public resources and to autonomy and self-determination? Furthermore, how is the cultural group that holds these cultural rights to be defined? If a cultural group is defined by individuals' sense that they belong to it, how can the process of recognition accommodate the fact that many individuals hold a number of cultural allegiances? They may identify with the cultural grouping only partly, or only in some aspects of their lives; they may find some of the values of the group intrusive or coercive. For instance, young women raised within close-knit cultural communities may have limited choice about the extent to which they live by the customs and values of the cultural group. In such instances, it may be intrusive to individual rights if school systems were to lock them into a group-based cultural identity and treat them accordingly.[13]

Should the state protect the rights of the individual against the right of the group? Governments are charged with a duty to protect cultural difference and identity, but they are also expected to settle ethnic and cultural strife. For some, the two goals need not conflict, since equal cultural recognition will promote tolerant coexistence; others hold that social settlement is best promoted by using schools to build a common national culture and identity. Government, has a legitimate interest in settling ethnic and cultural strife and in building citizens' capacity for tolerance and co-existence; it also has a responsibility to equip each child with civic skills and competence, and on this basis, is justified in treating children differently, as part of a general commitment to equality.[14] This still leaves the question of whether this common civic formation, pursued through the schools, should involve an insistence that all children, whatever their familial or community background, should be equipped alike with the skills of critical reason, even if this leads them to question the authority of their cultural norms and orthodoxies, or distance themselves, for some purposes, from the cultural traditions in which they have been raised.[15] This debate remains unresolved, at least at the level of education philosophies and cultural political positions. However, the clarity with which the Canada's debates on citizenship identify the issue can help to cast some light on parallel debates happening past its national borders with the United States.

Civics in the American melting pot

During the 1980s and 1990s, American cultural commentators proclaimed that the country was in the grip of "culture wars"; battles in the liberal academy, in the schools, in the arts and public cultural organisations over the perceived decline of cultural, educational and moral standards and the corruption of the American civic character by progressivism, cultural radicalism and relativism.[16] Writers took educators to task for failing to give students "cultural literacy", or familiarity with the basic facts and cultural references that a minimally educated person should know.[17] Social studies, it was argued, was empty of content. Students were encouraged to discuss social issues and to develop fervent opinions, but they were not being given the resources to understand the issues. They had little understanding of history, philosophy or literature; they had been denied a common cultural and civic heritage.[18] Social studies, in its socially critical mode, had done little more than promote relativism; the sense that there were no absolute truths or values, and that all ideas are open to question, including those taken to be the founding values of the American republic.[19] A voluminous American literature on the theme of "why schools are failing" proclaimed the failure of the American "common school", a lost tradition of assimilation within a common civic tradition linked by passionate commitments to liberal ideals of individual freedom balanced by responsibility. Civic education had to arrest this decline, it was argued, rebuilding personal commitments to common values and reshaping the American character.[20]

Coming into this still-continuing debate from Australia, bringing with us our own confusions about how American educational ideas and social studies techniques affected Australian civic schooling, it is hard to see why this is a "culture war". We might share the anxiety about young people's cynicism, apathy and political indifference, about their consumerism and computer-focused distraction from civic exchange. But Australian commentators, like their British and Canadian equivalents, tend to be more concerned about the elements of moral compulsion entailed in communitarian "virtue politics", especially when it is made compulsory in the school system.

The striking feature of the American debates is that even those commentators who advocate radical reform to American democratic life, in the promotion of civil society and active citizenship, recommend highly interventionist options. These range from the revival of compulsory national service to making each teenager do community service as part of their schooling. Such proposals are not far removed from the recommendations of socially conservative Christian activist groups.[21] This places them in close proximity, to activist Christian groups aligned with the political right. The "character education" movement, for instance, is a cluster of non-profit associations dedicated to conservative values. Educational progressivism, they argue, has led schools to focus on self-expression and "emotional therapy", rather than on its proper concern with character and ethics. They object to constitutional bans on the direct teaching of religion in American schools; these prohibitions, they argue, have inhibited teachers committed to treating moral issues in the classroom. Americans, they assert, do share common values, whatever the relativists and teaching profession might say, and public opinion is on the side of a return to character education in the civic virtues. Educators must "engage the heads, hearts and hands of their students so that students may come to *know* the good, love the good and do the good".[22]

This theme has been taken up, in different ways, by a network of civics institutes, think tanks and research agencies, dedicated to the dissemination of civic values, their Web pages stress the importance of free and private association between the civic-minded, as a remedy for government's inability to sustain moral standards. Some of these agencies are voluntary and community-based, linked to political and to church groups. Others are funded by a combination of corporate funding, entrepreneurial activity and government commissions. It may be the case that there is strong public support for such concerns. Certainly, there are many popular versions of the teacher as moral hero, who inspires disadvantaged individuals and communities, stymied by apathy and alienation, to strive for academic excellence and to build character, giving each individual freedom of choice. We might think of recent films such as *Music of the Heart* (1999), *Stand and Deliver* (1998) or *Dangerous Minds* (1995), where the teacher battles ·with apathetic students and belligerent, racially divided communities. He or she wins out by championing character and personal choice; in the end, these values serve to stitch divided communities together through self-respect and moral example, breaking the hold of the ghetto.

The venerable American educator R. Freeman Butts, heralding the release of the National Standards on Civics, remarked on this shift in American public opinion. He commented that "re-energising a sense of civic virtue and obligation" is "the single most important item on the agenda of American education". But it is a new agenda item: "There was a time, not so long ago, when the phrase civic virtue would have been laughed out of the classroom or off the campus."[23] The reforming fervor seems odd, given that Australians and Europeans tend to associate American schooling with one of the most assertive programs of patriotic sentiment, custom and ceremony. Americans themselves lay claim to a continuous civic republican tradition, welcoming a nation of immigrants into a common civic heritage of ideals enshrined in the Constitution and the deliberations of the Founders. The nation is conceived as "created by ideas" and as founded in an historical "experiment in ideas about government" inspired by civic republican writers, from Rousseau, De Tocqueville and J.S. Mill to John Dewey.[24]

Still, for all the confidence with which this tradition is asserted, civics experts represent themselves as fighting for a place in American schooling. Over the last few decades, debate on the cultural politics of schooling has highlighted the irrelevance of "national values" and liberal doctrine to the politics of race, class and gender experience. Education was not about freedom or equality, it was argued; it served to reproduce structural social inequality, while serving to persuade people to accept the cultural hegemony of the powerful.[25] Marxian, feminist and postcolonial theorists have introduced into the academy the model of schools as sites of cultural power, which promote liberal myths of equality of opportunity, while actually disempowering. Progressive teachers, alerted to these patterns, have sought ways to empower learners, working with cultural resistance to build agency and encouraging new cultural negotiations of identity and difference.

The "culture wars" is in part a reaction to these radical educational initiatives. Along with publicly funded arts programs and cultural institutions that have explored "resistant" and avant-garde experiments in culture, the American college curriculum has been lampooned for its "political correctness". Its expansion is seen as a failure of political will, helpless in the face of American liberal pluralism and humanism. The social virtues, it is said, must be rebuilt through the schools. There is a strong community base for a return to Christian schooling, including fundamentalist campaigns, in some states, to introduce legislation that might allow the direct teaching of Christian scripture, despite Constitutional prohibitions; currently, these campaigns are concentrated on legislative efforts to mandate the display of the Ten Commandments in all schools. Frustrated in their efforts to reform state schooling, however, many parents are turning to private schooling or home schooling as an alternative, often in a spirit of resentment against state interference and the provisions of liberal secular humanism.[26]

Letting communities and parents educate their own children could be seen as a form of organized cultural pluralism, with the state avoiding battles over the content of public education, permitting many ways of life. Parents can and have made the case that their children should be inducted into their own customs and beliefs — or indeed that they should be exempt from the legal compulsion to send their children to state schools in which they will be reared in values that are anathema to the community from which they come.[27] On the other hand, if parents and communities are given too much power in deciding the content of schooling and civic formation, how can the state education system be sure that they will not teach racism or militant cultural sectarianism, where there is no political pressure to do otherwise? Liberal theorists argue, in response to extreme communitarianism, that the social rights of the child must be preferred to the cultural rights of parents. The state education system has a duty to prepare citizens, and it should introduce them to universal principles such as critical reason and autonomy. If states abdicate this authority to parents, then they lose their most effective means to ensure that citizens learn mutual respect for one another.[28]

The broad pattern in the United States, then, is of a state education system struggling to find its way between sectarian associations, cut across by identification with religious faith, race, ethnicity and culture. From one point of view, this need not be a problem, given that part of the much-prized American civic republican legacy is freedom from state-imposed conformity, in the private and associational realms of civil society. Civil society has been supposed to be a mass of independent organizations and associations; the more they flourish outside the scope of state concern, the healthier the society will be. Tocqueville is conventionally cited as the authority on this; for him, the striking feature of the early American republic was that its flourishing civic associations and ethos of liberty provided a robust defence against the reach of the state. Nevertheless, his comments were made in the context of a warning against the excesses of associationalism; his observations contrasted the relatively cohesive American republic with the violent political sectarianism of France. Although Tocqueville's name has been used to encourage civic associational resistance to the state, he did not assume that an energetic associational life was enough, in itself, to preserve civil peace and maintain the rule of law. This, at least, is the argument of those who urge the need to retain public policies that foster cohesion, as a counter-balance to belligerent moral enthusiasms and secessionist tendencies.[29]

The Civitas experiment

We can get a very different sense of the capacities of civic associations in a quick excursion to perhaps the most successful and well-connected one in America. The Center for Civic Education, is a private research centre, curriculum development think tank and philanthropic agent sponsored by the US Department of Education, the Carnegie Foundation and the Disney Corporation, amongst others.[30] The Center has had extensive influence on both international and national debates on citizenship and civic education, running international conferences and workshops in Eastern Europe and Africa and within the States. It also produces curriculum models and resources, including the 1991 *Civitas* textbook, which developed models incorporated into the 1994 National Standards in Civics and Citizenship.[31] The Civitas model has had considerable international influence, in part through its deployment in Web-based resources and curriculum models.[32] Although the Center for Civic Education has focused its efforts on the new democracies, especially in Eastern Europe, its philanthropic globalism has also had some impact in Australia; *Whereas the People* cites it as an instance of a national framework of civic education that combines solid intellectual materials, including historical perspectives, with a practical focus on civic knowledge, values and skills. In many ways, its aims are not far removed from the Australian government's emphasis on getting the balance right between applied contemporary problems while drawing on history and philosophy.

Civitas is a remarkable document, not least for its efforts to be pluralistic and ecumenical.[33] In assembling extracts designed to represent the various traditions of American thought on democracy, liberalism, rights and responsibilities, it aims to give space to a variety of philosophical and political positions, from liberal theorists who see citizenship as limited to responsible voting, to communitarian advocates of grassroots participatory democracy as a generator of social change. The materials in the anthology range from examples of Supreme Court rulings to civil disobedience tracts, and the examples used include formal party politics, local government issues, neighborhood activities and environmental, feminist, anti-racist and human rights campaigns. Each example is discussed in philosophical terms and placed in historical context, but each is also used as an instance of civic activity and choice. There is a strong emphasis on building civic commitments and acting on them responsibly. This involves both civic virtue and "civic literacy", something best learned though practical democratic engagement, whether it be writing a letter to a politician, standing for the student representative council, circulating a petition, mounting a referendum or organising a large-scale campaign of civil disobedience.

The *Civitas* version of pluralism involves direct warnings, to educators, against using civic education for political indoctrination or for moral crusades. Civics, the writers stress, should not be "character education"; nor should it be an exercise in conformity. There are, they assert, common themes and problems in American democracy, and there is a "core of democratic values", but political debate should be treated as a process of vigorous discussion, in which citizens will find themselves negotiating conflicting political, moral, cultural, religious, racial and ethnic perspectives. Participation in debate is important, but schools must not indoctrinate students into participating. Instead, they must develop competence, a democratic orientation and the skills of "political self-government". Competent citizens are able to meet their obligations: to study issues; to vote and influence government policy; to work to improve the quality of government functioning; to limit governments to their constitutional authority; and to help their family, neighborhood, and community through voluntary service.

This is a normative position, based on the assertion of core moral and political principles, derived from the American tradition of liberal democracy. It owes much to a liberal philosophy: the ideal citizen is defined as one who is able to use his or her critical reason to take an ethical or political stance on public issues. She is equipped to understand the difference between approaching an issue in terms of the public good, as civic republicans tend to do, or with a liberal emphasis on individual rights and self-determination. She is prepared to defend the citizen's right to expect that political leaders will refrain from lying, but she is aware that sometimes the interests and security of the state prevent governments from making premature admissions and disclosures. She is attentive to different arguments, understanding the case for putting the public good above individual self-interest or freedoms in some cases (war, depression), and the need, in others, to balance between the rights of the individual and the claims of government or aggressive minorities. Her reasoned commitment to civic virtue is freely given, but shaped by the formative environments of school, home, faith and community.

Clearly, given the context described above, no one framework, however pluralist, will be uncontentious. The culture wars continue. Some critics see Civitas as minimalist and "mainstream", as an orthodox liberal celebration of individual civil and political rights that ignores structural inequalities. For all the "rights talk" in the document, it is argued, it has a weak idea of civic participation, one that ignores the reasons why people do not participate in the political system, that does not explore political and economic barriers to citizenship and that fails to empower future citizens to be critical of the system.[34] To others, Civitas seems overly liberal. Sandra Stotsky, for instance, praises it for its academic content standards, seeing them as an advance on cultural relativism. However, she regrets that it did not go further and assert an authoritative core of national values, founded in a common national language and culture.[35] Part of what is at stake in this debate, which still continues as the National Standards are implemented and revised, is the central issues with which we have been concerned: the role of government, of experts and of public funding in setting a common foundation for citizenship.

Liberal dilemmas

Amy Gutmann, perhaps the best known American liberal thinker on education, puts a strong case for governmental intervention in schooling, arguing against the continuing trend to defer all educational decision-making to local communities and parents as consumers. Civic formation, she argues, is too important to be left to associations and private concerns. Public schools are the primary institutions by which a democratic society educates future citizens, preparing them to share in responsible self-government. Teaching the elements of responsible self-government, which include mutual respect for basic liberty, opportunity and a commitment to deliberate about politically relevant issues, is a major reason for mandating and publicly subsidizing schooling for all children.

In response to those who urge the right of parents who seek a faith-based schooling for their children, Gutmann reminds her readers that the American constitution stipulates the neutrality of the state school system, prohibiting the teaching of religious doctrine so as to protect liberal freedoms, including freedom of conscience and privacy rights. Public schools have a responsibility to teach and practice religious toleration, but they are also justified in excluding some religious practices, where they conflict with liberal democratic principles. On the other hand, she argues, there are respects in which the school system is not neutral, to the extent that it sets up values. Citizens, she argues "should support an educational system only if it is not neutral between those ways of life that respect basic liberty, opportunity and deliberation, and those that do not. A liberal democracy should take its own side in arguments about teaching the skills and virtues that are constitutive of its own flourishing".[36] The guiding principles of democratic education are universal; they can be recognised as reasonable.

Gutmann does concede that there are circumstances in which democratic principles compete with one another, creating ethical and political dilemmas; she cites the case referred to in our previous chapter, where French schools objected to young Muslim women's insistence on wearing the traditional chador or scarf. In such a case, it might seem ethically or politically difficult to weight the relative claims of principles of (religious and cultural) freedom and of (gender) equality. Gutmann argues, however, that the two principles can be reconciled through critical reason; we can learn to tolerate religious difference, without acquiescing in gender segregation. The democratic solution to such cultural clashes, she argues, is to make them the focus of critical discussion for the students themselves, making the classroom a public forum, a place to learn and display informed moral choice and "public reasonableness". It is the school's primary duty to promote critical autonomy, she argues, to the extent of encouraging moral controversy; the teacher's duty is to give each child the opportunity to become a reasoning moral being, independent of the influence of parents, community or culture. Through democratic education, "children as future citizens should be enabled to choose between different cultures or versions of the good life". Multicultural heritage should be treated as a common resource; if students disagree with one another on the basis of cultural (and presumably religious) differences, they should be required to do so while behaving in a tolerant manner. Teachers, in leading the class and facilitating discussion, should model ways of balancing common civic values against "uncommon cultural appreciations". Universal principles need not be put aside out of respect for cultural particularism; all students can find common ground in respect for a robust set of human rights principles, such as those defined in United Nations declarations, which can be presented as internationally recognised values.

Nevertheless, Gutmann adds, there is no need to overstate the scope of universalist international consensus on these principles. Even if we could assert that all adults were committed to the same principles of liberty and justice, there would still be a need to educate children as future citizens of "separate sovereign societies". Keeping an emphasis, in civic education, on distinct national traditions makes moral sense, because "each sovereign society is a major political actor in bringing about better or worse conditions for its own citizens as well as other people significantly affected by its policies." The best way to achieve justice, on a global scale, is not to abolish patriotism, trying to make "citizens of the world", but to rear children to be "free and equal citizens of separate democratic societies". There is no world polity; if there were, it would be a tyranny. Civic life can be engendered on a local scale, without neglecting world politics; when children are introduced to international rights doctrines, they can understand them best if taught to "respect those closest to them".

Here, Gutmann's position is close to Eamonn Callan's and draws on a common legacy of liberal neo-Kantian thought.[37] Callan, it will be recalled, put a vigorous argument against the suggestion that schools should concentrate on minimal civic formation, since few individuals are able or willing to understand liberal democratic principles in a philosophical mode — through critical reflection alone. While admitting that critical reason is morally and intellectually demanding, Callan puts the onus back on the teacher.

For him, as for Gutmann, mindless patriotic loyalty is not good enough, and nor should teachers be content to let students claim that, for cultural reasons, they are disenchanted with democracy. Children can be persuaded to commit themselves to civic life, but the onus is on the teacher. Effective teaching should use "democratic play" (stories, history, literature, drama and students' reflections on their own experience) to build critical reason. Through emotion, modified by reason, all children can be given the "generous susceptibility to ... public emotions" that will bind them to democratic life.

Coming back to that argument at this point, the liberal philosophical approach to civic formation, through play and critical reason, might now look uncomfortably paternalistic. It might even look morally coercive — after all, should children really be required to make cultural controversies into a topic of public debate, however divisive or mortifying these might be? Must they own up to their own experience, even if all their cultural experience tells them not to confess their cultural discomfort in front of others? It might be said, of course, that we have already made the case that modern teaching cannot really dispense with these techniques of self-expression, discussion and the question-and-answer session; in the English-speaking world, they are the main ways we know to persuade individuals to reflect on their own conduct and reform themselves, and they are the staple of civic formation and moral education, at least in the school if not beyond. What the debate may have lost sight of, though, is that these are techniques. Some of course do hold that, if there were no obstacles, then all human beings would become the reasoning, critical and morally autonomous individuals that Western liberal philosophy has imagined into being and that Western moral education has fostered. From our historical and comparative perspective, though, this is surely beginning to look more unlikely. We have inherited and improvised some effective ways to make populations into citizens, bringing together a motley set of techniques that includes play, self-expression, discussion and critical reflection alongside memorisation, drill, tests and marching. We have come to prefer the former to the latter as a way of giving children civic habits. But we should not despise either the educational past or the possibilities that there are other ways of life.

There is of course a long-standing tradition of moral instruction in the school. But this has depended on maintaining a certain degree of distance from personal values and indeed from political ideologies. Although teachers have certainly been charged with the responsibility for modeling moral and ethical norms, and for introducing discussion of ethical or political issues within the classroom, they have done so in an indirect mode, as facilitators of discussions, as the observers of conduct or as non-directive guides to literary, historical or occasionally philosophical texts. In ethical formation, it is this capacity to teach without teaching which has made the teacher such a powerful and effective medium for moral formation.[38]

What we have, in the architecture and regimes of the modern Western classroom, is a working assemblage of techniques, which we can use in combination to persuade children to examine their own conduct, habits and assumptions and make some choices, within a normative framework. Who sets the norms? As we have seen, government in part, and partly for its own reasons, which are concerned with social settlement and the need to build the civic capacities on which civil peace depends, including the capacity to distinguish between private moral passions and conduct appropriate to a public sphere. These norms are of course vigorously debated in the various political forums that make up democratic cultures. The onus is still on teachers to negotiate their way through these political questions, but there is also an onus on government (through state education departments or school communities) to ensure that they have the means and support to do so.

Civics lessons for Australia

What can we bring back, from our long historical and comparative detours, to current Australian debates on citizenship and civic education? We can put some perspective on three main points of objection to the model of civics associated with *Discovering Democracy*. The first is that it aims to drill young Australians in information that is of little interest or relevance to them. Experts are too academic in their take on politics; they fail to see that "most Australians already possess a realistic understanding of the political process and their part in it". Second, they assume that greater knowledge about democracy will lead to greater involvement and participation, whereas "the causal chain works the other way".[39] Third, the program is seen as socially conservative, imposing social norms on a diverse population in the name of core values. It is "national and particularistic rather then universal and transnational".[40]

The first criticism carries the weighty charge of academic elitism, one that has become ever more sensitive in recent Australian political debate. Perhaps surveys that show young people to have low levels of political confidence are evidence of broader shift, a popular wave of distrust, sweeping politicians from the high ground of public opinion.[41] Such findings on Australian political attitudes were widely cited in the initial response to the revival of Australian civics, not surprisingly given the amount of press coverage of the "civic deficit" in young people. Those who feared that reviving Australian civic education actually meant importing American-style nationalism asked whether the results of such surveys of political knowledge and attitudes really meant very much. After all, American youth had been drilled in political and constitutional details for decades — did that mean they were good citizens?

Is it a problem if Australians are cynical about politicians, indifferent to constitutional debate and apathetic about national history? In a liberal democracy, people are free to be uninterested in politics. They are free to stay home from political meetings, or to express their contempt for politics and government, as long as they remain law-abiding. Those who distrust politicians may not just be mindlessly cynical; they may have a good understanding of politics and its limits. Even though the public expects politicians to be open, honest and driven by personal conscience, they also know that party-political life is imperfect and has its own particular pressures. Professional politics involves secrets and lies: labyrinthine decision-making, closed Cabinet discussions, caucusing and number crunching. It is partisan, factional and full of distrust. Skilful politicians take tactical advantage of their opponents' lapses. They exchange invective and accusations, calling on the rhetoric of moral denunciation and practicing the arts of hypocrisy, evasion and obfuscation. [42]

Furthermore, liberal democratic political institutions, both in Australia and elsewhere, are based on mechanisms of distrust.

Hence the development of legal and constitutional frameworks, of parliamentary procedures and administrative arrangements, which are designed to monitor parliamentary processes and politicians' conduct and to safeguard against rule by corrupt officials, by factions, or by interest groups.[43] In Australia, there are many such mechanisms of review and formal accountability, which monitor public spending and place pressure on politicians' honesty and on the transparency of government procedure. Apart from the constant monitoring of the press, including the broadcasting of Question Time, citizens have access to internal information, under the provisions of the Freedom of Information Act. However, these mechanisms are less visible than the antagonisms of parliamentary debate. They certainly do not seem to be well enough known to enable people to make a clear distinction between the workings of party politics and those of representative democracy and liberal democratic governance more generally. The problem, apparently, is not just that Australians are cynical about politicians and politics, but they also know little about political and electoral arrangements, constitutional provisions and law. This suspicion makes it difficult for policy makers and parliamentarians to have sufficient faith in the electorate to sustain sophisticated public arguments about complex matters of public policy, legal judgement and constitutional reform.

Political scientists have pointed out that it is quite unclear how much citizens really need to know by way of "facts" about political arrangements. It is generally assumed that information on government decision-making needs to be open and transparent, up to a point, since well-informed citizenries are less dangerous; less likely to be swayed by rabble-rousers, political extremists and special interest groups. But it is also often assumed that political, administrative and legal processes are beyond the ken of most citizens. This may not matter, political experts speculate, as long as democratic processes are not impeded by ignorance:

> At a mechanical level, it is worrying if there are different methods of voting for the House of Representatives and the Senate and when you wish to bring this to electors' attention a high proportion are unfamiliar with those names and cannot distinguish between the two chambers. Or if you rely on instructions as to how to vote printed on the ballot paper, and half the electorate says they had never noticed them there. Beyond that is a second-level problem. Perhaps electors know how to mark a

ballot paper correctly, that is to produce a valid vote, and are quite confident about their ability to do so. But they have no idea how that marking of preferences is translated into election outcomes, how the winner or winners will be actually selected by those votes. Perhaps they effectively abdicate any concern with such matters and merely copy a how-to-vote card provided by their preferred party. Are they still good citizens?[44]

The problem here is to distinguish between a chapter and verse drilling in political and constitutional documents, and an informed understanding of how Australia's political and legal systems work in practice. Even if students could be persuaded to learn all about political and electoral procedure and constitutional arrangements, does this really help them to come to understand how government and politics work? As Hal Colebatch points out, there may be little point in insisting on all students knowing the arcane complexities of the Australian Constitution, for instance, since the document alone is an unreliable source for information on Australian political arrangements; for instance, it makes no mention of the office of the Prime Minister. The Constitution has been modified by subsequent common law decisions and legislation. But even as he criticises crude efforts to assess current levels of political understanding, Colebatch raises the stakes; what we need is an informed but practical understanding of political and legal arrangements in Australia, of the models from which they derive, of the ways in which these have been adapted, and of the means by which they are being changed and challenged, not least by international law, treaties and agreements. Do citizens understand the system of liberal democratic checks and balances designed to monitor abuses of privilege? Are they familiar with the ideal — if not the practice — of a politically neutral bureaucracy, composed of unelected officials whose duties include carrying out the will of elected representatives of the people? Do they understand the arguments for and against the proposition that judicial bodies such as the High Court must be independent of parliamentary decision-making?[45]

Suzanne Mellor argues that students have such negative and apathetic attitudes to political participation that there is little prospect that formal lessons about politics and government, will make them more inclined to participate in the political process. Mellor conducted a study of the political attitudes of Victorian secondary students, which focussed on the extent to which attitudes to "power, politics and participation and decision-making" are affected by classroom and school climate.[46] Her study was modelled on Carole Hahn's ten-year study of political attitudes of later secondary school students in the US, England, Denmark, Germany and the Netherlands.[47] Compared with the international sample, Victorian students reported markedly low levels of political interest. These students are already "distanced from society", possibly by choice, and "it will be no easy task to get them back". The only real prospect lies in building students' own involvement in the decision-making civic environment of the classroom.[48] Mellor's interpretation of the results parallels Hahn's conclusion that, where students are given the experience of experience of open, participatory and negotiational classrooms, they develop more positive attitudes to politics and are more likely to express willingness to take political action on a matter of importance to them. It is this that will alert young people to their own responsibilities to act on powerfully held beliefs, while helping them to understand, through experience, that the opinions of the most vocal do not always dominate the outcomes of decision-making processes. Others support this focus on local issues, on experience and on the transformative potential of a fully participatory ethos in the school. But they also argue that citizenship education must build on students' strong moral interest in international issues, such as human rights and environmental protection.[49] Young Australians are now more cosmopolitan than an older generation can imagine, more connected to a global community of instant communication and digestible information and more willing to adopt attitudes unlimited by nationalism, xenophobia and cultural intolerance.

Advocates of civic education have a considered response. Stuart Macintyre, for instance, takes issue with those who argue that social education is primarily about identity, ethical issues and global values, while agreeing that there is a need for change. For Macintyre, the real problem is the current "mismatch" between young people's "ethical capacity", built through social education, and their "civic incapacity". Young people in Australia, he reflects, tend to have very strong ethical commitments (to human rights, to care for the natural environment), based in values like justice and fairness. They are comfortable with ethnic and cultural social difference and sensitive to Australia's international context and obligations; they are likely to accept the moral face of the Mabo decision, for instance. Yet, he adds, "if I were to ask them what tribunal made the Mabo decision and its present import, or the basis on which the Commonwealth was able to make decisions about logging some native forests and protecting others, they would find it hard to answer". Although it may be enough, for the business of government, for these young people to choose the parliamentary representatives "from whose work they feel so alienated", he maintains that this alienation is a "crippling deficiency", perpetuating the low regard in which politics is held in this country.[50]

The civic deficit

Questioning popular understandings of political arguments seems to cast doubt on ordinary citizens' political capacity. This is hardly a popular position at a time when the idea of the self-governing community has so much currency, and when there is so much suspicion of elite opinion. But ever since the emergence of modern democratic systems, political philosophers have dwelt on the fragility of liberal political systems, based as they are on the population's ability to bear their rights and exercise their liberties. Since their emergence, liberal democracies have seen themselves as vulnerable to corrupt governments and to dominance by interest groups and factions, whether political, social or economic.[51] The fear was that population was liable to be swayed by mob rule and strong majoritarian forces, threatening the liberty of minority groups and of individuals. For liberal political philosophers, the aim was to establish political, legal and constitutional procedures that were based on rules or guiding principles that were free from bias, that protected the liberties of the individual from majoritarian group interests and that drew on deliberation in various forums — political parties, pressure groups and advocacy groups amongst them.[52] Australian discussions, at the time of Federation, established equivalent limits and safeguards, as we shall see in the next chapter. These provisions were not designed to change lightly with trends in public opinion; the constitution, in particular, is heavily protected from amendment. Liberal political thought assumed that these procedures and principles should be based on reasoning that could appeal to all reasonable people, but it was not assumed that all citizens would be able to understand them. This is a more modern expectation, one that is the product of expanded education.

This is part of what is at stake in contemporary debates on parliamentary, legal and constitutional reform. Given that these institutions operate according to rationales that now seem arcane and outdated to many, can they be brought into accord with changing community expectations? We now tend to presume that political governance, bureaucracies and legal systems ought to correspond to the democratic ideal of popular sovereignty, or rule according to the will of the people. The present disenchantment with the "major political parties" which Pauline Hanson exploits, even as she acknowledges that she will never be in a position to govern is often expressed as a failure of the parties to listen or to represent the people's wishes. Similarly, the High Court is criticised both for being "out of touch" with popular sentiment or for encroaching upon the role of government. These views are uninformed by an understanding of the forms modern democracy has taken. As John Hirst's guide to Australian systems of law and government makes clear, there is an issue here about the extent to which governments have become responsible to parties, rather than parliament. Although the American federalists, concerned about factions, had the debate about separation of powers, Australia's constitution makers were more mindful of "sharing" power, as we'll see in Chapter 5. Nevertheless, the Australian system does require an independent judiciary. The present concern with public sector ethics and its attendant calls for codes of conduct tend to focus on the personal failings of elected officials. This deflects attention from the way our parliamentary system and public service delivers accountability through Senate committees and other routine mechanisms.

Without a knowledge of this history of debate — to recall John Hirst's comments, with which we began this book — it is very difficult to understand the complex political, legal and constitutional debates currently under way in Australia. The difficulty, in part, is that the cynicism and apathy discussed above are closely connected to ideal conceptions of democracy, which make it difficult to understand the imperfect assemblage of mechanisms and rationales that make up modern Australian systems of government. By extension, this makes it difficult for citizens to be effective advocates for reform; hence the persistent gap between "experts" and popular expectations of democratic politics.

These are some of the themes that we take up in the second part of this book. There, we move closer to the question of how we might think about democracy as educators working in a modern multiethnic Australian environment, as we negotiate political, economic and cultural change both within this country and around it. We begin by returning to the exploration of some of the distinctive features of Australian democratic settlements and arrangements, offering some worked examples of how historical understanding can help to make our understanding of current Australian political issues more pluralistic, better able to accommodate conflict and more prepared to tolerate imperfection. We put this to work in a revised assessment of current trends in Australian political life and public debate, drawing out the challenges facing those who take up roles as advocates, officials or informed citizens. Finally, we offer some suggestions, for educators and for concerned citizens in general, about ways in which we might aim for a more articulate democratic culture in Australia and for a more articulated conception of the elements that make up modern democratic life and citizenship.

Chapter 5

A Distinctive Democracy

A resilient Constitution

"Australia votes to keep Queen" proclaimed a billboard in a Tokyo train, following the 1999 referendum on the republic. In Australia, the outcome is interpreted differently. The move to a republic has merely been deferred; even the monarchist Prime Minister concedes this. And the Queen herself seems unperturbed by the idea that the Royal Family lives in Australia on borrowed time. Analysis of the referendum has focussed on the rifts it is seen to reveal, between urban elites and marginalised battlers, and within the republican movement itself. "Politics", in the sense of interest groups disputing over tactics and strategies, overwhelmed "public reasonableness" in the discussion of what the republic might be. Although opinion polls indicated support for the change, a sense of the electorate's Constitutional conservatism drove discussion of the "Yes" case. The "No" campaign did not invoke sentimental attachments to the Queen, instead it exploited public feeling against elites. The electoral success of One Nation has been attributed to this sentiment, and it seems to have been a winner for the "No" case. Public mistrust of politicians was exploited even by politicians: Peter Reith, a declared republican, urged a "No" vote.

Public confidence in political processes is critical in a democratic society. This chapter focusses on constitutional arrangements in Australia and shows how these arrangements balance national and popular sovereignty. It revisits the public debate about the framing of the Constitution in the nineteenth century, and discusses the ways it has been adapted to accommodate Australia's increasing independence. Its concern is to show how changes to the Constitution have provided a focus for discussion of the "common good", for debate and dissent.

The requirements for altering the provisions of the Constitution by referendum are stringent, and change has proved difficult to achieve. The Constitution sets out the powers of the commonwealth government, most of which are shared with the states. Some changes in these power-sharing arrangements can be achieved through legal interpretation and political concessions, but forty-two proposals for change have been submitted to referenda. Only eight have been successful. In the case of the 1999 referendum, complex questions of sovereignty were at issue. Minimalist republicans insisted the replacement of the Queen with an Australian Head of State was a "symbolic" change; "real" republicans exploited a populist view of direct democracy and the distrust of temporary majorities inherent in democratic systems. Support for a republic produced a vote against the minimalist model. Informed discussion of sovereignty and of the separation of powers disappeared in appeals to sentiment from the "No" case. The "Yes" case, however, may have underestimated the importance of sentiment. The change in legal terms may have been "minimal", but in other respects it was momentous. "Symbols" are powerful and emotional things.

The "No" case did not defend the monarchy, but neither did the "Yes" case offer a positive account of republicanism and federalism. The Australian Republican Movement's leaders were derided as "the café latte set". The organisation's "corporate" appearance left it open to criticism that it was elitist. This perception gave the "real" republicans' appeal to democratic principles some purchase, which was not countered by an informed account of modern republics. It could be argued that a media campaign in the context of a referendum vote is not the arena for such discussion. But it could also be that the ARM's support of the present arrangements indicates that the politicans and lawyers who led the movement were not well briefed on republican possibilities.[1]

It is interesting to look at the outcome in 1999 in the light of other referenda which involved democratic principles, rather than merely technical issues about "powers". In 1946 a wide range of social welfare responsibilities were transferred to the commonwealth, along with uniform tax-collecting powers.[2] Following the High Court's finding that the Communist Party Dissolution Act of 1950 was unconstitutional, the Menzies' government's proposals to add provisions which would allow the commonwealth to make laws about communism were defeated in 1951.[3] The 1967 referendum's two questions relating to indigenous citizenship were overwhelmingly affirmed. This extension of their rights was not a matter of the vote — Aboriginal people were eligible to vote in the referendum — but of the capacity of the commonwealth to make policy. As a result of the transfer of responsibility for Aboriginal affairs from the states to the commonwealth, Aboriginal people acquired the same "dual citizenship" as other Australians. Their exclusion from the census was also remedied.[4]

In 1988, a referendum to secure some minimalist changes was defeated, despite the fact that public opinion appeared to favour the propositions.[5] Four seemingly uncontentious propositions — regarding parliamentary terms, fair elections, the recognition of local government and the extension of rights to the states — nevertheless failed to attract majority support. This disparity might indicate an innate conservatism or a mistrust of public officials, but it might also be a sign that citizens differentiate between their personal opinions and their public duty, and might apply different standards to informed judgement. The deliberative poll conducted prior to the 1999 referendum suggests that expertise and transparency has a role in forming public opinion that advertising campaigns could take advantage of. This interpretation of public opinion is more optimistic about the workings of democracy, and suggests that the contemporary reliance on focus groups and opinion polling in policy development and political strategy is misguided.

The procedure for achieving constitutional change requires two things: that both houses of federal parliament pass legislation for the alteration and that a majority of all voters as well as a majority of states approve the change. This means that changes to the constitution rest with the people, not parliament. In the debates surrounding federation and the drafting of the constitution other methods were considered, and more extensive uses of referenda discussed. The hybrid nature of the arrangements adopted draw on the Westminster tradition, American federalism and the Swiss device of the referendum to achieve a system which balances minority and majority interests. Of all the parties to the federal compact, however, it is "the people" who are named first in the preamble. John Hirst asserts that this is a sign of public ownership of the Australian constitution, "that its people were and are directly involved in the making, accepting and amending of the constitution".[6] The federal movement comprised "representative men" rather than politicians. The Australasian Federal League, launched by Edmund Barton at a public meeting at the Sydney Town Hall in 1893 after the defeat of 1891, was "an organisation of citizens owning no class distinction or party influence", according to the *Sydney Morning Herald.* [7]

Although the record of failed referenda suggests that the constitution is resistant to change, this may be an indicator of resilience rather than rigidity. Constitutions produce and constrain power by defining its limits. The Constitution of the Commonwealth of Australia provides a framework for the enactment of legislation rather than policy prescriptions. Its references to God and to the Crown, its assumptions about race and constitutional monarchy, and its omission of any reference to the rights of the individual may not accord with contemporary values, but as a working document it has constrained temporary majorities and organised power sharing. The concerns of the framers — concerns shared by the earlier framers of the US Constitution — about restraining majorities and controlling factions, and with accountability of the executive — are not unfamiliar concerns now. Many of the supporters of the move to a republic wanted to preserve the essential features of the system as it stands. Their concern was that a directly elected president would have a claim to legitimacy which the current head of state does not. On the other hand, "real" republicans claimed that to agree to an appointed head of state was to cede too much power to politicians. Andrew Fraser argues that the minimalists wanted to preserve state sovereignty, rather than to extend popular sovereignty.[8]

Federation established formal relationships among the colonies where previously there had been none, and where each colony's primary relationship had been to the Crown.[9] A decision taken by the people of the colonies at a series of referenda, together with legislation enacted by the parliament at Westminster, established the self-governing Commonwealth of Australia. Independence, on the other hand, was an uneven development. Attachments to Britain were strong. The Crown is a palpable presence in the constitution, though mention of God was fiercely debated. "The people" of the new commonwealth were not called citizens: they were British subjects of a constitutional monarchy and remained so. The Nationality and Citizenship Act (1948) added the status of "Australian citizen" to the status of "British subject". When Western Australia, a latecomer to the "indissoluble" compact, wanted to secede in 1934, the imperial parliament declined to receive its petition, although it maintained that it did have the power to grant it.[10] The Statute of Westminster in 1931 conceded control over defence and foreign policy to the dominions of Canada, South Africa and the Irish Free State. Thereafter, the dominions were bound to Britain only by shared allegiance to the Crown. Although it had declined to call itself a dominion, Australia was more reluctant to relinquish the ties of empire and the mutual obligations entailed in defence. The Statute was not adopted by the Australian parliament until 1942.[11] The final vestiges of British imperial authority remained until the Australia Act of 1986 removed the provision for appeals to the Privy Council and affirmed Australia's status as "a sovereign, independent and federal nation".[12]

The work of the constitution, and of the proponents of federation, was to establish the terms of the agreement among the states and the commonwealth governments to share power. The basis of that agreement hinged on mutual interests in foreign policy, defence and trade. The process of reaching agreement embraced some other policy developments which have become central to Australian social history, notably arbitration and commonwealth responsibility for invalid and age pensions.[13] The division of powers was the most sensitive issue. The bicameral federal parliament adhered to the American model rather than to the unification represented by the single parliament at Westminster or to the Canadian model of confederation. The final document defined what were "federal" interests and specified the responsibilities of the new commonwealth government.

The extended campaign to achieve federation provides evidence of a similar concern to balance politicians' influence with popular will. Federation leagues together with the Australian Natives Association involved citizens in the movement. The Australasian Federation League limited the numbers of politicians on its Council, and excluded them from its executive.[14] Although the key figures in the movement, such as Parkes, Deakin, Griffith and Barton, were or had been politicians, the process involved the passage of legislation in the colonial parliaments to set up a constitutional convention. The delegates to the Convention were elected by eligible voters in each colony, a definition of the federal constituency which was codified in Section 41 of the constitution. At the time of the 1897 convention, this definition allowed women to vote in South Australia, and Aboriginal men in all the colonies except Queensland and Western Australia. Manhood suffrage had included Aboriginal people when the colonies became self-governing in 1850, but Queensland (in 1885) and Western Australia (in 1893) withdrew the right.[15] These voters elected "representative public men". The Convention debated and deliberated at arms length from the colonial governments.

The efforts to achieve responsible government in the 1850s have left behind evidence of the multiple sources of Australian political thinking.[16] In making representations to the British government, colonial leaders needed to make their arguments explicit. Many of the influential figures in these discussions were lawyers and journalists, and the newspapers of the day provided a forum for public deliberation. The adaptation of inherited tradition also extended to the law, and did not begin with the federal movement. As Bruce Kercher has pointed out, much Australian law is innovative and original, and does not derive simply or solely from English common law.[17] For example, the circumstances of the establishment of the first settlement meant that convicts enjoyed a "remarkable formal equality", being able to hold property, give evidence and to sue. The doctrine of attaint, which treated a convict as to all intents and purposes dead, did not apply until 1820, by which time it was difficult to roll back these advances. The Colonial Laws Validity Act (1865) provided that colonial governments could amend or repeal British laws which were not imposed explicitly on the colonies.

Michael Saward claims that "any political system claiming democratic legitimacy will also be distinctive — historically, culturally, and in the substantive values which it embodies or propounds beyond those internal to democracy".[18] The Australian traditions which were institutionalised through federation produced a form of economic or labour citizenship. In 1901, this citizenship excluded "aliens" but was soon extended to women. Marilyn Lake argues that the advocacy of women in post-suffrage campaigns was crucial to the establishment of a welfare state which supported "maternal citizenship".[19] The other aspect of post-federation citizenship was that it remained "empire citizenship" for so long. The extension of formal rights to migrants and indigenous people took most of the twentieth century to achieve. This widening net of citizenship will be discussed in Chapter 7.

Democratic traditions: citizenship and constitutionalism

"Citizenship, in any muscular form, was not a primary concern of our constitution-makers".[20] Consequently, Peter Beilharz argues, we can't look to the heritage of federation to help us think about the new forms citizenship might take. The Australian tradition of "labour citizenship", set in place at the end of the nineteenth century and consolidated into the 1950s, is too narrow. Beilharz would have us revive civic republicanism or "social liberalism" as a way of extending and strengthening citizenship. This definition of "muscular citizenship" implies support of positive liberty. Where liberal traditions prize negative liberty — freedom from interference and the right to pursue the good life — republican traditions go a little further, looking to secure protection against interference: "To be positively free...may require freedom to participate in the collective self-determination of your community...freedom from the internal obstacles of weakness, compulsion and ignorance as well as from the external obstacles presented by the interference of others; and even the achievement of a certain moral perfection".[21] If this tradition demands more of government, it also expects a lot from citizens.

It is often taken to be a flaw in the constitution that it does not explicitly underwrite some of the basic democratic freedoms. Section 116 prevents the commonwealth from making laws in respect of religion, though an argument against explicit reference to God was lost. Equal protection provisions were purposely omitted. The High Court has been called upon to determine the extent of constitutional protection of freedom of speech, often through its determinations in respect of defamation actions. A series of decisions in 1990s relating to political broadcasts established an implied right to freedom of political speech.

How could people who proudly considered themselves British subjects also think they were citizens? Nineteenth century reform movements which pressed for the extension of political rights were built on the exercise of civil freedoms of speech and association. British subjects had had civil rights from the time of the glorious revolution: they were protected from arbitrary arrest and imprisonment; they had a right to trial by judge and jury; and their property was protected from entry without a warrant.[22] At public meetings and in local associations, reformers organised to extend the franchise and reshape constituencies. We may believe that we have the advantage of rights which are more "formally perfect", but John Hirst claims that the citizens who joined the movement for federation or for votes for women had "in fuller measure than we…a sense of how open the political order was to change".[23] If the people who framed and voted on the constitution had a stronger civic consciousness and a stronger sense of their capacity to shape their polity than we do now, it is nevertheless generally agreed that civic republicanism was eclipsed by liberal traditions in late nineteenth century Australia. It could be that acceptance of this view depends on an ahistorical understanding of the traditions. In other times and places, notably seventeenth and eighteenth century Britain, the two were "perfectly compatible", as Stephen Holmes has shown.[24]

Holmes points out that "constitutionalism is the key concept for understanding the interdependence of liberalism and democracy".[25] The dominant strands of liberalism emphasise privacy and negative liberties; the separation of political and private spheres; limited government and the neutrality of the state, which allows the pursuit of various ways of life and of commerce and enterprise, without excessive intervention and regulation. The core liberal values of freedom, individualism and justice are supported by the creation of institutions which seek to constrain the concentration of power and to provide checks and balances against its abuse.

Constitutions both limit and construct power, providing a framework for decision making. "Liberal constitutions are crafted to help solve a whole range of political problems: tyranny, corruption, immobilism, unaccountability, instability, and the ignorance and stupidity of politicians".[26] Temporary majorities are constrained by constitutions. Distrust of the powerful is implicit in these arrangements; a point that puts claims about current cynicism about politicians in some perspective. Rather than seeing distrust as a measure of the ignorance or apathy of citizens, it might be better understood as integral to liberal systems. The framers of Australia's constitution were alert to the need to balance the interests of the smaller colonies against the more populous, particularly New South

Wales. The different electoral procedures for the House of Representatives and the Senate were designed to achieve this, as were the standards for achieving a successful outcome in referenda to change the constitution. This constitution emphasises mechanisms and structures to achieve separation of powers within the bicameral parliament and power-sharing among the federal and state governments.

The national population constituted through federation enjoyed a "dual citizenship", as members of the federation but also as citizens of the states. This duality is enacted through the different voting procedures for the House of Representatives and the Senate. The citizens whose interests were recognised in these deliberations were largely white and male, though provisions relating to the definition of eligible voters anticipated the extension of the franchise to women. The interests of Asian people already resident were recognised to some extent, and separated from deliberations about restrictions on "alien" immigration. The concern to achieve balance among states produced the decision not to count Aboriginal people in the census; this had a pronounced effect in South Australia, where the Aboriginal population was numerous and had previously been included in the manhood suffrage.

Liberal traditions have shaped Australian political culture. At the time of federation, those traditions had a social or welfare dimension, which, as the previous chapter has noted, has been significantly reconfigured, in Australia as elsewhere. In Chapter 6, the new emphasis on mutual obligation, duties as well as entitlements, will be discussed. Here, the key feature of liberalism to be taken up is constitutionalism, as it defines the relationship of citizens and the state. This discussion will also open out some of the tensions between liberalism and republicanism in Australian democratic institutions. But first to the question of rights.

The 1990s saw a number of attempts to have the High Court interpret "implied rights" in the constitution. In the case of *Lange v the Australian Broadcasting Corporation*, the Court clarified the limits on freedom of communication provided for in the constitution. Such communication is protected to the extent necessary for "the effective operation of that system of representative and responsible government provided for by the Constitution".[27] Protection of political speech has to be balanced with concern for the reputation of public figures: good candidates will not present themselves for election otherwise. The effect of the free speech cases was to encourage a view that "the High Court would be willing to find a whole catalogue of freedoms and rights implied in the Constitution or at least a catalogue of restrictions on legislative power which would have carved out an enhanced zone of individual liberty".[28]

This zone has not opened up. Members of the stolen generations have brought cases for damages, claiming that the removal of children in the Northern Territory violated constitutional rights to freedom of movement and association. In the case of *Kruger v The Commonwealth* (1997), "no justice was prepared to find that the Constitution created private rights enforceable directly by an action for damages".[29] The judges agreed that the susceptibility of a power to misuse does not render that power invalid. However, their judgement left a way open for individual actions for damages. In August 2000, Lorna Cubillo and Peter Jenner sought damages against the commonwealth in the Federal Court. The Court acknowledged the existence of the stolen generations, and Justice Maurice O'Loughlin accepted the claimants' evidence that they had suffered ill treatment and abuse while in institutional care. Yet the Court could provide no legal remedy for their claim. The lack of documentary evidence relating to the Protector's determination of the children's interests and the apparent consent of Cubillo's mother weighed against a favourable judgement. The outcomes in these cases make it plain that a political, rather than a legal, solution must be found.

The framers of the constitution adopted and adapted British common law traditions, in which individual rights are not protected by statute, rather than the American model, where constitutional amendments protect rights. The American system gives the judiciary the power of interpreting these provisions. The 1898 Constitutional Convention did not cede such power to the judiciary. It rejected a proposal to include a guarantee of due process and equal protection. As the *Kruger* judgement concluded: "the Constitution contains no general guarantee of the due process of law. The few provisions contained in the Constitution which afford protection against government action in disregard of individual rights do not amount to such a guarantee."[30]

But how did it come about that the framers chose not to guarantee due process and equal protection? Was it a matter of their great faith in the democratic process and their sense of the responsiveness of the political order to reformers? Provisions for equal protection and due process were included in the US Constitution after the Civil War ended slavery, to protect African Americans. This connection was discussed at the Constitutional Convention, where a strong coalition of interests ran in the opposite direction. Opposition to the inclusion of equal protection succeeded on the basis that it would prevent colonies from excluding Asians (especially Chinese) and Africans; and that factories legislation in the colonies which allowed discrimination against non-white labour would be null and void.

Recent High Court decisions have drawn attention to the diverse sources of Australia's legal inheritance which impact on citizenship, particularly the *Mabo* and *Wik* decisions about property rights. These judgements will be discussed at length in Chapter 7. The Court's role in these cases was controversial. If the constitution were to turn its face to the twenty-first century and to capture what is distinctive about Australian democratic traditions and new forms of citizenship, how might this be achieved? The preamble drafted by John Howard and Les Murray, and intended to capture contemporary aspirations, was comprehensively rejected. In the Vincent Lingiari Memorial Lecture in Darwin, Malcolm Fraser renewed the debate about a Bill of Rights, saying that this might be the only way to address the patent failure of indigenous policy to protect the rights of Aboriginal people.[31] Commenting on the outcome of the Cubillo and Jenner claims, Fraser maintained that it was clear that the commonwealth had failed in its duty of care to the children it removed.

To return to Peter Beilharz's comment, is there anything to be salvaged from the heritage of federation? Does the republican tradition offer a way of thinking about new forms of citizenship? Or does it depend on a dangerously authoritarian moral communitarianism, as some contemporary critics claim?

The long process of debate and publicity which accompanied the drafting of the Constitution finally succeeded in 1899, though by no means all of those eligible to vote did so. Nevertheless, the process and its outcome allowed "the sentiment and the rhetoric of public will, public affection and public commitment to the constitution to grow".[32] This sentiment was exploited by the delegates who went to London to persuade the British parliament to enact the legislation which brought the Commonwealth of Australia into being. Helen Irving argues that federalists and republicans shared common ground in this process of publicity and debate, even though the empire loyalties of the federalists were at odds with republicanism. Republican views, expressed in journals like *The Boomerang, The Republican, The Australian Nationalist, The Bulletin* and *The Dawn*, favoured the idea of central government. Although republican voices were muted as only two of these journals (*The Bulletin* and *The Dawn*) survived to 1901, key figures among the federalists were not unsympathetic to republican sentiments. They were impressed by the American federalists, Hamilton, Madison and Jay, whose model was adopted, and they "must also have been aware of republicanism as an ideal, as a type of society, as a relationship between citizen and government, a set of principles governing both civil and political behaviour".[33] But J.A. Froude's interpretation of the republican ideas of James Harrington was even more influential. Writing in England in the seventeenth century, Harrington described a "commonwealth" which was "based on a widespread dispersal of property,... with decentralised, participatory assemblies for the citizens, and with a separation of powers, and rotation of office, all designed to prevent the concentration of power in the hands of any one social group".[34] After a visit to Australia and New Zealand, Froude published *Oceana, or England and her Colonies* in 1886. The "commonwealth" he describes chimes with the politics of the Australian federalists, incorporating self-determination with empire loyalty and dependence. Stephen Holmes cites Harrington's *Oceana* and Trenchard and Gordon's *Cato's Letters* as evidence of an earlier compatibility of liberalism and republican thought: "they effortlessly combine a commitment to popular sovereignty with an acceptance of both constitutional limitations and, within the bounds of justice, the private pursuit of personal interests". [35]

In contrast to liberalism's emphasis on the individual, privacy and freedom, civic republicanism emphasises civic participation and public good. This tradition demands a great deal of citizens: that they contribute to decision making, whether as representatives or as informed observers, and that they call representatives and officials to account for their conduct in public life. It may be that this is to expect too much. In the 1920s Walter Lippman remarked that the "current disenchantment" with politics had been produced by the misguided pursuit of the "ideal of the omnicompetent, sovereign citizen".[36]

Democratic values have been given expression at various times and places: in the Athens, in the New England town, and in contemporary Switzerland. These are highly ordered, exclusive societies. In some Swiss cantons, according to Patricia Springborg, the franchise is still restricted to men who vote with swords by their sides[37]. And the New England town meeting was convened infrequently and controlled by selectmen, "older, richer members of the church, regularly returned to office", who set the agenda.[38] Nor were they autonomous or unconstrained in their decision making. Except in Rhode Island, the town meeting was accountable to the governor or the court system. These arrangements were not egalitarian or democratic, in the sense that they provided a space for dissent and disagreement or for argument about the public good. Rather, they aimed to achieve consensus and order, and depended on the assent of the governed.

Advocates of a civic republicanism often cite Alexis de Tocqueville's observations of democracy in America to support their enthusiasm for community participation. De Tocqueville's work was also well known to the federalists. He was impressed by American enthusiasm for forming associations, and his description of the skills and capacities this encouraged have become a trope in discussion of civic education. We will take a closer look at this in Chapters 6 and 8. But de Tocqueville was also critical of democratic mass culture. He found less evidence of independence of mind and freedom of discussion in America than in France, and put this down to the "very formidable barriers" which majoritarianism raises to the liberty of opinion. Communities founded on common beliefs do not easily find room for dissenting voices.

Critics of communitarianism dismiss civic republicanism as something which can only work in small, homogeneous societies. Renewed interest in building social capital and community involvement in decision making, together with optimism about the democratic possibilities of the Web, has revived civic republicanism. How can we live together with our differences?[39]

Alastair Davidson counters some of the communitarian objections by reinterpreting the tradition.[40] He interprets *"res publica"* as the public visibility of decision-making and deliberation, and sees the critical difference between classical and contemporary republicanism in terms of the separation of the private realm of interests and emotions and the public realm of politics. Davidson's benchmark is not direct participation but transparency and accountability in public life, a requirement that is only partly fulfilled by present procedures. Ministerial accountability, scrutiny of the administration of departments by Senate committees, the establishment of codes of conduct and registers of Member's interests, together with the recent passage of Freedom of Information legislation are elements of a raft of measures designed to meet concerns about public sector ethics.

Davidson, in common with feminist scholars and political theorists like Norberto Bobbio, identifies a more philosophical dimension to the problem: the notion of the secular, neutral public sphere, and the language of rationality in which its business is conducted. Emotions, passions and "personal interests" are quarantined in the private sphere by this liberal model. In a pluralist society, recognition and understanding of differences is not within the scope of debate in this "public sphere". The cold reason so prized by this model, and which is taken to produce "clarity" in public debate, is at odds with the objective of inclusiveness. The best it can produce is indifference.

A Republican future?

Since the Australia Act of 1986 finally proclaimed Australia as a sovereign nation, the Constitution has been deemed to reflect more of the past than the present circumstances. "There are still signs on its face of Australia's former colonial status. The link with the monarchy is one, however it may be interpreted now".[41] The Preamble preserves its history as an Act of the imperial parliament. The document's silence on the role of the head of state is another remnant of that link. The republicanism debate was formally activated by the establishment of the Republic Advisory Committee which produced an options paper in 1993. The Committee's report outlined the implications of methods of appointment of a head of state, including the codification of the reserve powers.

The rejection of the republican model offered in 1999 hinged on the method it proposed of appointing and dismissing a head of state, and the relative powers of the president and the prime minister. The choice between a head of state as an independent constitutional umpire and a president who became a political player took a back seat in the debate. Rather than emphasise the virtues of a bipartisan method of selection which required more consultation than the present process of appointing a governor-general, the direct electionists emphasised the agency of politicians. As well, the confusion about who the present head of state was — the governor general, or the Queen of Australia? — was unhelpful to the minimalist case.

Though the definition of "things federal" was one of the key topics for deliberation among the participating colonies on the Federation Council, and the bicameral parliament provided both a House of Representatives and a "states' house", the Senate, the constitution does not address the powers of the head of state. These powers devolved from the monarch to the governor-general, and so lay outside the domain of the framers, who were subjects of Her Majesty. The first three chapters of the constitution describe the functions of the parliament, the executive and the judicature and define the separation of powers among them. This arrangement introduces a tension within the constitution between "responsibilist" and federalist impulses.[42]

The 1975 "constitutional crisis" exposed this tension. The memory of this crisis and the bitterness of the divisions it produced may have been fresh in the minds of some of the key figures in the republican debate, and thus urged them to caution. But the events of 1975, when the Senate's determination to block supply lead to the dismissal of a government which still had the confidence of the House of Representatives, cannot be overlooked in a debate about the redefinition of the role of a president, and the codification of powers. In 1975, before withdrawing the commission of the Prime Minister, the Governor-General, Sir John Kerr, sought the confidential advice of a High Court judge, who confirmed his maximalist interpretation of the "reserve powers". Writing about these events, Paul Kelly argues that a proper use of the reserve powers required Kerr (and the Prime Minister he dismissed) to take a different course. Citing the British constitutional theorist, Walter

Bagehot's, definition of the "outer limits of the power of the sovereign under the Westminster system as the right to be consulted, the right to advise, the right to warn", Kelly "transforms the idea of sovereign rights...into duties".[43] By this argument, the Prime Minister had an obligation to consult with, or at least keep the Governor-General informed of, his strategy for handling the crisis, and Kerr should have advised and warned "openly and frankly of the course of action he intended to pursue in the absence of a political resolution to the deadlock of the houses"[44]. Instead Kerr took advice secretly and acted without warning, even though Whitlam might still have reasonably expected to win the day politically. The unfolding of these events in secrecy, with the final act involving an unsuspecting prime minister and a knowing leader of the opposition, are exemplary of the private acts that Alastair Davidson takes to be antipathetic to republicanism.

The link with the past, and with the monarchy — even with a "Queen of Australia" — was the unspoken issue in the 1999 republican referendum. There is widespread agreement that the answer to a simple question would have indicated popular support for a republic, and that the referendum foundered on the model and the method of appointment of a head of state. But the referenda which have been successful have had bipartisan support; in this case, the questions were being put in the face of the implacable opposition of the Prime Minister, and with other members of the government firmly behind the "No" case. As well, agreement on a model clearly required more discussion, and not in the context of an adversarial campaign.

If the move to a republic is "inevitable", how can it now be progressed? The important questions now are concerned with the legitimacy of the process which secures an outcome, and the legitimacy of the outcome itself. How can the process of determining a form of republic be properly democratic? And how can the method of appointment and definition of the powers of a head of state preserve the division of powers set out in the present constitution (assuming this is desirable)? It may be that such a process would produce more radical changes to the "federal compact" than the rejected model entailed.

The deliberation on these issues at the Constitutional Convention in 1998 was foreshortened by the Prime Minister's demand that the assembly should decide on a "preferred model". The commonly held view that Australians are cautious about constitutional change and the indications of popular support for a republic seemed to favour a minimalist model. Yet the proceedings at the Con Con exposed both the complexity of the issues and the depth of feeling they evoked. The proceedings were managed with considerable aplomb by the seasoned politicians in the chair. Individuals displayed passion and gravity, exasperation and anger. Steve Vizard's account of the proceedings suggests that the appearance of civility was readily disrupted when antagonists met informally.[45] Tempers frayed in public, too, especially when the minimalist model narrowly won majority support. Subsequently, the matter was taken back to the political arena and subject to political expediency. This is in stark contrast to the protracted deliberation which produced the constitution in the first place, and to the campaign which achieved such unprecedented success in 1967, when the referendum was passed with a "Yes" vote of 90.77%.[46]

Writing during "Australia Week", the celebration in London of the passage of the Constitution Act, Mark McKenna suggests that attention to processes, rather than symbolism, should be the focus of further attempts to secure a republic. "Despite the brief period of intoxication which surrounded the Con Con festival in 1998, many Australians felt that the bipartisan model which came out of the convention lacked democratic legitimacy.... Before we argue again about the sort of republic we want to become, we should first try to reach agreement on the democratic processes which will give legitimacy to the final decision".[47]

McKenna recommends a process rather like the federation process: first, a plebiscite to secure agreement for the change and an indication of preferences about the appointment of a head of state; then, the election of a convention, charged with the responsibility of developing a model. As with the federation process, this would remove deliberation from the arena of party politics, which clearly contaminated the recent referendum campaign. The model would be subject to public debate and discussion, a process which was conflated with the campaign in 1999. "Any vision of constitutional reform in Australia," he concludes, "needs to be enticing, hopeful, inclusive and substantial".[48]

Chapter 6

The Scope of Politics

The account of Australia's political history that we have given in the previous chapter is shaped by contemporary interest in the republican debate and the Centenary of Federation. It was a story of independence achieved through legislation, acts of parliaments in Britain and Australia over several decades: the Constitution Act in 1901, the Nationality and Citizenship Act (1948) and the Australia Act (1986). Legislative measures may be dull when compared to revolutions, and the gradual relinquishment of "empire citizenship" seems timid and unimaginative, or worse, cringing and "forelock tugging" at this distance. The public's lack of knowledge of Australian political history has often been put down to this: that parliamentary deliberation is not the stuff of colourful folklore and that we expect our political leaders to fade into obscurity. As Mary Kalantzis said of the constitution, an "uninspiring division of powers" is an unpromising starting point for a national celebration of federation. But histories shaped by present preoccupations have to acknowledge the risk of describing the past through a rear view mirror.

The focus on "identity" in accounts of Australian nationalism has tended to emphasise culture rather than politics. Benedict Anderson's idea of the nation as an "imagined community" which calls up strong allegiances or "comradeship" to the extent that members will die for the community, has influenced historians' attention to the field of culture.[1] They have turned to images, myths and celebrations and to forms of mass communication and publicity to account for the ways national character and sentiment are constructed. It is now widely accepted that identity is "invented",[2] and the analysis of this process turns on dynamics of exclusion, marginalisation, oppression and dispossession. Identity, whether singular "national" identity or pluralised and multi-ethnic, tends to be seen in terms of cultural belonging, rather than political settlements.

Like the histories of identity formation, this chapter is also framed around the idea of the nation and nation-building in the period since federation. At the end of his book, *The Coming Commonwealth,* published in 1897, Robert Garran observed:

> When a constitution has been framed and adopted, the work of the Australian union will have begun, not finished. The nation will be a nation, not of clauses, but of men and women; and the destiny of Australia will rest with the Australian people rather than with the Australian constitution. The work now at hand — the making of a constitution — is great and important, but it is the beginning, not the end.[3]

The outcome of the framers' work, as we have already seen, was an arrangement for sharing power. The political institutions and political culture which organised Australian citizenship and identity after federation were constituted through this arrangement. The constitution mapped the parameters within which national agendas could be debates and national futures imagined. This chapter will describe the constitution of a democratic polity, a nation of "men and women" in Australia since federation. First, though, a disclaimer: this discussion of "the scope of politics" is not about specific domains of policy making, such as economic policy, trade or foreign policy. We are not addressing these issues as "experts", but as "citizens". Nor are we going to arbitrate on party politics and ideologies. Rather our focus is on describing the shifting locations of politics and political debate and action. The political knowledge and capacities we are addressing here are about understanding agendas, making judgements about issues and understanding where decisions can be made and influenced. We turn first to the political settlements which followed federation and then to the current reorientation of Australian political life, usually attributed to "globalisation", a complex convergence of internationalisation, economic reform, and technological change. The discussion is shaped by questions about the extent of national sovereignty, or the power of the nation and national governments to determine "destiny", to use Garran's word. The chapter is organised around three headings: "Settlements" sketches in Australian social democratic traditions; "Reorientations" considers the extent of government in late modernity; and "Transformations" considers some prospects for new forms of internationalised citizenship.

This discussion will climb down from the lofty heights of Kantian moral laws and critical reason, a region inhabited by many of the educationalists cited in Part 1. The attraction of Kantian ethics for democrats is its notion of autonomy. Freedom for Kant is not primarily freedom from oppression or arbitrary rule, or even the freedom which comes from consenting to be governed. Real freedom is achieved when one acts not from necessity but in accordance with a law that one recognises and respects as prescribed by reason. In Kant's moral philosophy the legislation and the subject of law are one and the same person. Humans are capable of this self-government because they are both rational and self-conscious. It might seem that Kantian standards are too high. Kant's ethics, however, are not confined to moral philosophy and its theories of universal law. In the *Groundwork for a Metaphysics of Morals* (1785) he acknowledges the contingent and empirical terrain that ethics has to work on: the impulses and inclinations of humans and the shifting actualities of social and political life. Though humans are capable of the idea of reason, making that idea concrete in the conduct of every day life is another matter. Social and political life inhabits a realm, apart from the theoretical realm of moral philosophy. Indeed, according to Kant, setting up a state can be accomplished "even by a nation of devils". The task "does not involve the moral improvement of man, it only means finding out how the mechanism of nature can be applied to men in such a manner that the antagonisms of their hostile attitude will make them compel one another to submit to coercive laws, thereby producing a condition of peace with which the laws can be enforced".[4] This excerpt from *Perpetual Peace* (1795) might give some clue as to why Kant is often understood to reduce politics to law or jurisprudence. This is a mistaken view, according to Peter Berkowitz, who claims that "rather, Kant limits the *philosophical investigation* of politics to what reason, independent of experience, can clarify about the principles according to which human beings ought to organise their collective lives".[5] Such an investigation, Kant understood, does not account for all the dimensions of politics; it needs to be supplemented by a "practical anthropology" and an empirical ethics.

Kant wrote quite a lot more about moral theory than he did about practical politics, so at this point we are turning to Aristotle to supply the "practical anthropology" of political life. This discussion hangs on a notion of "politics" as "an activity through which an aggregate of many members, with diverse ends, deals with the problem of self-government".[6] The outcome of this process is not a unity of interests, but an agreement about common interests. The approach to national identity via politics rather than culture, then, can accept and maintain the continuing existence of diversity and difference. Indeed, the Aristotelian notion of the *polis* is predicated on difference: "A *polis* which goes on and on, and becomes more and more of a unit, will eventually cease to be a *polis* at all. A *polis* is by nature some sort of aggregation".[7]

There are gains and losses in turning from Kant to Aristotle. Kant's good citizen is democratic, egalitarian and benevolent. This individual is more attractive to us than Aristotle's aristocrat, devoted to self-perfection.[8] But Aristotle's politics does not share Kant's emphasis on "reasons of state". The previous chapter's discussion of federation made clear that the process was driven by a careful balancing of the separate colonies' interests and the definition of 'things federal". In the process of "deconfessionalisation" and unification involved in states like Germany, discussed in Part 1, quite different considerations take priority.

Bill Brugger describes a republican idea of good government as "one which selects all that is best in divided interests and distils them in the name of the public interest or the common good".[9] The word "commonwealth" captures this idea. Some features of contemporary political culture — the rise of neo-liberalism, the global economy, the spread of technology and identity politics — have been described as the public interest being overwhelmed by private interests. The second part of this chapter will discuss the implications of these changes for civic participation and politics.

Settlements

The constitution's power sharing arrangements attempted to balance the "divided interests" of the states and the new commonwealth. The enterprise of nation building hinged on establishing institutions to support economic and social citizenship: tariff protection, wage regulation and welfare measures. Restrictions on immigration were also designed to protect the labour market. Immigrant workers' willingness to work cheaply posed a threat to wages and conditions.

Wage arbitration also had pay-offs for industry, helping to produce a stable workforce. The "ameliorative" liberalism of these arrangements was underwritten as well by the constitution's provision for age pensions. In Chapter 5, we noted Peter Beilharz's view that the constitution was not concerned with "muscular" citizenship, and that the labour citizenship that emerged was very "narrow".

For much of the twentieth century, "industrial citizenship" was largely the province of white male workers. Arbitration assumed and constructed a gender difference in setting different pay rates for men and women. Equal pay for women was not granted until 1972, but even now, women's earnings do not match men's. Aboriginal people claimed both the right "to work for full wages" and the right to unemployment relief in the 1930s. Universal unemployment relief was introduced by the Lang government in New South Wales in the 1930s, but Aboriginal workers, some of whom were members of unions and the ALP, were denied their right by the officials who administered the payments.[10] The Pilbara strikes of 1946 protested wages and conditions, but union support of wage equality for pastoral workers was about providing employment for white workers.[11] Post war immigration policy was designed to procure a workforce for national projects. British migrants were preferred and given assisted passages, until an agreement with the International Refugees Organisation resulted in a significant influx of "aliens". Assistance to refugees was conditional upon their agreement to be placed in work at the government's direction and to stay in those jobs for two years. The designated jobs did not take account of the workers trade skills or professional qualifications. Immigration increased the nation's workforce more efficiently than natural increase: two "not gainfully employed" people were added with every three migrants; whereas a natural increase of three people added fifteen "not gainfully employed".[12]

Arbitration had some benefits for women: they were able to secure minimum wages and conditions. But the "settlement" which followed federation protected men's interests and positioned women as mothers and dependents. The judgement in the Harvester Case in 1907 sought to determine a fair standard of remuneration to "allow for the matrimonial condition for an adult man" in a civilised community. A "living wage" had to meet the needs of a worker, his wife and three children.[13] The "family wage" also set a standard for masculinity: the "breadwinner" who kept his dependent family in "frugal comfort".

This construction of the worker as "family man" was linked to a notion of "maternal citizenship". In 1904, a Royal Commission on the Decline of the Birth-Rate and on the Mortality of Infants in New South Wales was set up in response to alarm at the apparent threat to the growth of the white population posed by women's reluctance to bear children. Various measures were put in place to remedy the decline and to educate mothers in childrearing ("mothercraft") and domestic hygiene. Maternity hospitals and clinics, staffed by expert nurses, were designed to ensure the production of healthy babies. Payment of "child endowment" direct to mothers provided an economic incentive.[14]

The working-class family was subject to regulation and expert intervention; by contrast, the middle-class family was represented as the centrepiece of civilised life. In 1942, Robert Menzies appealed directly to a constituency of such families in his radio broadcast to the "forgotten people", listening on the radio in their "homes material, homes human and homes spiritual". These private citizens embodied values which, Menzies claimed, Australian democracy disparaged: "ambition, effort, thinking, and readiness to serve". In this wartime speech, he denounced "false class war", at the same time as he defined the middle class as the taxpayers who funded the social benefits of the class he called the "leaners". The "mass of unskilled people" were "almost invariably well-organised, and with their wages safeguarded by popular law". The "forgotten people" were homeowners, with "habits of frugality"; fathers whose "instinct" was to be with their wives and children, and to raise their children as "lifters"; believers whose dependence on God was combined with a "fierce independence of spirit".[15]

Independence of spirit was hardly compromised by welfare dependency, however. The years of depression and wartime austerity gave way to prosperity in the 1950s. Up to the 1960s, social welfare was directed mainly to the aged and the young. Pensions and other benefits and the high rates of home ownership supported the retired. Families were supported by free education, and access to health services baby clinics and immunisation. Care of children, the sick and the elderly largely fell to women, who also provided voluntary community service. Unemployment relief, introduced in the 1930s, was typically a short term and limited measure. This was the "wage earner's welfare state", where industry subsidy and tariffs protected domestic markets and employment.[16] The "well-organised workers" were not the sole beneficiaries of the Australian settlement: this was an instance of "aggregated" interests finding a solution to the problem of self-government. The diverse interests which were represented then by the "breadwinner", business and government have radically changed in character, and the same solutions are no longer appropriate. Contemporary advocates of an open Australia have to find new solutions.

The forms of citizenship we've described so far were thin and exclusive, but the "social capital" that accrued to the wage-earner was significant. Richard Sennett describes that capital as "character". He shows how it was linked to the routines of industrial work and community life. For the blue-collar "breadwinner", work had "one single and durable purpose: the service of his family". That purpose motivated commitment, but work itself reinforced the disposition to delayed gratification and to recognise mutual obligation which social life requires. Sennett suggests that time is the "only resource freely available" to members of low socio-economic groups. The routines of work, of saving and of family and community involvement gave people a way of managing this resource. The outcomes of this self-government for the worker and the community were "more than economic".[17] Sennett's point is not nostalgia for the old forms of work and family. It is to ask how new forms of work, with their flexible routines and spatial mobility can be compatible with "civic" purposes: building trust, commitment and mutual obligation. We will return to this question later in this chapter. But what are the pressures for change?

Universal entitlement to limited welfare benefits could be honoured in times of full employment and when women were carers. Some of the changes to welfare provision have been a consequence of changing demographics, but rising levels of unemployment and welfare dependency present a more intractable problem. Young people who have never been employed, communities where unemployment is the result of economic downturn and the closure of industries and Aboriginal communities where there is no infrastructure or existing enterprise: these are the issues in urgent need of solutions.

Social policy has been able to address some of the new demands. From 1960, women's participation in the workforce increased. Increasing participation in education meant that more women looked to establish economic independence. Family law reform in the 1970s made provision for "no fault" divorce, and anti-discrimination and equal opportunity legislation saw increasing numbers of married women in paid employment. Child-care became an important dimension of social policy. The provision of community based care and support for sole parent households were measures addressed to this need. Means testing, and compulsory superannuation, were introduced as an ageing population put pressure on the provision of pensions. Increasing longevity and technological advances in medicine have increased demand on health care services. Family income support has been extended. Targetted programmes have had the unwelcome side effect of marginalising beneficiaries (such as "single mothers") as "exploiters" of the system.

The recent trend in social policy has been to introduce measures to encourage personal responsibility, to refocus thinking on "obligations" rather than "entitlements". These measures may help to arrest what Sennett calls "the corrosion of character" but welfare dependency is not however a personal issue. The effects of long term unemployment and dependency are felt across the community, and effective solutions will invoke the common interest. Noel Pearson despairs that in the indigenous community welfare — "sit down money" — is having a devastating impact. He has been making the case that partnerships between community, government and business are required to give Aboriginal communities the capacity to create capability and start new enterprises. Other commentators agree that the key to a solution is not more welfare, but getting communities to care for themselves, to create wealth and to make jobs. The political question is how to strike the balance between what governments owe to citizens and what citizens owe to the community. The political vocabulary of "mutual obligation" makes choice the responsibility not just of prudent consumers but also of good citizens.[18]

Reorientations

Some of the apparent disenchantment with politicians and governments seem to stem from a perception that these issues are beyond the influence of politics. The unravelling of "the Australian settlement" and "the end of certainty"[19] are linked to the influence of free market economics and neo-liberal philosophies. There is plenty of evidence of the force of these philosophies, and of arguments that Australians have to change their thinking, relinquish nostalgia for the old protectionist economy, become entrepreneurial, embrace new technologies and become global citizens. This is a version of what Australians' "best interests" might be that sets itself against the traditions of social democracy that underpinned industrial citizenship. Have those traditions, and the institutions which grew out of them, become hopelessly outmoded? Shifts in government policy in the direction of economic reform — deregulation, privatisation, competition — and the requirements of new forms of accountability — to international financial markets, to the UN, to environmental agencies — look to some like "a hollowing out of the state", the retreat of government.[20] These reorientations in domestic policy and institutions and in international relationships raise questions about the extent of national sovereignty.

Michael Pusey described the move to smaller government as "economic rationalism".[21] In international debates, the term used is "neo-liberal" or "advanced liberalism". The term describes a set of strategies for governing national economies and social welfare states. Classic liberal thought emphasises the advantages of market competition, and advocates limited government intervention. Similarly, in social policy, liberal thinkers take a "laissez faire" approach. This position is informed by a distrust of government intervention and an emphasis on individual choice, liberty and self-determination. Neo-liberal philosophies have had a significant impact on public policy in the US and Britain. They have also been influential in Australia, where economic rationalist agendas have been shaping public policy since the 1980s.

A series of public policy changes are associated with neoliberalism. First, this tendency is associated with the relinquishment of sovereignty over the national economy in the face of a perceived "globalisation" of economic relations. Floating the currency, reducing tariffs and changing rules about foreign investment are signs of this. Second, it is linked to a tendency to prefer market solutions over government intervention. This tendency has been evident, for instance, in education policy, where private providers play an increasing role. The arguments for opening access to fee paying domestic students and for increasing students' choice of institution emphasise the private benefits of education and justify decreasing public funding. Third, neoliberal approaches are associated with privatisation. Strategies adopted in Australia include reducing public sector employment, privatising publicly owned companies such as Telstra and contracting out government services. Private agencies have largely taken over the business of job placement. One of the concerns about this trend is that private business will "cherry-pick", tendering only for those contracts which promise to be profitable. What obligation does business have to provide service where there is little or no profit — telecommunications in the bush, or difficult cases of long-term unemployment? The response of one banking executive, when challenged about the closure of rural branches, that the bank was not in business to promote social interaction, has been difficult to live down. It also ignored the cost of closures to rural people forced to transfer their commercial and retail transactions to towns with a bank.

Rural and regional communities have felt the impact of economic reform and competition policy to a disproportionate degree. Income has declined with commodity prices and farm debt has increased. In 1998, 36 of the 40 poorest electorates were in rural and regional areas. Unemployment in non-metropolitan areas is high, especially among youth. Higher death rates, and especially the incidence of suicide, are cause for alarm. Health services, education provision, and poor communications add to the disaffection that rural people have expressed in voting patterns and in consultations with Human Rights Commissioner, Chris Sidoti. As Sidoti observed:

> Human rights include the right to an adequate standard of living. The enjoyment of this right requires, at minimum, adequate food and nutrition, clothing, housing and necessary care and support such as health and medical services.... When allocating public funds, when developing or cutting programs, all levels of government ought to give

primary consideration to the people they serve. As one person told us: "Governments must acknowledge the fact that *people* live in rural communities and need to be recognised as being part of society rather than part of an economy".[22]

In neo-liberal strategies, two processes are occurring. On the one hand, governments draw back from their commitment to fund some social services, such as health, education, or childcare. The aim is to reduce the state's direct responsibility to meet potentially unlimited needs and rights claims. The alternative is for citizens to be less dependent on welfare payments, assistance and services. Instead, government agencies set up networks, encouraging people to manage themselves, make their own decisions and sometimes to fund their own choices. The objective is "to steer rather than row".[23]

These reforms are not only about smaller government, they have profoundly altered the configuration of the polity. The public sector has got smaller, and public servants are now employed on different terms, which impact on the way policy advice is tendered to governments. Although ministers have traditionally had their own advisors, political appointments are now being made to head departments. Consultants on contracts have a different and limited obligation to serve the public interest. In the workplace, reform has resulted in downsizing and restructuring. The influence of the Arbitration Commission has declined as wages and conditions are negotiated and enterprise bargains struck. Enterprise-based agreements could encourage efficiencies and be the means to identify common interests. However, the trend is away from collective bargaining and toward individual contracts. The recent attempt by the Commonwealth bank to introduce 22,000 individual agreements, is evidence of this trend.

According to Eva Cox, the effect of privatisation and the decline of national protection has eroded "what makes us social" in Australia, undermining trust, making it difficult to identify common interests and defuse conflict between different communities, defined by ethnicity, class and religion. This applies not only to commercial interactions but also to social relations and attitudes to institutions. Economic systems and social relationships profoundly affect one another. The real problem, Cox argues, is to find the proper mix of market, community and government solutions. Australia must find its way back to its egalitarian community-minded traditions — as a way to social solidarity, trust and economic health. Cox made these arguments in her Boyer lectures in 1995. Her argument has resonances with discussion elsewhere. In the US, Robert Putnam provoked academic and public debate when he published "Bowling Alone", describing the decline in associationalism and social capital[24]. Putnam's article was prompted by a striking statistic, which suggested that although bowling continued to be a popular past time for Americans, membership of teams had sharply declined. His concern was that the signs of social alienation apparent in rising crime rates and urban decay could be traced to this decline in membership of clubs and voluntary organisations.

In Britain, the "Third Way" describes an alternative to the standard political choices between the new right and the left: between market liberalism and the social-democratic welfare state. Translated — however partially — into the programmes of Tony Blair's New Labour, this has meant a combination of neo-liberal economic reform programs and community-oriented social programmes, emphasising often traditional moral obligations. Parents, for instance, will now be required to read with their children; a curriculum for the pre-school years has been developed and home schooling is being encouraged. The citizen is represented not as passively dependent on social welfare to realise rights and entitlements, but as actively engaging in citizenship responsibilities and in the negotiations on which a pluralist society depends.

The Labour backbencher Mark Latham has been an advocate of the "Third Way" in Australia. He argues that Australian party political debate no longer works as a contest in which the conservative defenders of capitalism, market competition and stable patterns of privilege face off a socialist party championing the interests of labour and the "working man". Nor can it work as an opposition between strategies based on state spending and planning (on the one hand) and the advocacy of unfettered market competition on the other. For one thing, states can no longer afford the escalating costs of social welfare. For another, even those who prefer neoclassical economic models based on market liberalism actually advocate a combination of market and state interventions, generating "quasi-markets". The problem is how to maintain the basics, providing sufficient security to maintain social settlements, while avoiding dependence, and targeting social welfare provision and building a commitment to "mutual obligation". Public policy must find the middle ground between state coercion and market freedoms — a middle ground to be found in the "reciprocal" obligations between states and citizens and between different communities and business.

Most recently, Australian governments have edged away from an emphasis on market competition in social services, turning instead to the powerful political rhetoric of community. The watchword is "mutual obligation", a reassertion of community values such as taking responsibility for oneself, one's family and one's neighbourhood. This reorientation and the political necessity for it, was powerfully evident in the convening of the "Rural Summit" in 1999.

Prime Minister John Howard's office has released a series of statements about "compassionate conservatism", explaining the current government's approach to social policy. Citing a liberal tradition of thought, the statements emphasise the connection between choice and responsibilities. Individuals are not isolated: instead, they are stitched to families and beyond that to community and civic society through forms of mutual responsibility. These are rarely formalised, but they are (or ought to be) based on a common understanding. The problems of unemployment, alienation, dependence on government and distrust of it stem from a skewing of this balance of rights and responsibilities. Programmes such as the "Work for the Dole" scheme, for instance, are designed to draw on young people's sense of responsibility and obligation.

A key aspect of these reforms is the renewed importance of what some call the "third sector" in social governance — voluntary and community sector agencies such as church groups and charities. From employment assistance to aged care, this sector has a newly important role, since it is increasingly able to tender as a provider of government services. Agencies such as the St Vincent de Paul Society, Meals on Wheels, the Salvation Army and other church groups have taken on an increasingly important role in sustaining social networks. The movement of responsibility for welfare provision to arrangements like this is also occurring in the US, where it has prompted debate about the principle of separation of Church and State.

Some have welcomed what looks like a shift in Australian politics towards an emphasis on community and civil society. If nothing else, they argue, these shifts present an opportunity to make the case for more participation in institutions and community. "Community" has a potent electoral appeal, linking people into work and into domestic life. It promises "ownership", participation and "empowerment", as a remedy for passivity and dependence. Some communities have responded energetically. There have been many stories of local communities cooperating to replace banks with alternative facilities. At Boonah, in South East Queensland, the Rural Development Institute and the local council have built community partnerships to develop new enterprises and worked with the students in local schools to address youth issues. The "Riverland" region around Mildura is also a success story. In Cape York, Noel Pearson has convened a summit to advance the Cape York Partnership Plan, involving already established local organisations, business and government. This builds on ground established by the Cape York Peninsula Development Association, which has brought together Aboriginal groups, pastoralists and environmentalists to develop a land use strategy. The land councils, as we will see in the next chapter, have already had to adapt indigenous values to bureaucratic decision making processes. The appeal of "community" in these instances evokes a tradition of cooperation which in the past built local institutions. Associational democracy is being revitalised and transformed in these local contexts.

Transformations

Much of the discussion so far has described a philosophical shift. But we began by suggesting that politics works with more mundane materials: it is about diverse interests and commitments, and difficult processes of forging common ground. The ground is always shifting. The changes that are occurring now, and are described by "globalisation" cannot be confined to an idea of international financial markets and footloose capital. Information technology has had an impact on communication that has changed spatial and temporal relationships, as well as economic and political ones. The industrial age, it is sometimes said, has given way to the information age. Geographical location no longer anchors capital or labour in the ways it once did. Time zones are blurred: we live in a wired, 24 hour society.[25] In this "borderless" world, new lines of accountability challenge national sovereignty. International organisations make policy and set benchmarks, in human rights, environmental issues, and finance. The Web allows endless possibilities for connection for those who have access. Much of the discussion is still breathless and prophetic. Our interest here is in the ways citizenship is transformed in this environment. What are the prospects for democracy and good government in this information environment? In what ways can it enhance civic capacities? Does it offer opportunities to revitalise politics, to facilitate the good government which "selects all that is best in divided interests and distils them in the name of the public interest"?

Privatisation has appeared to some to have narrowed the scope of politics; to others it has intensified and politicised private life. The visibility of interest groups and identity politics can be cited in support of both positions. The connectedness and openness of the Web is said to realise democratic values of equality and liberty. Regulation is difficult, and to date has been concerned with protection of privacy and detection and policing of criminal activity. The "shareware" ethic of the early developers of the Web has come into conflict with the commercial interests of ebusiness. "Information" exchanged on the Web comes in many varieties. Because business has been quick to capitalise on, if not yet profit from, these opportunities, issues related to contracts and protocols have been prominent: ownership of patents and intellectual property, the protection of privacy in financial transactions through encryption, Microsoft's violation of anti-trust laws, for example. Regulation of "adult" sites and of political speech has provoked debate about freedom of speech. These issues highlight the libertarianism of many of the Web's advocates.

To fully explore the democratic possibilities of the Web, and its potential for transforming politics would require the kind of "practical anthropology" Kant descibes. As yet, we have only patchy knowledge of how people use the Web. Yet it is clear that it can enhance the capacitiy of citizens to be informed, and to organise political activity. Government departments and agencies are providing documents such as discussion papers and policy guidelines online, and it is possible to do such things as lodging tax returns and tertiary admission applications electronically. Lobby groups and individual citizens can make immediate contact with representatives: witness the campaign to exempt tampons from the GST. This example also contains a caution: registering protest, however well organised, does not guarantee a policy change. Dissenting groups, however, have organised impressive support via the Web: the world wide demonstrations at meetings of the World Trade Organisation and the World Economic Forum required no local meeting halls or coordinating committees.

If the workings of democracy require informed citizens, willing to engage with politics and to make considered judgements on public matters and of the conduct of public officials, then the problem may now be information overload. Americans made it clear that they did not want to read the voluminous Starr report, posted on the Web prior to the impeachment of Bill Clinton. They had seen enough of the televised testimony. Even the most practised Web navigator turns up information of dubious quality, and a great deal of political comment on the Web is gossip or rant. Media organisations are extending their online capacity; but the quality of commentary has not necessarily improved. Michael Schudson suggests that the competent citizen in the information age is a "monitorial" citizen, able to access information, to take soundings and to probe further as the circumstances require: "Monitorial citizens scan (rather than read) the informational environment in a way so that they may be alerted on a wide variety of issues for a very wide variety of ends and may be mobilised around those issues in a variety of ways."[26]. These citizens are watchful. They may subscribe to mailing lists that keep them informed about areas of particular interest. They seek and use information as they need it, and make decisions accordingly. They make discerning use of other people's expertise to interpret events. They trust experts to be reliable. This means that the institutions which conserve information — libraries, for example — and which protect the public interest and the "right to know" — the press and journalists — also have to adapt to the new environment. This requires resources and a new look at media regulation. Content heavy sites are expensive to maintain and screen text difficult to read and often slow to download. The need for knowledge workers, who can process, validate and package information is only just beginning to be recognised. The individual searcher after truth will have to morph into an adept networker.

Knowledge workers are needed in this new environment, but it is not entirely a new world. Changes to the nature of work and the emergence of new industries requires new skills, flexible routines and different forms of attachment to the workplace. The fastest new industry, the call centre, illustrates some of the downside of the technological world. Here monitoring and benchmarking show how the imperatives of "flexibility" organise this service industry. As Richard Sennett explains, flexibility has three structural aspects: "discontinuous reinvention, flexible production, and the concentration of power without centralisation".[27] Call centre workers are not connected to each other, or to even to a company: in the US, they may even be in jail. The customer who phones to report a lost credit card, or to inquire about a travel itinerary, may not care that they are speaking to someone in another state or even another country. Indeed, many customers are probably happy that, for example, an insurance company in New York can have documents drawn up overnight by their data enterers in Ireland and deliver a contract for electronic signature by start of business the next day.[28] Consumers accessing the Web through their mobile phone as they decide which rug to buy, may feel that they are exercising ethical choices if they log into a site to check out who made it, with what kind of dyes, and who is profiting;[29] but they would have to ignore the resources expended in the production of their computer, not to mention forget their commitments to recycling. Andrew Ross points out that the "elite cadres" of knowledge workers are joined in the IT workplace, wherever it may virtually be, by another workforce of "sweatshop" labour.[30]

Networking can, nevertheless, provide some ways of renewing the "arts of association" that de Tocqueville claimed was essential to vital democratic life. His impression of the variety of voluntary associations in America, and the importance of civil society in educating people for democracy are well-known: "In democratic countries knowledge of how to combine is the mother of forms of other knowledge, on its progress depends that of all the others".[31] "Knowledge of how to combine" is the key, because voluntary associations are just that. People are bound into many associations involuntarily: in families, religious and ethnic groups and so on.[32]

These are significant attachments, and mostly enrich private life, but they do not necessarily transmit knowledge of *how* to associate. They teach how to belong. Knowledge of the arts of association is often gained through membership of insignificant communities.[33] These communities bring together people from diverse backgrounds around a common interest: choirs are an example, but the activity of the group can be more complex and more temporary. The Woodford Folk Festival, held annually in Queensland, is an example of such an association. Here the folk tradition embraces all kinds of performers and performances, in an event held over a week in January each year. This event has grown from small beginnings and has depended largely on the contributions of volunteers. It has negotiated various "inclusions": different folk traditions have been added to the original Anglo-Celtic and indigenous culture has been incorporated in ways which preserve its autonomy.[34] Virtual association promises to extend voluntary association and to be inclusive of more participants. But the political uses of the Web have to embrace more than the lobby and to look to ways to reinvent politics.

"Significant" or "moral" communities cohere because they are grounded in shared beliefs and offer their members a sense of belonging. Members identify their interests with those of the group. Shared language, rituals, practices and institutions underwrite forms of identification. In the context of increasingly heterogeneous populations, the term "identity" has been extended and multiplied. The "confessions" or religious affiliations which liberal pluralism confined in the private realm are no longer the only or most powerful communities and identities. The liberal disposition to secularisation holds that the state should not interfere with the freedom to pursue a particular way of life, nor promote or preserve particular versions of the good life. This version of pluralism is challenged by the contemporary tensions between "equality" and "difference".

The communities which form around identity, however, can be closed and exclusive. "We" does not necessarily express tolerance and respect. The "aggregate" which is the polis coheres in a different way. It depends on the "arts of association", not the processes of identification. The "common interest" does not pre-exist; it is established through deliberation, negotiation and disagreement. It is the outcome of these processes, and is never finally determined. Democratic deliberation assumes that all participants are equal, in the sense that they are able to know their own interests, and claim the rights and entitlements that accrue to them as members. Living together in a *polis* requires an additional capacity to identify, recognise and respect the rights and interests of others and to evaluate and arbitrate on competing claims. The next chapter traces a history of indigenous rights claims; in order to show how the recognition of indigenous citizenship continues to reshape the Australian *polis*.

Chapter 7
Histories for Citizenship

History has been at the centre of current discussions of citizenship and of Australia's future. The celebration of Federation has renewed attention to our changing relationship with Britain, as Australia has cast off colonial ties and Britain has looked for a place in the new Europe. The negotiation of new relationships with Asian neighbours has recalled a history of the commerce and trade on the northern coastline. The "rediscovery" of Asia has brought to light an alternative geography of contact: rather than a west or east coast awaiting European discovery, extensive contact with Asia focussed on the region from Broome to the Gulf of Carpentaria and the Torres Straits.[1] Perhaps most controversially, history has been involved in the movement toward recognition of indigenous rights and reconciliation with indigenous people. Above all, history has been political.

While history has had this exciting public life, a renewed amateur interest has been evident in the popularity of family history. Yet in the schools history is in decline. How is history important to citizenship education? This chapter offers two approaches to this question. It traces a history of citizenship through a case study of the political struggle which secured the extension of rights to indigenous people over the twentieth century. It also considers how doing history enhances political knowledge, extends civic and political competences and perhaps even, as Inga Clendennin claims, encourages civic virtue.[2]

This chapter and the next turn to some applied questions about the knowledges, competences and values a civics curriculum might address if it is to discover democracy in its modern and postmodern guises. The case study focusses on the twentieth century history of a key democratic value: equality; and way that value is expressed through rights claims. As we trace indigenous people's political campaigns, we emphasise the formation of organisations and affiliations to promote citizenship goals; the adoption of civic identities[3] as advocates, representatives and leaders; the variety of domains of political action; and creation of new institutions to facilitate the exercise of rights.

Extending the web of citizenship.

Nineteenth century social movements culminated in the extension of political rights to women and the widening of economic citizenship through such measures as the age pension, maternal and child welfare and unemployment benefits. Aboriginal people were almost entirely excluded from this citizenship. Their eligibility to vote was unevenly distributed and readily obstructed, until in 1962 they achieved the right to vote in federal elections. If the "Australian century" was about "political struggle in the building of a nation" as a recent anthology with that title suggests,[4] the domain in which that struggle took place was not bounded by any simple conception of the nation.

The twentieth century also saw the rise of totalitarian regimes and of an "international community". In the aftermath of World War II, the UN Declaration of Human Rights provided a framework within which rights consciousness emerged as the focus of political claims. By 1968, a watershed year for contemporary social and civil rights movements, "a consensus had crystallised that [the Declaration] constituted a part of customary international law".[5] The increasing recognition of land rights claims from 1972 involved four sources of law: "international law, Aboriginal traditional law, common law as declared by the High Court, and statutory law as legislated by Australian parliaments within their constitutional limits".[6]

Rights talk has become a powerful language of citizenship and has extended the reach of government into many spheres of life. But equality, as R.H. Tawney pointed out in 1931, is not just a matter of formal rights. It also requires that

> each member of a community, whatever his birth, or occupation, or social position, possesses in fact, and not merely in form, equal chances of using to the full his natural endowments of physique, of character, and of intelligence. In proportion as the capacities of some are sterilized or stunted by their social environment, while those of others are favoured or pampered by it, equality of opportunity becomes a graceful, but attenuated, figment.[7]

The acceptance of this view, that equality has little substance if it is not supported by measures to secure basic standards of health, education and economic and social welfare, has seen the ascendancy of the "rights-regarding citizen". This citizen is visible in a political domain that extends into "private" life, in debates about abortion, euthanasia, and questions of race, ethnicity and sexuality. Michael Schudson claims that American political experience at the end of the twentieth century was defined by a "tripod of mutually reinforcing social forces — the expansion of government, the proliferation of rights, and the intensification of private social life".[8] In the US, the sphere of government so expanded is federal. Rights claims pursued through the courts there have raised legal questions about the application of the Constitution in state jurisdictions. The questions this raises for Schudson are about the effects of rights consciousness on public life — does it reinforce the culture of private individualism, or does it energise public life?

In Australia, the assertion of rights claims since the 1960s has involved some High Court interpretation of the Constitution, particularly in regard to implied freedoms of speech and association. These issues were raised in Chapter 5. The High Court's decisions in *Mabo* and *Wik* will be discussed below. Prior to *Mabo*, land rights were the subject of federal and state legislation. In the case of claims advanced by Aboriginal people, which are the concern of this chapter, and of claims made by women and minority groups, there has been contention about how Australia's obligations as a member of the United Nations have been realised through domestic policy. Australia has ratified most of the UN's core human rights treaties. Yet, in the eyes of prominent jurists like Michael Kirby, Australia has been "one of the few countries to stand substantially outside the body of human rights jurisprudence".[9] In the *Mabo* judgement in 1992, international law, and especially human rights law, was cited as "a legitimate and important influence on common law". Any expectation that this influence should have weight was explicitly denied in 1995. In a Joint Statement, the Foreign Minister and the Attorney General declared: "It is not legitimate, for the purpose of applying Australian law, to expect that the provisions of a treaty not incorporated by legislation should be applied by decision-makers".[10]

Despite the tensions created around the issue of national sovereignty, the ethical force of international obligations is real. The provisions of some treaties have been incorporated by legislation. The International Convention on the Elimination of All Forms of Racial Discrimination (1965) was implemented in Australia by the Racial Discrimination Act 1975. The commitment to these obligations has also been institutionalised by the establishment of bodies like the HREOC. Australia signed the International Convention on the Rights of the Child in 1990. The HREOC's investigation of the separation of Aboriginal children from their parents began in 1995. In 1991, Australia acceded to the first Optional Protocol to the International Convention on Cultural and Political Rights, which allows individuals to communicate with the Human Rights Committee in the event that domestic remedies have been exhausted. ATSIC and other NGOs participate in the Working Group on Indigenous Populations. Mick Dodson is positive in his assessment of the Group. It has been able to "use existing structures and transform them to meet our needs and aspirations" as well as to "transform the way many of us approach the whole struggle".[11]

Another tension which emerges in "rights talk" relates to the sharing of power between the Commonwealth and the states. The Aboriginal Land Rights Act (Northern Territory), enacted by the Fraser government in 1976, was subjected to repeated challenge (44 in all) by the Northern Territory government. More recently, the federal government has refused to intervene in the case of the Northern Territory's provisions for mandatory sentencing, which impact most severely on the Aboriginal population, who already suffer disproportionately in the justice system. Following the passage of legislation relating to the *Wik* decision, the responsibility for developing native title regimes has been passed to state governments.

This chapter's discussion of the politics of indigenous citizenship will show how rights claims were framed with regard to these institutional locations. While rights claims have a moral force, they are given substance only within the context of institutional arrangements. Australian institutions have been able to recognise economic and social rights which accrue to industrial citizenship. Claims based on "natural rights" are more problematic. These claims have appealed to UN charters and conventions, and to public opinion.

The discussion is in two parts: first it attends to claims for "equal citizenship", and takes as its cut off point the successful referendum of 1967; then it takes up the question of claims which require the recognition of "group rights". Liberal democratic regimes find it easier to accommodate individual rights than they do to recognise group or cultural rights. This was as much a problem for the UN as for any national government: the proviso that only the singular "nation-state" could be the subject of UN agreements was an obstacle to its engagement with indigenous "populations".

One of the themes of this discussion will concern the role of experts in advancing or advising on indigenous rights claims, and in institutionalising gains. Justice Woodward and "Nugget" Coombs played a crucial role in the establishment of land councils to represent indigenous interests. Historians were important in the *Mabo* and *Wik* cases; anthropologists made interventions in the Hindmarsh Island case, and in earlier campaigns for "advancement" and "uplift" of Aboriginal people. William Ferguson, of the Aborigines Progressive Association, writing to the Sydney *Daily Telegraph* , 15 October 1937, gave some advice about experts:

> Some of your professors write wonderful books about us and our customs. But...you never read them or try to learn about us or understand us.....
>
> We do not want anthropological studies and books about the length of our toenails and the size of our heads.
>
> We want you to realise that we are your brothers....You have taken everything away from us but given us nothing in exchange. Is that right? As one of your scholars has said, you owe us not benevolence, but atonement.[12]

Ferguson's appeal has a particular resonance in the context of Reconciliation. The final section of this chapter looks at the role that historians have played in the "politics of recognition". And Chapter 8 takes up the place of moral sentiments in public debate.

Indigenous politics and citizenship to 1967.

In 1967, more than 90% of voters in a majority of states approved two propositions in a referendum which has come to be seen as a crucial recognition of indigenous citizenship. The constitutional changes were minimal, but their symbolism was significant. The deletion of apparently discriminatory references to Aboriginal people was perceived as an endorsement of civil and political rights. In hindsight, what is remarkable about this referendum is that so little change really occurred: the power of the commonwealth government to make "special laws" in respect of Aboriginal people was not acted upon for some time. At the time of drafting, the clause was intended to allow the commonwealth to act to exclude non-Europeans. After 1967, the expectation has been that the power would be used in a positive way. Initially, the incumbent coalition government set up a small office, but it was not until the election of the Whitlam government in 1972 that a Department of Aboriginal Affairs was established. The Racial Discrimination Act was proclaimed in 1975, and the Aboriginal Land Rights (Northern Territory) Bill passed the House of Representatives on November 6 1975, just days before the dismissal of the Labour government. The Bill became law in 1976.

The campaign which secured overwhelming support for the referendum — in only a few electorates in Queensland and Western Australia was there significant opposition — was not, as many believe, about giving Aboriginal people the vote.[13] Nor did it significantly alter the shared responsibility of the states and the commonwealth for Aboriginal affairs. Neither was it the first sign of public support for such a measure. In 1944, the fourteen point referendum included a proposal to "provide the Commonwealth with the power to make laws ... with respect to ... the people of the aboriginal race". Had this proposal been the subject of a separate clause, it is likely it would have carried.[14] Where the 1944 proposal was seen as a welfare question, by 1967 success was a sign of Australia's international standing in a world where the civil rights movement was at its height, and where anti-apartheid feeling was strong. As then Attorney-General, Billy Snedden, realised, the removal of these apparently discriminatory references would "appeal to the broad public conscience".[15] Chicka Dixon made the appeal to natural rights explicit in the *Sun-Herald:* "I want to be accepted by white Australians as a person....We want to be human like everyone else".[16] Though the outcome would make little difference to Aboriginal people's relation to government, the notion of welfare was talked up by the press and by the referendum's supporters. That support was mobilised in large part by FCAATSI, an organisation of indigenous and non-indigenous people, led by Kath Walker, Faith Bandler and Joe McGuinness. The success of the campaign was a sign that indigenous citizenship was being exercised in a powerful and effective way.

The referendum campaign was not the first sign of indigenous political activism. Aboriginal people used a variety of strategies, including petitions, delegations and strikes, to press the issue of their unequal status. From the mid-nineteenth century, Aboriginal protest began to be heard. They petitioned the Queen for status as British subjects. In the 1880s, they walked off a reserve at Coranderrk. Bain Attwood and Andrew Markus observe that this action and the identification of common interest was based not on "tribal" affiliations but on colonial political formations, such as occupancy of a reserve.[17] Until the 1950s, their political organisations tended to have exclusively Aboriginal membership, and were limited and local. European supporters of Aboriginal rights formed separate associations. Anthropologists were prominent in these humanitarian organisations, but feminist groups were also engaged, especially by issues such as the separation of children and sexual exploitation of Aboriginal women by white men.[18]

Campaigns for "equal citizenship" gathered momentum from the 1920s. Initially, the focus of these campaigns was conditions "under the Act". Protection Acts applied in almost all states, but activism was concentrated in New South Wales, Victoria, South Australia and Western Australia. The effect of the various regimes was to deny the rights of freedom of movement and association. The Protector had legal guardianship of all children to age 21, had the authority to approve or to prohibit marriages, and controlled access to and from reserves. Aboriginal people "exempt" from the Act were awarded "certificates of citizenship" which required that ties to extended family and tribal associations be renounced. This citizenship could also be revoked for various offences. Under the Western Australian Natives (Citizenship Rights) Act of 1944, for example, the certificate could be suspended or cancelled by a magistrate if the holder was "not adopting the manner and habits of civilised life" or was "twice convicted of an offence under the

Native Administration Act 1905-1941, or of habitual drunkenness".[19]

The provisions of the Protection Acts remained in place up to 1962. In 1934, the Western Australian government appointed Henry Moseley as Royal Commissioner to "Investigate, Report and Advise upon Matters in relation to the Condition and Treatment of Aborigines". Marilyn Lake argues that this was a response to feminist agitation. Among the witnesses were several Aboriginal women, who detailed the treatment endured at Moore River. One, Emily Nannup, "wanted answers: I want to know the reason for my children being taken from me".[20] She got little satisfaction from Commissioner Moseley.

Margaret Tucker, a "half-caste" woman, voiced her concerns in the wider public domain. In the *Worker's Voice*, she pleaded: "Help us to protect ourselves from the clutches of the Aborigine Protection Board". She described conditions at Cummeroogunga: the people were issued with rotten rations; the cows drank from contaminated dams; trachoma was rampant. Worse, "the people at Cummeroogunga lived in constant fear of their children being taken from them by the Board, and being placed in homes". On one occasion, the men had been sent rabbitting. Immediately they were out of the way, police arrived and bundled the children into cars, to take them away "for the Board to dispose of".[21]

Margaret Tucker wrote in the *Worker's Voice* in 1939. On January 26 in the previous year, 1938, Aboriginal people marked the sesquicentenary of the arrival of the First Fleet with a Day of Mourning. A resolution passed unanimously at a public meeting:

> We...hereby make protest against the callous treatment of our people by the whitemen during the past 150 years, and we appeal to the Australian nation of today to make new laws for the education and care of Aborigines, and we ask for a new policy which will raise our people to full citizen status and equality within the community.[22]

The rhetoric of "uplift" and "advancement" was widely used in these campaigns, by both Aboriginal groups and Europeans. William Cooper stated the objects of the Australian Aborigines League in 1936: "the ultimate object of the League shall be the conservation of special features of Aboriginal culture and the removal of all disabilities, political, social or economic, now or in the future borne by aboriginals and secure their uplift to the full culture of the British race".[23] Those "special features" of Aboriginal culture had been destroyed by the removal of people from their land and the separation of families. Cooper's assertion that they should be conserved was at odds with the prevailing view that policy should "smooth the pillow" of a dying race.

Almost ten years earlier, the Australian Aboriginals' Progressive Association had petitioned the New South Wales' government for repatriation. They demanded that: "all capable aboriginals shall be given in fee simple sufficient good land to maintain a family;" that "the family life of the aboriginal people shall be held sacred and free from invasion and that the children shall be left in the control of their parents"; and that control of aboriginal affairs "be vested in a board of management comprised of capable educated aboriginals under a chairman to be appointed by the government". When the petition was brushed aside, Fred Maynard urged the Premier, J.T. Lang, to take a personal interest in Aboriginal advancement: "I wish to make it perfectly clear on behalf of our people, that we accept no position of inferiority as compared with European people....We are, therefore, striving to obtain full recognition of our citizen rights in terms of absolute equality with other people in our own land".[24]

Heather Goodall has demonstrated the importance of continuing claims about land in Aboriginal politics in New South Wales.[25] These claims first achieved recognition in the federal arena, in the 1976 Act, which was the culmination of strike action in the Central Desert. At the same time as the Referendum campaign, begun in 1958, was reaching its height, Vincent Lingiari led a walk off at Wave Hill Station in 1966. At issue were better wages and working conditions, but also "their right to be Gurindgi".[26]

The Gurindgi left Wave Hill and walked westwards to their own land at Daguragu, where they built stockyards. The strike became a ten year struggle for land rights. In an anthology published in 1998 for the Central Land Council, *Take Power like this old man here,* an oral history of the strike is combined with an account of the processes which transformed the claims into rights. The memory of Vincent Lingiari going to Darwin in "dirty-bugger clothes" to talk to the Northern Australia Worker's Union, and of his firm resolve in talks with the Vesteys, has passed into folklore:

That old man there, Vincent Lingiari, he was a really hard man, he had a strong heart. And this same three — Donald Nangiari, Vincent Lingiari and Captain Major — they been talk really hard to Vesteys. Because Vesteys been treating these people all over Australia just like a dog....

But this old man been kicked from a mule. They put him on a plane to go to Darwin because he been breakem. Dirty bugger clothes and everything. And that's the way he gone and see them.[27]

The political skills of Vincent Lingiari and the determination of the people who reasserted their claim to Daguragu saw results. In the first weeks of the Whitlam government, the Woodward Royal Commission was appointed to report on Aboriginal Land Rights in the Northern Territory. By 1973 it recommended the establishment of land councils as a means to formulate claims and protect the interests of traditional owners and to represent those interests in negotiations with government. In August 1975, Gough Whitlam handed over the deeds to Gurindgi land, which had been purchased with money from the Aboriginal Land Fund. In 1986 the lease was converted to freehold title.

Renewed political pressure was brought to bear in the aftermath of the Whitlam dismissal. Land rights legislation had been introduced, and the Fraser government enacted it. But in the interim, a land rights march in Alice Springs in March 1976 demonstrated the depth of public support. Wenten Rubuntja, the Chairman of the Central Land Council, led a deputation around the country and to a meeting with Malcolm Fraser.

Protest, political organisation and the moral force of rights claims lay behind the success of this political struggle. The recognition of land rights, initially confined to Crown land in remote areas, marked a beginning. Justice Woodward's recommendations about the substance of those rights created a new indigenous legal persona: the "traditional owners". This collective identity and the determination of the extent of group rights has been the focus of indigenous politics since the 1990s.

Indigenous citizenship: cultural rights.

Land rights were first recognised through commonwealth and later state legislation. Justice Woodward's definition of "traditional owners" was adopted in this legislation and in the procedures for making claims. That definition was based on a submission from the Northern Land Council, which included a paper by the anthropologist R.M. Berndt. Berndt's paper described Aboriginal people's spiritual connection to the land, and this was expressed in the definition of "traditional owners":

> A local descent group of Aboriginals who have common spiritual affiliations to a site on the land, being affiliations that place the group under a primary spiritual responsibility for that site and for the land, and are entitled by Aboriginal tradition to forage as of right over that land.[28]

While this definition was an important recognition of cultural difference, the definition presented some difficulties. It meant that Aboriginal people's access to land and ceremonial uses of it were privileged over any economic or political interest they might have in land, and over a right to limit the access of other parties, particularly mining companies. Other dimensions of the definition were also open to interpretation: lines of descent, the way responsibility for the site had been demonstrated especially in the case of people who had been removed from their land, and the question of different groups' claims to the same land.

Aboriginal people's participation in land rights negotiations also presented some problems. The land councils brought together different groups, but their traditions lacked a machinery for decision-making which was compatible with bureaucratic procedures. Nugget Coombs, Chair of the Council for Aboriginal Affairs from 1968 to 1976, saw the necessity for them to adapt their capacities for forming alliances, sharing authority and adopting complementary roles to contemporary issues. He recommended that processes should allow time for consensus to emerge, and that representatives should be chosen using Aboriginal processes, rather than elections. This meant that "non-Aboriginal colonial authority would have to make room for Aboriginal decision-making, and Aboriginal people would have to acquire, by trial and error, the political skills to make collective decisions and to abide by them."[29]

Making land rights claims, then, involved the establishment of new institutions and the adaptation of administrative practices to new constituencies. Land Rights legislation did adapt to some extent. The Queensland Aboriginal Land Act 1991 extended the definition of "traditional owners": "if there are no traditional owners of the land, it can still be claimed by those claiming an historical affiliation, or if there be no historical occupiers, others can make a claim on the basis of need".[30]

The next step in giving substance to land rights claims came with the High Court's *Mabo* decision. This established that "native title" existed and had survived the colonial imposition of common law. Until *Mabo,* the doctrine of *terra nullius* had been accepted. This doctrine was enunciated by the Privy Council in 1889, in the case of *Cooper vs Stuart:*

> There is a great difference between a case of a Colony acquired by conquest or cession, in which there is an established system of law, and that of a colony which consisted of a tract of territory practically unoccupied, without settled inhabitants or settled law, at the time when it was peacefully annexed to the British dominions. The Colony of New South Wales belongs to the latter class.[31]

The High Court recognised that the land was occupied prior to European settlement and that the people who occupied it did have a system of settled laws, including a system of title, which might involve communal, group or individual rights to land. It also determined that native title was extinguished when the Crown granted land to another person or when the government took over land for a public purpose. Native title could still exist on vacant Crown land. The Court, however, did not give content to native title rights, observing that the kinds of uses of land and water were varied and localised.

The Native Title Act 1993 recognised native title rights and interests and put in place a means for indigenous people to have their claims heard, by establishing native title tribunals. Where native title exists, the Act accords native title holders the same rights as other title holders. They are entitled to be compensated, as are other title holders, if their land is resumed for a public purpose. But additionally, they are entitled to be consulted before their title can be extinguished, and they have a right to negotiate with mining companies.[32] The legislation also sought to protect native title from extinguishment by state governments. The *Mabo* ruling left a further uncertainty over the status of titles granted after the Racial Discrimination Act 1975. The legislation resolved this problem by validating those titles and compensating traditional owners for loss of title.

A further question remained, to be taken up in the *Wik* judgement. This was concerned with the co-existence of native title and other titles. This time the Court determined, in a much narrower decision than in *Mabo*, that native title could co-exist with pastoral leases. The co-existence of leases had not been an issue in *Mabo*, because there were no pastoral leases on Mer. The Wik and Thayorre peoples, from Cape York, did not make a native title claim. Rather, the issue was the status of pastoral leases on their traditional lands. Aboriginal people in these remote areas had worked and lived on pastoral properties. These leases, over two separate properties, had a history. The Mitchellton lease had been surrendered in 1921; the Holroyd lease had originally been granted for pastoral purposes, though that condition had lapsed.[33] Whereas the *Mabo* decision had found that native title was a form of title that had equivalents in English property law, what came out in *Wik* was that pastoral leases were peculiar artefacts of colonialism. Large tracts of sparsely occupied land did not exist in England. Historical documents were produced in evidence which purported to show that pastoral leases were never intended to give exclusive possession, and that the rights of Aboriginal people to use the land were specifically preserved. A majority of four of the seven member Court decided that, in the words of Justice Kirby:

> Pastoral leases give rise to statutory interests in land which are *sui generis*. Being creatures of Australian statutes, their character and incidents must be derived from that statute. Neither of the Acts in question here expressly extinguishes native title. To do so very clear statutory language would, by conventional theory, be required. When the Acts are examined, clear language of extinguishment is simply missing. On the contrary, there are several indications which support the contention of the Wik and the Thayorre that the interest in land which was granted to the pastoralists was a limited one: for "grazing purposes only", as the leases stated.[34]

The Court found that native title was extinguished on the mining leases around Weipa, but it could co-exist with title on pastoral leases. Not only could native title continue to exist, it might even be revived on land to which other people had been given rights. What followed from Wik was political deliberation about rights: how to balance rights of native title holders with the right to mineral exploration, and rights of leasees to "improve" pastoral properties.

If native title holders had the right to negotiate with mining companies, how did this compare with pastoralists' rights?

These questions required a political solution, and achieving that solution raised questions about the role of the Senate. In circumstances where the Independent Senator from Tasmania, Brian Harradine, held the balance of power and where the government could use the possibility of a double dissolution and a "race" election, the debate was volatile. Three principles were applied for balancing competing claims of pastoralists, miners and traditional owners: justice, certainty and workability.[35] The High Court's failure to consider how the Racial Discrimination Act impacted on their assertion that in cases where pastoralists' rights were in conflict with Aboriginal rights, Aboriginal rights must yield, created uncertainty. Some pastoralists, and the leader of the National Party, thought the only certainty lay in extinguishment. In the event, the responsibility for establishing regimes was turned over to state governments.

In its *Mabo* judgement, the High Court also pronounced on the issue of sovereignty: it was adamant in its view that "the Crown's assertion of sovereignty over the Australian continent was unchallengeable in any domestic court".[36] The British annexation of Australia was legitimate. This was not the first time this question had been before the Court. In 1977 Paul Coe instituted an action, claiming that the Aboriginal people had exercised "exclusive sovereignty" over the land before it was "wrongfully" claimed for Britain, and that as a conquered people they had never ceded their rights. Nor had the British terminated them or entered into a treaty. Consequently, dispossession had been "unlawful".[37]

Coe's action did not succeed, but on Australia Day, January 26 1972 the idea of Aboriginal sovereignty was made visible in the tent embassy erected on lawns of parliament house in Canberra. On that day, the Prime Minister, William McMahon, made a statement about new directions in policy, a "statement which can be interpreted as the moment when "assimilation" was renounced as government policy and replaced by ... it is not clear what".[38] This change in policy direction goes by different names: self-determination or self-management, but its social and institutional forms are still evolving. Patrick Dodson argues that the "for their own good" approach still directs government policy, and that there will still be "unfinished business" until a "comprehensive framework agreement" is legislated:

> It is needed for two additional reasons, what I will refer to as the "unfinished business". The first is to deal with the conditions of our existence as Aboriginal Australians within the Australian society, and the second is in order for us to survive as Aboriginal peoples in keeping with our own laws and customs within our own traditions and values. This is our Aboriginal unfinished business, questions concerning the survival of our being as a consequence of having been subjugated and disadvantaged through the necessities of defending our interests and meeting our needs since the arrival of Governor Phillip; "to be Gurindji" in the words of Vincent Lingiari. Such an agreement should define, and set out a path, to resolve all the matters of unfinished business between the parliament and the Aboriginal peoples.[39]

Dodson goes on to list some heads of agreement that a document able to form the basis of self-determination should address. Since he stood aside as Chair, the Council for Aboriginal Reconciliation has consulted about and drafted a document of reconciliation, which was handed to the Prime Minister at Corroboree 2000. This document comprises a symbolic declaration with attached action plans, "map[ping] out the detailed steps that need to be taken by governments, organisations and individuals from both indigenous and wider communities to solidify a real practical commitment to reconciliation".[40] The political process of achieving policy agreement which gives substance to self-determination is still unfolding.

According to Tim Rowse, "the essential problem of a post-'assimilation' vision of nationhood [has been] how to conceptualise and institutionalise the possibilities of Indigenous autonomy".[41] Is there room for self-determination within the structures of the nation state? Sovereignty does not necessarily imply a single, absolute authority. Indeed, liberal democracy is premised on the separation of powers. The federal model already involves the sharing of sovereignty between the commonwealth and the states. In Europe, as Henry Reynolds notes, the federalist model has attracted interest, as the establishment of the European Union moves some elements of sovereignty upwards to a supranational level and other elements have been devolved to regional level. "If sovereignty could be divided one way in 1901 there can be no reason, in principle, why it cannot be cut again to create a new level of government that would allow Aboriginal and Islander communities to run their own internal affairs in ways already apparent in the external territories of Cocos-Keeling, Christmas and Norfolk Islands."[42]

The recognition of native title was an acknowledgement of an indigenous system of property law. Frank Brennan describes Aboriginal people's relationship with "clan, Dreaming and land...[as] law in its fullest sense". This view, he points out, was articulated in 1971, in the Gove Land rights case. Mr Justice Blackburn declared that Aboriginal society was governed by "a subtle and elaborate system...remarkably free from the vagaries of personal whim or influence...a government of laws not of men".[43] The incorporation of customary law into the criminal justice system is one sign of the ways that some measure of autonomy might be conceptualised and institutionalised. Customary law's provisions for "payback" have been recognised in cases of assault. To date this has happened at the point of sentencing, where courts can exercise some discretion.[44] Mandatory sentencing has constrained the courts' discretion with tragic consequences. Further adaptation of customary law to the problems facing the juvenile justice system may offer some hope.

Public history

In *Mabo*, Justices Deane and Gaudron asserted that "the full facts of the dispossession" have a critical bearing on assessing the legitimacy of the propositions that New South Wales in 1788 was, for legal purposes, an unoccupied territory and that the Crown became "the full and beneficial owner", whose ownership was unaffected by Aboriginal claims.

> Long acceptance of legal propositions, particularly relating to land, can give legitimacy and preclude challenge. But these two propositions have been associated with dispossessing the Aboriginal peoples; and that prevents them from acquiring the legitimacy which more than 150 years would otherwise give them.[45]

History also played a role in the *Wik* judgement, where acceptance of the historical evidence that pastoral leases were a colonial artefact was significant. The majority accepted that the history of granting pastoral leases was evidence of an intention to preserve traditional rights.[46] Justice Gummow dissented, placing no reliance on this history, because there was no "established taxonomy to regulate such uses of history in the formulation of legal norms".[47]

Historians have emerged alongside anthropologists as a source of expert advice in the arena of indigenous politics and law. Henry Reynolds has played a significant and public role in the High Court's deliberations; Peter Read has been an advocate and activist, establishing Link-up, an organisation which reunites families in partnership with separated children. The HREOC published the stories of members of the stolen generations on its website. Elsewhere, history has been integral to a process of public commemmoration and reparation. In Europe, memorialising the Holocaust, the scandal of the Vichy government, and the phenomenon of "survivor's shame" in those who were liberated from the concentration camps, have all been the subject of ongoing public contention, because these acts of memory have also brought discomforting emotions to the surface of public life.

There has been division among historians, and considerable public debate, about "black armband history". In a review of recent histories in the *Australian's Review of Books,* Marilyn Lake posed the question in terms of how history's task has shifted: in modern times, it was "to serve, even create, the nation" now it seems "a shame job" forcing the "recognition that nation-building rested on the dispossession of the Aborigines and the violent destruction of their communities".[48]

In *Why Weren't We Told?*, (one of the books Lake was reviewing) Henry Reynolds recalls those nationalist histories, in which Aborigines were banished from the text to a "melancholy footnote". Revisionist history, on the other hand, is

> written in the hope and expectation of reform, crafted in the confidence that carefully marshalled, clearly expressed argument can persuade significant numbers of Australians to change their minds and reconsider their sympathies. Beyond that confidence in individuals is a firm belief in the capacity of Australian democracy to respond to new ideas which in time can reshape policies and recast institutions, laws and customs.[49]

The historian, Reynolds contends, also has a duty as a citizen. That duty is to find, in the archives and other sources, the evidence which, once subject to the accredited methods of the discipline, can reveal truth and put it into the public domain. Inga Clendennin similarly insists on the importance of "*true* stories". In her Boyer lectures, she performed a practice of history, telling her audience on the public broadcaster stories of Australia's colonial past, and of the present. She told the stories, but extended the idea of "doing history" to the acts of imaginative indentification she engaged in. She asked her listeners to participate in similar acts of identification. She described the elements of the "intellectual and imaginative exercise" of retrieving these incidents from the documents: thinking about the event and its consequences; making sober judgements about the actors, their motives and character; imagining "the thoughts and feelings of the silent players in the scene" and "clarifying and examining our own responses to what happened".[50]

This kind of examination, Clendennin claims, can be "conducive to civic virtue". It can elicit a recognition of the other, and a realisation of the lessons the past offers. It can prompt questions about responsibility, debt and reparation, and guide future action. In short, it can give us a means to address questions of ethics and values, as well as politics and community. Clendennin makes large claims for the moral effects of "narrative imagination", and for the historian as a public intellectual. She expects her listener to respond to the force of moral law and to exercise critical reason. Like Eamonn Callan, she suspects sentiment; this is the point of her insistence that the stories are *true*. How can public discussion and debate of contentious issues foster "civic virtue"? This is a question we explore further in the next chapter.

Chapter 8
Articulate Citizens

In this final chapter, we return to questions about the cultivation of "civic virtue". We've suggested that the exercise of critical reason demands a great deal of citizens. Yet sentimental patriotism is an unsatisfying alternative. What is required to support "good" citizenship in a pluralist multi-ethnic society? Can we talk meaningfully about a "common culture"? In a society where people pursue different ideas of the good life, how can we live peacefully and well together? These are questions which we approach now with a particular caution, given the twentieth century's evidence of the destructive force of ideas about ethnic belonging and of religious and moral beliefs. We have already noted how dangerous communitarian ideals can be, but is the liberal indifference to difference sustainable in the contemporary context of cultural diversity? This chapter will take on these issues from the perspective of applied ethics, rather than moral and political philosophy. This means that we will pitch the discussion at the level of the practical wisdom and skills required of responsible citizens, rather than attempt to occupy the higher ground from which discussions of perfection — whether of systems of government or human achievement — begin.

In this chapter, we sketch out an idea of "articulate citizenship". This is something of a hybrid. "Articulate citizens" have a practical awareness of the contexts — social, economic, governmental — in which they operate. They are disposed to "do the right thing" and to respect the rights and dignity of others as well as to know their own interests. They make connections. They also strike a balance, recognising that enlightened self-interest does not demand saintly self-sacrifice to the common good.[1] Their civic and political identities exist alongside other dimensions of identity, to be engaged as necessary, but not always taking priority. We are using "articulate" here then, in its sense of "joining together". But we are also aware of its connotations of "eloquence". This goes against the grain of Australian stereotypes: the "national character" is laconic, taciturn. It also flies in the face of characterisations of contemporary political culture, as an "argument culture"[2] or a "culture of complaint"[3] which engenders a "politics of grievance"[4]. We don't wish to suggest that "higher standards" of public speech are what are required here, though some commentators wistfully suggest that this is needed. We do, however, want to question some assumptions about what public debate can do.

"Articulate" does not signify some standard to be attained. Rather, we want to use it to represent the skills and capacities that go with a lower order of civic virtue than critical reason. This is a practical wisdom that is enacted in the skills of speaking, negotiating, listening, disagreeing; and the capacity to make connections, not just with other interested parties, but across disciplines, across policy domains, across cultures. Implicit in our discussion so far is the question of where and how good citizenship can be articulated and realised. This chapter focusses on the realm of civil society as the space where the line between private life and the expansive domain of politics is negotiated.

Civic Virtues

In the last chapter, we concluded with Inga Clendennin's claim that doing history was conducive to civic virtue. She agrees with Martha Nussbaum that the capacities necessary for "responsible citizenship" are

> An ability to critically examine oneself and one's traditions; an ability to see beyond immediate group loyalties and to extend to strangers the moral concern we "naturally" extend to friends and kin; the development of ... the "narrative imagination": the ability to see unobvious connections between sequences of human actions, and to recognise their likely consequences, intended and unintended.[5]

These are virtues that have to be learned, and Clendennin contends that the disciplines and methods of history teach them. She also insists that historical documents (*true* stories) both produce the distance which allows critical examination of one's own traditions and extend empathy from kin to strangers. The examples we draw on in our discussion come from experience that is closer to home and from everyday popular culture. The "truth" of these experiences, performances and texts is not amenable to the kinds of tests of reliability and accuracy that historians apply.

There are many versions of the "civic virtues", some of which we'll outline here. But the point to be drawn now is that civic virtues can be differentiated from "moral virtues" and particularly "critical reason" on the basis that they can be learned. Peter Berkowitz invokes Artistotle's distinction between moral and intellectual virtue to make this point. Moral virtue involves "right reason" but intellectual virtue is "exercised in practical judgement as well as in theoretical contemplation". More importantly, intellectual virtue comes from teaching; whereas "right reason" requires moral knowledge and capacities of a much higher order.[6]

Political stability depends on citizens with grounds for mutual trust, a capacity for friendship, and a shared sense of justice. These civic virtues need not be linked to any particular idea of what human nature might be (as moral virtues are), but can instead be linked to how we perform our obligations in our various roles as citizens. Those obligations attach to our social relationships as members of families, as friends, and as neighbours; to economic relations in our identities as workers and householders; and to our political identities as members of communities and voluntary associations, as jurors, voters, representatives, advocates, delegates and so on. In each of those roles we have particular and limited obligations. These roles have an ethic attached to them which requires that persons occupying them are able to recognise the limits of their duty; to discern the rights and interests of others; to understand the policy and legal contexts which constrain action, and to understand processes and procedures of accountability. In short, doing the right thing in the right way toward the right people and for the right reasons.[7]

We are not going to consider the particular ethics of any of this wide array of roles here. Rather we will focus on the more general obligations of the citizen to take an interest in public affairs, and consider how these obligations are played out in the public sphere of discussion and debate. Citizens are not obliged to participate in public life to the extent of becoming officeholders, or even to formulate an informed position on every issue. If they exercise only their minimal obligations — to be law abiding, to vote — then the necessary virtues might be cast as civility, public reasonableness and a commitment to hold public officials accountable for their conduct.[8]

Citizenship does not exhaust the possibilities of life choices. We are stressing the option to minimise public involvements because the attractions of private life and the rewards it offers are not to be lightly dismissed. Most people do not get deeply excited by politics; and many who do are not attractive people. This is not simply to denigrate politicians as power hungry and unprincipled. It is to say that an interest in power, its operations and institutions is not distributed evenly across the population. Berkowitz explains the appeal of Aristotelian political science in terms of its modest and moderate aims:

> Aristotelian political science does not seek to transform imperfect regimes, such as democracies and oligarchies, into regimes devoted to human excellence; rather, it aims to institute measures so as to enable imperfect regimes to honour their principles and to moderate their unwise tendencies. The single greatest expedient for preserving a regime, says Aristotle, is the one most neglected by actual regimes: education in virtues that serve as a counterpoise to the characteristic bad habits and reckless desires which regimes tend to foster in their citizens.[9]

Bad habits and reckless desires compromise liberty. General virtues like loyalty, prudence, generosity and temperance constrain those desires. They can be translated into *civic* virtues in different ways. A rule based ethic, according to J.B. Schneewind, poses the question as "what should I do?" and focusses on the act: "is this being done in the right way?" The central question in a virtue centred approach is "what sort of person am I to be?" or "is this what a good person would do?"[10]

A common culture?

The state has an interest in cultivating civic virtue, even though it must do this indirectly. It requires citizens who will take their obligations seriously and who will cooperate in the establishment of cohesive law-abiding communities. In pluralist societies, this requirement has been translated into a need to foster and support a common culture. State interventions in educational and cultural policy are one means of promoting a common culture, but attachments to shared values and meanings occur at the level of participation in the popular culture. Ideas of Australian identity and national character have emphasised independence, egalitarianism and mateship. The meanings of these traditions have been grounded in the experience of the bush worker and in the Anzac tradition, rather than in political history and government. They have been robustly criticised as racially exclusive and masculinist. This contestation has been critical to their survival. The traditions have been transformed by the incorporation of resistant elements. Opinion is divided about this outcome. Is inclusiveness optimal or even desirable? Does it erase difference and maintain dominance? Should diverse and even rival traditions be supported?

> Historically, virtually every liberal democracy has, at one point or another, attempted to diffuse a single societal culture throughout all of its territory. Nor should these efforts at assimilation be seen purely as a matter of cultural imperialism or ethnocentric prejudice...The sort of solidarity required by the welfare state requires that citizens have a strong sense of common identity and common membership, so that they will make sacrifices for each other, and this common identity is assumed to require (or at least be facilitated by) a common language and history. Promoting integration into a common societal culture has been seen as essential to social equality and political cohesion in modern states.[11]

Will Kymlicka distinguishes three ways the state can deal with multiculturalism: marginalisation, integration and self-government. Marginalisation is the choice of some groups to isolate themselves in their community, whose religious or moral beliefs justify their withdrawal from all but unavoidable contact with the common culture (the Amish, for example, but also and more alarmingly, fundamentalist cults). Integration, Kymlicka argues, is the appropriate policy in immigrant nations, since people have chosen to make a new life in a new country. In keeping with the principles of liberal pluralism, integration assumes that a common culture will shape social and political relations, and that the state will not intervene in cultural or religious expression in private life. Self-government for indigenous peoples has properly become a matter for public debate in settler societies, like Canada, New Zealand and Australia. In these instances, colonial administrations supplanted societies with settled systems of law and culture. Those societies have suffered territorial dispossession and the destruction of their cultures and should now be compensated and supported in achieving self-determination.

In Australia, the exclusionary White Australia policy and assimilation have given way to pluralist multiculturalism. The common culture has accommodated ethnic difference to a limited degree. Citizenship in a common culture has been supported by education and social policy. The state has promoted free compulsory and secular education in English since the middle of the nineteenth century. Since the 1970s support for ethnic cultures has included establishing the multilingual television service, SBS, and a commonwealth office of multicultural affairs. Multicultural policy has been designed to achieve integration.

As we've already suggested, giving content to the notion of indigenous autonomy is a problem still to be addressed. In the area of language policy, some support has been given to maintaining indigenous languages and to funding for schooling in indigenous languages, particularly in South Australia. The House of Representatives published a report, *Language and Culture — A Matter of Survival,* in 1992. Currently a National Indigenous English Literacy and Numeracy Strategy is in place for 2000-2004, but a Senate report into the effectiveness of education and training for indigenous people, *Katu Kalpa,* made no recommendations about indigenous languages.[12] The Northern Territory government discontinued a bilingual education policy in 1998. Concern about the disappearance of indigenous languages is especially acute given the legal imperatives of native title regimes, that "traditional owners" demonstrate the continuity of their affiliations to land and culture.

State subsidy of a "national" culture has a longer history. The Commonwealth Literary Fund began as a pension scheme for writers, before its expansion and transformation into the Australia Council under the Gorton government in 1968. Institutions like public libraries, museums, the Australia Council and the Australian Film Institute, as well as public broadcasting support a common culture. National celebrations focus attention on questions of values and character in a powerful way. We've already alluded to the proposals for the commemoration of the Centenary of Federation. The annual ceremonies on Anzac Day provide an illustration of the way these values accommodate change and difference.

The Anzac legend has been an important strand of the "common culture". After the enormous loss of life in World War 1, memorials were raised in local communities, in France and Britain, as well as Australia, to commemorate the soldier citizen. The figure bowed over reversed arms was not only common property, he was also set apart as a member of a military order. This exclusiveness was protected by the RSL, which has firmly maintained ownership of the public ceremonial, and determined rights of participation in the parade. Popular mythology and oppositional nationalism fashioned an understanding of the circumstances of Australia's war history — that the AIF served in an imperial force in a "foreign" war, that Australian forces were sacrificed to foreign interests — which produced ambivalence about these celebrations. Alan Seymour's play, *The One Day of the Year,* (1962) expressed bitter generational divisions about the sanctity of the tradition. The introduction of conscription during the Vietnam war and the long delay in recognising the veterans of that unpopular war in public ceremonial, indicate some of the problems in adapting this tradition within mainstream culture. But it has adapted and incorporated difference and diversity. The service of Aboriginal people and women has been recognised. The ugly episodes of enemy internment have been acknowledged. And the experience of war has been extended to include the homefront.[13] The contribution of women, for example in the Land Army, anti-War and anti-conscription protests, and the remembrance of the victims of war are now part of the tradition. One sign of this is that an anti-war song, "The Band Played Waltzing Matilda", has become an anthem for Anzac Day.

In recent years, there has been a revival of public interest in these observances, with increasing crowd numbers at the traditional dawn services, marches and wreath laying ceremonies. At Gallipoli in April 2000, on the 85th anniversary of the landing, a new memorial was dedicated to the soldiers who lost their lives there. In his address John Howard described the inheritance of Anzac, but differentiated the ideals of the soldier citizen from those appropriate to the present time. "The inheritance we claim today is not a fallen sword, nor have we come to extol a warrior's code", he said. Instead, "we come to draw upon their stirring example of unity and common purpose, to believe that, whatever our differing circumstances, we are all companions with each of our countrymen and women, and together we travel a single path".[14] The audience who heard this speech included large numbers of young Australian backpackers, en route to Europe. This generation, children and grandchildren of Vietnam veterans, is rediscovering the meanings of Anzac. At North Mackay High School in Queensland, students undertook a "civics excursion" to Gallipoli, Belgium and France. Their trip was documented on ABC TV's *Australian Story*.[15] These students set out to do history in the way Inga Clendennin describes. They turned to the documentary evidence to find the "true story", and they extended their narrative imagination in an effort to understand the experience of young people of their own age who volunteered to fight and to understand the meaning of their loss for their families. The excursion became a community project, as the students collected oral history from surviving family members. On the trip, they met a reciprocal obligation to share their experience: 100 year old Amy Taylor, who had mourned her brother Herbert in the years since his death, saw a photograph of his grave for the first time.

Is this a sentimental attachment to culture and community of the kind Eamonn Callan deplores? Should we be suspicious of this evidence of traditions recuperating resistance — even to the extent that battlefields become tourist attractions and protest songs part of Anzac folklore? The strategy of inclusiveness does disarm resistance. But it is also easy to overlook the investments which propel the struggle for inclusion. The opening ceremony at the Sydney 2000 Olympics has been praised for presenting Australia without the cringe, and criticised for political correctness. Aboriginal protocol took precedence in the welcome, and Aboriginal custodianship of the land was acknowledged. Behind the scenes stories suggest that the "Awakening" segment of this extravagant spectacle did not simply fall into place. Funding had to be fought for, and "creative" arguments won, before the traditional stories could be staged. The organisers' preference for "dot paintings and flaming boomerangs" gave way to strenuous advocacy in support of representing a "surviving, vital culture". Non-Aboriginal audiences saw that Aboriginality is not one thing, but "incredibly diverse". Stephen Page and Rhoda Roberts, the directors of this performance, brought together 330 women from the central Desert, 200 young people from four Arnhem Land communities,

100 Torres Strait Islanders and 400 dancers from urban and rural New South Wales. Its message was not only for the Australian and international audience but was also directed to urban youth, to give them an opportunity to be part of the kinship system. Addressing the young dancers drawn from high schools in New South Wales at a rehearsal, Rhoda Roberts told them: "We want to show respect for elders and what we are about... We want to show the world we are one nation... we are all one mob".[16]

The opening ceremony displayed Australia's common culture as a work in progress. Meanings are not settled, but contested and transformed. It played freely with stereotypes and iconic figures, while minimally interpreting them for the international audience. The "Tin Symphony" celebrated inventiveness and innovation, as well as the myths of bush culture. The mix of solemnity and wit even pervaded the singing of the national anthem. And the failure of the mechanism as the cauldron rose underlined how difficult it can be to make meanings hold together. Meanings hold together only for as long as they are useable. The parochial or patriotic crowds at the Olympics will discard their wigs and banners until the next time. The fervour will dissipate, as will some of the friendliness and cooperation.

It is worth recalling an earlier public ritual of recognition, to reinforce the point that understanding is contingent and never final. In 1975, Gough Whitlam handed over the lease for Daguragu to the Aboriginal owners. In a poignant gesture, the Prime Minister poured soil into Vincent Lingiari's hands. Lingiari generously responded: "We are all mates now".[17] Mateship has been celebrated as a "together against the odds" sentiment, and it has been decried as exclusionary, not egalitarian. But words get new meanings when they pass into new contexts and are used by new interpretive communities. What did Vincent Lingiari understand mateship to be? How does his usage transform its meaning? Can his meaning survive if the circumstances in which he uttered it — a ritual expression of recognition and reciprocity — are not sustained in the mundane exchanges of everyday life? Restoring the original egalitarian associations of "mateship", transforming its connotations of "mutuality" and "reciprocity" to accommodate diversity, presents a challenge for public discourse. The failure of the proposed preamble to the constitution, and its attempt to invoke "mateship", suggests that this is not such a malleable term.

The exchange of public reasons

Dissenting talk is as critical to the determination of the common good as any public spectacle of unity. Is all dissent to be tolerated? Complaints about political correctness imply that public speech is being unreasonably constrained. It's also common to hear the view that speech has become uncivil, racist and xenophobic, and above all selfish. Jennifer Hewitt reflected on the character of public discourse in a recent edition of the *Sydney Morning Herald*. She observed

> an unprecedented degree of emotional turmoil and feverish debate in a country more noted for its inarticulate stoicism and its unblinking acceptance of the "it's just how things are" approach. No worries, indeed. Instead, the whole country seems to have spent the past few years arguing loudly about everything from Aborigines to immigration to the United Nations to racism to welfare to refugees to single mothers and even lesbian mothers.[18]

The public sphere is full of the clamour of voices, if we think of the popularity and influence of talk back radio hosts, the regular publication of opinion polls on almost every issue and the increasing access to the Internet. Judith Brett has argued that these voices find a theme in the "politics of grievance".[19] While the "shock jocks" whip up these feelings and resort to law and order and a return to traditional values as solutions, they also spurn elite opinion. Beyond the "sense of grievance and barren comfort of complaining", civic virtue requires a willingness to engage in discussion, to participate in the "public exchange of reasons".[20]

Does a disposition to "public reasonableness" enhance the likelihood of agreement? In many instances of public debate, it is evident that the parties cannot agree, and are not disposed to achieve agreement. Disagreement is not always resolved even where there is good will. Toleration might be an appropriate response to some situations; in other circumstances toleration may not appear to be neutral or impartial. The Liberal Party disendorsed Pauline Hanson because her views about race contravened the party's policy. She gained election as an independent and elaborated those views in her first parliamentary speech. John Howard's refusal to repudiate her views divided public opinion. Many read his tolerance as a tacit endorsement. The debates about reconciliation and about the High Court decisions on native title have also raised questions about the extent of toleration of racist speech. The National Farmers' Federation's television "Twister" advertisement, screened when the 10-point plan was being debated in parliament, aroused strong reactions not only because of its representation of "inequality" but because it projected its sentiments onto children. We turn to this question here, not in order to arbitrate on racist speech, but as a way of considering how political communities debate and deliberate about the common good, and how the exchange of public reasons takes place. Recalling Alastair Davidson's argument that transparency and openness is the key to public accountability, and that the neutrality of public language poses a problem for communication in plural societies (Chapter 5), this discussion will be attentive to liberal standards of neutrality and to the effects of public emotion.

Public spheres of controversy animate democracy. In contemporary culture, there has been some reaction against this, which particularly focusses on the media and politics. Casting disagreement invariably as antagonism, staging differences of opinion as confrontations, looking for sound bites rather than informed discussion: these are elements of what Deborah Tannen has called "the argument culture". Technologically enhanced aggression is a feature of this culture: the anonymity allowed by the telephone, email and the Internet encourages a lack of restraint, even rage. The recorded message, the call centre operator and the radio "shock jock" are all manifestations of the disconnectedness which, Tannen argues, allows hostility to erupt unchecked. Tannen draws attention to the contrast of Western traditions of argument and disputation with Indian and Chinese traditions, which emphasise exposition. "The aim was to 'enlighten an inquirer', not to 'overwhelm an opponent'." And the preferred style reflected "the earnestness of investigation" rather than "the fervour of conviction".[21]

William Galston argues that the importance of public discourse to citizenship in liberal democracies is not just about the obligation to participate or the right to express views. The disposition of public reasonableness also requires "the willingness to listen seriously to a range of views which, given the diversity of liberal societies, will include ideas the listener is bound to find obnoxious ... [and] willingness to set forth one's own views intelligibly and candidly as the basis for a politics of persuasion rather than manipulation or coercion".[22] The desire that public discourse should be persuasive rather than coercive is more difficult to realise than this appeal might allow, however. Being candid, listening seriously, speaking intelligibly: these are standards that many public commentators and public intellectuals fail to meet. Deliberation on matters of public importance, whether or not they involve moral principles, is a fraught process. Persuasion does not depend solely on right reasons, but also involves the participants' willingness to reach agreement.

Debate about reconciliation has found a focus in the contentious issues of an official apology to the stolen generations, and the recognition of indigenous peoples' status in the nation. Words, symbols and meanings have been critical here. The constitutional preamble drafted by John Howard and Les Murray stumbled over words. "Mateship" as an expression of national values was ridiculed in some quarters; this is a word whose egalitarian associations have been considerably diminished. Finding a word to convey indigenous peoples' status and relationship to the land also precipitated debate: were they custodians or stewards of country, or did they merely occupy it? Parliament has recorded its "deep and sincere regret" for the policies which tore apart Aboriginal families and the Prime Minister has made a personal apology, but an official "sorry" has not been forthcoming. As the Council for Aboriginal Reconciliation prepared to hand over its draft document at Corroboree 2000, its Deputy Chair, Gustav Nossal, conceded that this would have to await the next prime minister. Opinion polls report that many Australians endorse John Howard's position, and think it's time to "move on". A Newspoll survey conducted for the Council for Aboriginal Reconciliation revealed that respondents warmed to sentiments of "equality, unity and a desire for resolution" in the draft document. However, even among those "who say they support most of the contents ... a significant proportion find sticking points concerning the apology, original ownership or colonisation without consent".[23] Shadowing all this discussion is "Hansonism". The anxieties and grievances which found a fierce, if quavering, voice in the leader of One Nation have not dissipated. One Nation is in disarray; but the sentiments which galvanised it are still registering. Populist feeling and elite opinion are still seen to be at odds, and this gap continues to be exploited in media commentary.

These comments take this discussion into the realm that liberal tradition quarantines from the public domain: the realm of morality. The achievement of liberalism was to establish a secular public domain; the separation of church and state was to guarantee public neutrality. The legitimate pursuit of private interests and the expression of moral and religious belief were separated from the concerns of the state. Civil harmony was achieved by the refusal of the state to intervene in private life, and by the practice of toleration. This indifference to differences is challenged by demands for cultural rights, and by the increasing heterogeneity of multiracial and multiethnic societies. Do we need something more than "tolerance" and is it going to be produced by public debate?

How has "elite opinion" sparked and shaped debate? An array of leaders in politics, the judiciary, the churches, academia and the indigenous community have contributed to the "open-ended conversation" about reconciliation. Their opinions do not always chime and at times they have been emotional. It is this public expression of emotion, and the reactions it provokes, which interests us here. Since the *Mabo* decision in 1992, the native title debate has been a catalyst of public emotion, some of it expressed in the opinions of the Justices, much of it in opposition to the roles of the unelected members of the bench. The fallout has often been hostility and antagonism but there have also been very public changes of heart.

Leadership on these issues has emerged on both sides of politics. Paul Keating's Redfern Park speech inaugurated the year of indigenous peoples; Malcolm Fraser's recent Vincent Lingiari Memorial Lecture reminded us that his government had enacted land rights legislation drafted by the Whitlam government. Fraser's speech called out divisions in liberal party thinking on indigenous issues. Prominent advocates for indigenous claims have also come from the churches. Frank Brennan has published extensively on the *Mabo* and *Wik* decisions. At Easter, members of the Anglican clergy and congregation boycotted the inauguration of Peter Carnley as Primate, following the publication of his meditation on the meanings of the crucifixion in the *Bulletin*. Speaking about forgiveness, Carnley suggested that Christ might not be the only means of reconciliation with God. This gesture toward inclusiveness was not welcomed by many orthodox Anglicans. Public intellectuals have also attracted controversy. The academic Robert Manne resigned as editor of *Quadrant* in controversial circumstances in 1997. The management committee was disturbed by the journal's "political correctness": "It had become far too obsessed with questions of Aboriginal justice". Reflecting on the circumstances of his removal, Manne has written that he set out to create "a forum where complex, open-ended conversation could take place". His policy divided readers as well: some responded "warmly"; others sent hate mail, expressing "visceral anger".[24] Is Manne's faith in the value of "conversation" naïve? Jeffrey Wallen suggests that "conversation" is an interaction between intimate equals and is more likely to close down debate than to open it to fresh opinions.[25] Mark Davis has produced a savage account of the "gangs" who protect each other's reputations and interests in the confined circles of Australian public intellectuals.[26] Wallen maintains that conducting a conversation is too often seen as itself an affirmation of democracy:

> Getting people to talk to each other does not, however, produce a functioning democracy. A conversation about "who we are" is no substitute for discussing the economic, political and social problems that are the evidence of how far we still are from the ideals of democracy ... .Any fuller articulation of the problems ... would shatter the pretence that understanding someone else's perspective offers an adequate means for addressing these questions.[27]

Conversation, however, can be a step toward acknowledging differences and establishing trust. It need not be, in Wallen's words, "weak and tepid". The directness and intimacy of informal speech and action can be very powerful in the public domain. A number of recent instances demonstrate this. On 28 May, 2000 many thousands of people walked across the Sydney harbour bridge to express their hopes for reconciliation. Many more joined them in similar walks in other cities. This demonstration of support coincided with Corroboree 2000 and recalled the sea of hands which commemorated Sorry Day in 1997. Jamie Mackie describes the emotion the walkers evoked: "It was the spontaneous, Brown's cows quality of it which I found most moving, enjoyable and weirdly characteristic of this marvellously casual country."[28]

In their judgement in *Mabo*, Justices Deane and Gaudron drew attention to their own unrestrained language, as they reflected on the "full facts" of Aboriginal dispossession. They described the effects of colonial settlement on indigenous culture: "the conflagration of oppression and conflict ... spread across the continent to dispossess, degrade and devastate the Aboriginal peoples and leave a national legacy of unutterable shame". They declared that "the nation as a whole must remain diminished unless and until there is an acknowledgment of, and retreat from, those past injustices".[29] Does such language compromise their judgement or does it reinforce its legitimacy and significance? This was a risk the Justices acknowledged. The *Mabo* judgement produced a fundamental change in the Australian legal system and in the political culture. This use of language does not shrink from that. But it also accomplishes more than simply declare a position: it invites engagement and indicates a course of action.

Resourceful citizenship

In Chapter 1, we noticed "community" as a key theme of 1990s popular culture, citing examples of television series which centred on small town life. *SeaChange* has outrated *60 Minutes*, consistently winning bigger audiences in its Sunday timeslot. We could risk speculating here, that this as a sign that on Sunday nights at least, audiences are turned off by the questionable ethics of the "exposé" genre in current affairs, and prefer to watch people work out how to put lives together. A casual survey of television — "domestic" popular culture — is evidence of the intensification of private life. Infotainment captured viewers in the 1990s, with an emphasis on home improvement and holidays. The enthusiasm for DIY seems to have waned, while travel programmes continue to flourish. Even cooking programmes now incorporate exotic locations and local excursions. The ABC's *Gardening Australia*, produced in Tasmania, promotes sound environmental values and home-grown egalitarianism (how can composting co-exist with class distinctions?). It appeals to audiences who share its presenters' values of neighbourliness, thrift and self-reliance. But elsewhere on television, time-poor suburbanites are taking off for the weekend, leaving the experts to swarm over desolate backyards, blitzing sad examples of DIY handiwork and replacing them with gazebos and water features. This is the generation who work the double shift and outsource domestic duties. They are networkers who add value by connecting to resources. In the current idiom of industry policy, we could say that citizens need resources if they are to create capability.

Working Dog, the creators of *Frontline*, turned their attention from the exposé of current affairs journalism to domestic do-it-yourselfers with *The Castle* (1997). After *Frontline's* bitter satire of media ethics, they poked fun at suburban dreams. But the film also celebrated Darryl Kerrigan's resourceful defence of his right to his castle. In his DIY life, Darryl relies on the *Trading Post* and his devoted if dysfunctional family to assemble his idiosyncratic version of the dream. His defence of that right cannot be sustained by these personal resources. He needs his neighbours and experts. His need extends the competence of the bumbling local solicitor, wins public sympathy and the support of a more expert legal representative. Darryl has just enough civic competence to know his "rights". He knows nothing of the legal system (despite having a son in jail), and he doesn't consider the "public interest".

Frontline told us we were being treated like mugs. It exposed the seductions of television, the opportunities it offers for the greedy and the cynical. At the same time, it showed us how slick and clever the techniques which fool us are, and in exploiting them itself, it invited us to appreciate the potential uses of media entertainment. In Darryl we saw that suburban seclusion, and the attractions of private life are no bad thing. There is more to life than political engagements — there's fishing weekends, and sponge cake, and home improvement projects. These things don't turn us into complacent dullards (though, in the example of Darryl's family, we see that they very easily *could*). Yet even if we are disarmed by the Kerrigans, and suspend our judgement on their pleasures, we still have to notice that their house was to be resumed for a public purpose. NIMBY politics is usually in the news because it is being played out around the interests of a more affluent class of property owner. Urban professionals restoring inner urban properties object to aircraft noise, or owners of outer suburban acreage protest that a road or a rubbish dump will detract from their quality of life. These groups have become expert in organising protests, and in exploiting their political clout.

We might say that *The Castle* celebrates the right to be a private citizen. But when we see Darryl settling back into his house under the flight path, we see an "isolationist" to recall Kymlicka's term. Private rights have public costs.[30] How do we calculate the public cost of the "right" to home ownership, or of exclusive rights of access to the foreshore, for example? The film does not pose these questions directly: they would never occur to Darryl.

Rob Sitch and Tom Gleisner, two of the film's creators, made a return to television with *A River Somewhere*, a travel documentary which showed them indulging their passion for fishing at the same time as it indirectly promoted environmental values. As members of *The Panel*, they participate in a low-key discussion of "public affairs" with guests who include sports stars, celebrities and the occasional politician and public intellectual. The conversation turns to subjects that would be on the agenda in pubs and living rooms in most towns and cities. These people exchange banter, and ask the odd searching question of their expert guests. The panel don't have the answers, and their opinions are sometimes off beam. They are not omnicompetent citizens but they know how to become informed. They are articulate citizens, at ease in a networked world.

Bibliography

Adams, P. ed. *The Retreat from Tolerance. A Snapshot of Australian Society.* Sydney: Australian Broadcasting Commission, 1997.

Albala-Bertrand, L. "First lessons from the research phase: what education for what citizenship?" *Educational Innovation and information,* no. 90 (1997): 2–8. Available from http://www3.itu.int:8002/ibe-citied/purpose.html

——. "International project; what education for what citizenship? " International Bureau of Education, UNESCO (1997). Accessed 1997. Available from http://www.3.itu.int:8002/ibe-citied/the_project.html.

Alexander, D. "From citizen to individual: a study of changing influences on citizenship education in Queensland from 1968–1988". PhD diss., University of Queensland, 1987.

Alexander, Don and Lloyd Logan. "The informed citizenship project: one instance — two expressions". Paper presented to Connections 97 Conference. Sydney University, July 1997.

Anderson, B. *Imagined Communities: Reflections on the origin and spread of nationalism.* London: Verso, 1991.

ANOP Research Services. *Young People's Attitudes to Postcompulsory Education.* Canberra: Australian Government Printing Service, 1994.

Apple, Michael. "Power, meaning and identity: critical sociology of education in the United States". *British Journal of Sociology of Education* 17.2 (1996): 125–144.

Arnold, J., P. Spearritt, et al., eds. *Out of Empire: the British dominion of Australia.* Melbourne: Mandarin Books, 1993.

Attwood, B. and A. Markus. *The 1967 Referendum, Or when Aborigines didn't get the vote.* In collaboration with Dale Edwards and Kate Schilling. Canberra: Australian Institute of Aboriginal and Torres Strait Islander Studies, 1997.

——. *The Struggle for Aboriginal Rights: A Documentary History.* Sydney: Allen and Unwin, 1999.

Aulich, T. "A Response to Gilbert". *Ethos* (1992): 8–11.

——. (Chair). *Education for Active Citizenship in Australian Schools and Youth Organisations.* Senate Standing Committee on Employment, Education and Training, 1989.

——. (Chair). *Active Citizenship Revisited.* Senate Standing Committee for Employment, Education and Training, 1991.

Australian Curriculum Studies Association. "Civics and Citizenship Education". *Curriculum Perspectives* 16.1 (1996).

Australian Federation of Societies for Studies of Society and Environment. *Discovering Democracy Civics and Citizenship Education.* Report on the outcomes of the initial teacher focus groups on Curriculum Corporation draft unit overview and outlines and unit writers guidelines, 1997.

Bader, V. "The cultural conditions of transnational citizenship". *Political Theory* 25.6 (1997): 771–814.

Bailey, P. *Bringing Human Rights to Life.* Sydney: Federation Press, 1993.

Ball, S. *Education Reform: A Critical and Poststructural Approach.* Buckingham: Open University Press, 1994.

Barber, B. *An Aristocracy of Everyone: the Politics of Education and the Future of America.* New York: Ballantine, 1992.

Barcan, A. *Social Science, History and the New Curriculum.* Sydney: Workers' Educational Association of New South Wales, 1971.

——. "History in a pluralist country: Response to Stuart Macintyre". *Australian Journal of Education* 41.2 (1997): 199–212.

——. "The curriculum as social studies". *The Australian Quarterly* 60.4 (1998): 448–477.

Bartelson, J. *A Genealogy of Sovereignty.* Cambridge: Cambridge University Press, 1996.

Batstone, D. and E, Mendieta. *The Good Citizen.* New York: Routledge, 1999.

Baubock, R., ed. *From Aliens to Citizens: redefining the status of immigrants in Europe.* Aldershot: Avebury, 1994.

Baykan, A. "Issues of difference and citizenship for 'new identities': a theoretical view". *Innovation: the European journal of social sciences* 10.1 (1997): 61–67.

Beem, C. "Civil is Not Good Enough". *Current* no. 388 (1996): 22–27.

Beilharz, P. "Republicanism and Citizenship". In *The Republicanism Debate*. Eds. W. Hudson and D. Carter. Sydney: NSW University Press, 1993. pp. 109–17.

Bell, D. A. "Civil Society versus Civic Virtue". In *Freedom of Association*. Ed. A. Gutmann. Princeton: Princeton University Press, 1998. pp. 239–72.

Bell, G., ed. *Educating European Citizens: citizenship values and the European dimension*. London: David Fulton, 1995.

Bellah, R.N. *Habits of the Heart: individualism and commitment in American Life*. Berkley: University of California Press, 1985.

Bennett, S. *White Politics and Black Australians*. Sydney: Allen and Unwin, 1999.

Bennett, T. and C. Mercer. "Improving research and international co-operation for cultural policy". In *Intergovernmental Conference on Cultural Policies for Development*. Stockholm, Sweden, 1998.

Berkowitz, P. *Virtue and the Making of Modern Liberalism* Princeton: Princeton University Press, 1999.

Berland, J. "Politics after nationalism. culture after 'culture'". *Canadian Review of American Studies* 27.3 (1997): 35–52.

Berlet, C. *Eyes right!: challenging the right wing backlash*. Boston, Mass.: South End Press, 1995.

Black, J.H. "Government as a source of assistance for newly-arrived immigrants in Canada: some initial observations". In *Education for democratic citizenship: a challenge for multi-ethnic societies*. Ed. R.S. Sigel and M.H Hoskin. Hillsdale, New Jersey: Lawrence Erlbaum Associates, 1991. pp. 167–192.

Bloom, A. *The closing of the American mind*. New York: Simon and Schuster, 1987.

Board, P. "The development of secondary education in Australia". In *The Education of the Adolescent in Australia*. Ed. P.R. Cole. Melbourne: Melbourne University Press, 1935.

Board, P. *Whither Education*. Sydney: Angus and Robertson, 1939.

Boyte, H. and N. Skelton. "The Legacy of Public Work: Educating for Citizenship". *Educational Leadership* 54.4 (1997): 12–18.

Branson, M. "The education of citizens in a market economy and its relation to a free society". Paper presented to the

International Conference on Western Democracy and Eastern Europe: Political, Economic and Social Changes. East Berlin: Center for Civic Education, 1991.

———. "Rights: An international perspective". Paper presented to the First Plenary Session of the Annual Leadership conference of the Center for Civic Education. Marina del Rey, California, 21 June 1991.

———"What does research on political attitudes and behaviour tell use about the need for improving education for democracy?" Paper presented to the International Conference on Education for Democracy. Serra Retreat, Malibu, California, 3 October 1994.

Brennan, F. *Legislating Liberty: A Bill of Rights for Australia?* St Lucia: University of Queensland Press, 1998.

———. *The Wik Debate: Its Impact on Aborigines, Pastoralists and Miners.* Sydney: University of New South Wales Press, 1998.

Brennan, M. "Schools as public institutions: students and citizenship". *ACE News*, Nov 1995 (1996): 10–11.

Brett, J. *Robert Menzies' Forgotten People,* Melbourne: Macmillan, 1992.

Brindle, P. and M. Arnot. "'England expects every man to do his duty': the gendering of the citizenship textbook 1940–1966". *Oxford Review of Education* 25.1 (1999): 103–124.

Brubaker, R. *Citizenship and Nationhood in France and Germany.* Cambridge Mass.: Harvard University Press, 1992.

———. *Citizenship and Nationhood in France and Germany.* Cambridge Mass: Harvard University Press, 1992.

Brugger, B. *Republican Theory in Political Thought: Virtuous or Virtual?* Basingstoke: Macmillan, 1999.

Bulbeck, C. "Republicanism and post-nationalism". In *The Republicanism Debate.* Eds. W. Hudson and D. Carter. Kensington: New South Wales University Press, 1993. pp. 88–96.

Butt, P. and R. Eagleson. *Mabo, Wik and Native Title.* Sydney: The Federation Press, 1998.

Butts, R.F. *The Morality of Democratic Citizenship: Goals for Civic Education in the Republic's Third Century.* Calabasas, California: Center for Civic Education, 1988.

——. "The time is now: to frame the civic foundations of teacher education". *Journal of Teacher Education* 44.5 (1993): 325–335.

Butts, R.F., D.H. Peckenpaugh, and H. Kirschenbaum, eds. *The School's Role as Moral Authority*. Washington: Association for Supervision and Curriculum Development, 1977.

Callan, E. "Beyond sentimental civic education." *American Journal of Education* 102.2 (1994): 190–222.

——. *Creating Citizens. Political Education and Liberal Democracy*. Oxford: Clarendon Press, 1997.

Cameron, L. and M. Varma, "Citizens for a new century". *Canadian Ethnic Studies* 29.2 (1997): 121–136.

Cannon, A. "Civics or religion?" *US News & World Report* 128.8 (2 August 2000): 36.

Capling, A, M. Considine and M. Crozier. *Australian Politics and the Global Era*. Melbourne: Addison, Wesley, Longman, 1998.

Carr, W. and A. Hartnett. "Civic education, democracy and the English political tradition". In *Beyond Communitarianism: Citizenship, Politics and Education*. Eds. J. Demaine and H. Entwhistle. London: St. Martin's Press, 1996. pp. 64–82.

Castles, F. "Seeing Australia in the comparative perspective". In *Teaching Young Australians to be Australian Citizens*. Ed. D. Horne. Melbourne: National Centre for Australian Studies, Monash University, 1994.

Carter, A. "Nationalism and Global Citizenship". *Australian Journal of Political History,* 43.1 (1997): 67–81.

Carter, J. "New civics". *Parliamentary Patter* 22 (1994): 3–4.

Center for Civic Education. *National Standards for Civics and Government*. Calabasas, California, 1994.

Center for Civic Education. "About the Center for Civic Education". Accessed March 1995. Available from http://ericr.syr.edu/Civnet/partners/Center/excsum.html.

Character Education Enquiry. *Character Education Poll*. Melbourne: Character Education Enquiry, 1945.

Character Education Enquiry. *Character Education in the home, school, church and club, being report of a conference held at Seaforth, May 1948*. Melbourne: Character Education Enquiry.

Character Education Institute. *Character Education Curriculum*. San Antonio, Texas: Character Education Institute, 1996.

Charlesworth, M. ed. *Religious Business: Essays on Australian Aboriginal Spirituality*. Cambridge: Cambridge University Press, 1998.

Chatterjee, P. *The Nation and its Fragments. Colonial and postcolonial histories*. Princeton: New Jersey, Princeton University Press, 1993.

Citizenship Education Research Network. *Towards a research agenda for citizenship education in Canada*. Alberta: Canadian Society for the Study of Education, 1998.

Civics Expert Group. *Whereas the People: civics and citizenship education*. Canberra: Australian Government Printing Service, 1994.

Clendennin, I. *True Stories*. Boyer Lectures. Sydney: ABC Books, 1999.

Cohen, R. *Frontiers of Identity: the British and others*. London: Longman, 1994.

Cole, M. and D. Hill. "'New labour', old policies: Tony Blair's 'vision' for education in Britain". *Education Australia*, 1998. http://www.edoz.com.au/edoz/archive/issues/blair.html

Cole, P.R. *The Education of the Adolescent in Australia*. Melbourne: Melbourne University Press, 1935.

Colebatch, H.K. "Political knowledge and political education". *Australian Quarterly*, (Spring 1995): 13–23.

Coleman, J.A. "Under the cross and the flag: reflections on discipleship and citizenship in America". *America*, 11 May 1996, 6–15.

Congress, United States of America. *Goals 2000*: Educate America Act, 1994.

Connell, W.F. *New Directions for Character Education*. Melbourne: Character Education Enquiry, 1951.

Connell, R.W., D.J. Ashenden, S. Kessler, and G. Dowsett. *Making the Difference: schools, families and social divisions*. Sydney: Allen & Unwin, 1983.

Cox, E. *A Truly Civil Society*. Sydney: ABC Books, 1994.

Craven, R. "Indigenous Aboriginal studies: an essential component of citizenship education". *The Social Educator* 14.3 (1995): 31–35.

Crawley, A. "Canadian cultural policy — bridging the gaps: Or the cultural activist — a laboratory specimen". *Canadian review of American studies* 27.3 (1997): 99–110.

Crick, B. (Chair). *Education for citizenship and the teaching of democracy in schools; final report of the advisory group on citizenship*. London: Qualifications and Curriculum Authority Department for Education and Employment, on behalf of the Citizenship Advisory group, 1998.

Crittenden, B. "The revival of civics in the school curriculum": comments on the report of the Civics Expert Group: Curriculum Corporation commissioned paper, 1995.

Cunningham, K.S. and W.C. Radford. *Education for Complete Living: the challenge of today*. Melbourne: Australian Council for Educational Research, 1938.

Curriculum Corporation. Discovering Democracy School Materials Project: Draft Conceptual Design Paper, 1997.

——. *Introducing Discovering Democracy School Materials Project*. Carlton Vic: Curriculum Corporation, 1997.

——. *Internet-based collaborative projects in civics*. Accessed 23 June 2000. Available from http://www.curriculum.edu.au/democracy/connect/collabor/collab.html.

——. Can young people influence government? 2000: http://www.curriculum.edu.au/democracy/connect/, 2000.

——. Federation and Centenary celebrations. Curriculum Corporation. 2000: http://www.curriculum.edu.au/democracy/connect/classact/fedceleb.html, 2000.

——. Our Nation; then and now. 2000: http://www.curriculum.edu.au/democracy/connect/classact/ournatn.html, 2000.

Damoisi, J. *The Labour of Loss: Mourning, Memory and Wartime Bereavement in Australia*. Melbourne: Cambridge University Press, 1999.

Davis, G. and M. Keating. *The Future of Governance: Policy Choices*. Sydney: Allen and Unwin, 2000.

Davies, I. "What has happened in the teaching of politics in schools in England in the last three decades, and why?" *Oxford Review of Education* 25.1 (1999): 125–140.

Davidson, A. "*Res publica* and Citizen". In *Crown or Country: The Traditions of Australian Republicanism*. Eds. D. Headon, J.

Warden and B. Gammage. Sydney: Allen & Unwin, 1994. pp. 161–74.

——. *From Subject to Citizen. Australian Citizenship in the Twentieth Century*. Cambridge: Cambridge University Press, 1997.

de Cuellar, J.P. *Our creative diversity*. Report of the World Commission on Culture and Development. Paris: UNESCO, 1995.

De Garis, B. "Federation". In *The Australian Century: Political Struggle in the Building of a Nation*. Ed. R. Manne. Melbourne: Text Publishing, 1999.

Demaine, J. "Beyond communitarianism: Citizenship, politics and education" In *Beyond Communitarianism: Citizenship, Politics and Education*. Eds. J. Demaine and H. Entwhistle. London: St. Martin's Press, 1996. pp. 6–29.

Demaine, J. and H. Entwhistle, eds. *Beyond Communitarianism: Citizenship, Politics and Education*. London: St. Martin's Press, 1996.

Dening, G. *Readings/Writings*. Melbourne: Melbourne University Press, 1998.

Department of Education, Training and Employment, South Australian. *The ABC of being a critically literate citizen*. Teaching civics and citizenship education in Studies of Society and Environment and English for years 4–7. Seacombe Gardens SA, 1998.

Doig, B., K. Piper, S. Mellor, and G. Masters. *Conceptual Understanding in Social Education*. ACER Research Monograph no 45. Melbourne: Australian Council for Educational Research, 1993.

Donnelly, K. "Whereas the People... Civics and Citizenship Education: A response". Curriculum Corporation commissioned paper, 1995.

——. "Disneyland and teaching civics". Unpublished paper, 1996.

——. "The Eureka Stockade or the Boston Tea Party?" *EQ Australia* 3 (1996): 37–38.

Dunn, J. "How democracies succeed". *Economy and Society* 25.4 (1996): 511–528.

Dunn, S. and V. Morgan. "'A fraught path' — education as a basis for developing improved community relations in Northern Ireland". *Oxford Review of Education* 25.1 (1999): 141–154.

Edwards, B. and M.J Foley. "Editors' introduction: escape from politics? Social theory and the social capital debate". *American Behavioral Scientist* 40.5 (1997): 550–561.

Edwards, T. and G. Whitty. "Parental choice and educational reform in Britain and the United States". *British Journal of Educational Studies* 40.2 (1992): 101–117.

Elliott, B. and D. MacLennan. "Education, modernity and neo-conservative school reform in Canada, Britain and the US". *British Journal of Sociology of Education* 15.2 (1994): 165–185.

Englund, T. "Education as a citizenship right — a concept in transition: Sweden related to other Western democracies and political philosophy". *Journal of Curriculum Studies* 26.4 (1994): 389–399.

Erebus Consulting Group. Evaluation of the Discovering Democracy Program. Canberra: Department of Education, Training and Youth Affairs, 1999.

——. Evaluation of the Discovering Democracy Program. Canberra: Department of Education, Training and Youth Affairs, 1999.

Etzioni, A. *The spirit of community; the reinvention of American society*. New York: Simon and Schuster, 1993.

European Commission. *Accomplishing Europe through education and training; report of the study group on education and training*. Luxembourg: Office for Official Publications of the European Communities, 1997.

——. *Education and active citizenship in the European Union*. Luxembourg: Office for Official Publications of the European Countries, 1998.

Everitt, A. "Designer global culture". *New Statesman and Society* 9.388 (1996): 31–3.

Evrard, Y. "Democratizing culture or cultural democracy? (State intervention in culture)". *Journal of Arts, Management, Law and Society* 27.3 (1997): 167–175.

Fearnley-Sander, M. and T. Sprod. *The pedagogy of civics and citizenship education*: Curriculum Corporation commissioned paper, 1996.

Featherstone, M., ed. *Global Culture, Nationalism, Globalisation and Modernity*. London: Sage, 1990.

Fleischacker, S. "Insignificant Communities". In *Freedom of Association*. Ed. A. Gutmann. Princeton: Princeton University Press. pp 273–313.

Fogelman, K. "Education for citizenship and the National Curriculum". In *Beyond Communitarianism: Citizenship, Politics and Education*. Eds. J. Demaine and H. Entwhistle. London: St. Martin's Press, 1996. pp. 83–91.

———. "Citizenship education in England". In *Citizenship, education and the modern state*. Ed. K.J. Kennedy. London; Washington, D.C.: Falmer Press, 1997. pp. 85–95.

Foley, M.W. and B. Edwards. "Escape from politics? Social theory and the social capital debate". *American Behavioral Scientist* 40.5 (1997): 550–562.

Foucault, M. *Discipline and Punish: the birth of the prison*. Harmondsworth: Penguin, 1977.

———. "Omnes et singulatum: towards a critique of political reason". In *The Tanner Lectures on Human Values*. Ed. S. McMurrin: University of Utah Press, 1981.

———. "Governmentality". In *The Foucault Effect: Studies in Governmentality*. Eds. G. Burchell, C. Gordon and P. Miller. London: Harvester and Wheatsheaf, 1991. pp. 87–104.

Fraser, A. "Strong Republicanism and a Citizen's Constitution". In *The Republicanism Debate* Eds. W. Hudson and D. Carter. Sydney: NSW University Press, 1993.

Frazer, Elizabeth. "Introduction: the idea of political education". *Oxford Review of Education* 25.1 (1999): 1–22.

Gaita, R. *A Common Humanity Thinking about Love and Truth and Justice*. Melbourne: Text Publishing, 1999.

Galeotti, A.E. "Citizenship and equality: the place for toleration". *Political Theory* 21.4 (1993):585–596.

———. "A problem with theory; a rejoinder to Moruzzi". *Political Theory* 22.4 (1994): 673–8.

Galston, W. *Liberal Purposes: goods, virtues and diversity in the liberal state*. Cambridge, Cambridge University Press, 1991.

Gates, H. L. Jr. *Loose Canons: notes on the culture wars*. New York: Oxford University Press, 1992.

——. "Critical Race Theory and Freedom of Speech". In *The Future of Academic Freedom*. Ed. L. Menand. Chicago: University of Chicago Press, 1996. pp. 119–59.

Geras, N. *The Contract of Mutual Indifference: Political Philosophy after the Holocaust*. London: Verso, 1998.

Gilbert, R. "Active citizenship and identity politics". *Ethos* (1992): 2–7.

——. "Where are the people? Education, citizenship and the Civics Expert Group Report". *Curriculum Perspectives* 16.1 (1996): 56–61.

——. "Identity, culture and environment: education for citizenship for the 21st century". In *Beyond Communitarianism: Citizenship, Politics and Education*. Eds. J. Demaine and H. Entwhistle. London: St. Martin's Press, 1996. pp. 42–63.

——. "Issues for citizenship in a postmodern world". In *Citizenship, education and the modern state*. Ed. K.J. Kennedy. London; Washington, D.C.: Falmer Press, 1997. pp. 65–82.

Gilbert, R. and P. Low. "Discourse and Power in Education: Analysing Institutional Processes in Schools". *Australian Educational Researcher* 21.3 (1994): 1–42.

Giroux, H.A. *Schooling for Democracy: critical pedagogy in the modern age*. London: Routledge, 1988

Gitlin, T. *The twilight of common dreams: why America is wracked by culture wars*. New York: Metropolitan Books, 1995.

Glendon, M.A. and D. Blankenhorn. *Seedbeds of virtue: sources of competence, character, and citizenship in American society*. Lanham, Md.: Madison Books, 1995.

Goldfarb, J. C. *Civility and Subversion: The Intellectual in Democratic Society*. Cambridge: Cambridge University Press, 1998.

Goot, M. "Civics, survey research and the republic." *Australian Quarterly*. (Spring 1995): 25–39.

——. *Hanson's heartland; Who's for One Nation and Why? Two nations: the causes and effects of the One Nation Party in Australia*. Melbourne: Bookman, 1998.

Gordon, K. and R. Land. "Student action: social and economic planning in a school community". In *Education for*

Responsible Citizenship. Classroom Units for Primary and Secondary Teachers. Ed. R.Land. Adelaide: The Social Education Association of Australia, 1997. pp. 43–56.

Goudie, Y. *Citizenship and school ethos*: Curriculum Corporation commissioned paper, 1996.

Grahl, J. and P. Teague. "Is the European social model fragmenting?" *New Political Economy* 2.3 (1997): 405–427.

Grattan, M. *Reconciliation: Essays on Australian Reconciliation.* Melbourne: Black Inc., 2000.

Greeley, A. "Coleman Revisited: Religious Structures as a Source of Social Capital". *American Behavioral Scientist* 40.5 (1997): 562–574.

Green, A. *Education and state formation: the rise of education systems in England, France and the USA.* London: Macmillan, 1990.

———. "Education and state formation in Europe and Asia". In *Citizenship, education and the modern state.* Ed. K.J. Kennedy. London; Washington, D.C.: Falmer Press, 1997. pp. 9–26.

Green, V.A. "The globalization of citizenship education: a Canadian perspective". Paper presented at Connections 97 Conference. University of Sydney, 1997.

Grimshaw, P., M. Lake, et al. *Creating a Nation.* Ringwood: McPhee Gribble, 1994.

Gutmann, A. "Challenges of multiculturalism in democratic education". *Philosophy of Education,* 1995.
http://www.ed.iuc.edu/COE/EPS/PES-Yearbook/95_docs/gutmann.html

———. *Democratic Education.* Cambridge MA: Princeton, 1987.

———. ed. *Freedom of Association.* Princeton: Princeton University Press, 1998.

Guy, R. "All aboard the civics bandwagon". *The Age*, 26 March 1996, p. 13.

Hahn, C. "Citizenship education: an empirical study of policy, practices and outcomes". *Oxford Review of Education* 25.1 (1999): 231–250.

Harber, C. *Political Education in Britain.* London: Falmer Press, 1987.

Harwood, R.C. "Originating civic faith. Self-trust in America". In *Vital Speeches of the Day*. Address to the Health Resources and Services Administration and Bureau of Primary Care at a symposium in Bethesda Maryland, 1999.

Hebert, Y. "Citizenship education: towards a pedagogy of social participation and identity formation". *Canadian Ethnic Studies* 29.2 (1997): 82–97.

Held, D. "Democracy, the nation-state and the global system". *Economy and Society* 20.2 (1991): 138–172.

Held, D. and A. McGrew. "Global transformations". *ReVision* 22.2 (1999): 7–14.

Hindess, B. *Freedom, Equality and the Market: arguments on social policy*. London: Tavistock, 1987.

——. Taking socialism seriously. *Economy and Society* 20.4 (1991): 363–379.

——. "Imaginary presuppositions of democracy." *Economy and Society* 20.2 (1991): 172–192.

——. "Citizens and peoples". *Australian Left Review* 140 (1992): 20–23.

——. "Citizenship in the modern West". In *Citizenship and Social Theory*. Ed. B. Turner. London: Sage, 1993. pp. 19–35.

——. "'The Greeks had a word for it': the polis as political metaphor". *Thesis Eleven* 40 (1995): 119–32.

——. "Divide and rule". Paper presented to the Culture and Citizenship conference. Brisbane, 1996.

——. "Democracy and disenchantment". *Australian Journal of Political Science* 32.1 (1997): 79–92.

——. "Governing cultures". *Southern Review* 31.1 (1998): 149–162.

Hirsch, E D. *The schools we need. And why we don't have them*. New York: Doubleday, 1996.

Hirst, J. "Can subjects be citizens?". In *Crown or Country: The Traditions of Australian Republicanism*. Eds. D. Headon, J. Warden and B. Gammage. Sydney: Allen and Unwin, 1994. pp. 118–124.

——. "History and the Republic", *Quadrant* (September 1996): 38–43.

Hirst, P. "The international origins of national sovereignty". unpublished working paper, 1996.

Hobson, P and R Crewell. "Parental rights, education and liberal tolerance". *Discourse* 14.1 (1993): 44–51.

Hoepper, B. "Australians as global citizens": Curriculum Corporation commissioned paper, 1996.

Holmes, S. *Passions and Constraint: On the theory of liberal democracy.* Chicago: University of Chicago Press, 1995.

Holmes, S. and C.R Sunstein. *The Cost of Rights: Why Liberty Depends on Taxes.* New York: W.W. Norton, 1999.

Hoy, A., ed. *Report on the Teaching of History of Civics in Victorian Secondary Schools.* Melbourne: Australian Council for Education Research, 1934.

Hughes, C.A. "The good citizen: past and futures for citizenship education". *Australian Journal of Politics and History* 42.1 (1996): 1–9.

Hughes, P. "International best practice in civics education". In *Whereas the people...civics and citizenship education. Report of the Civics Expert Group.* Ed. Civics Expert Group. Canberra: Australian Government Printing Service, 1994. pp. 173–84.

Hunter, I. *Culture and Government: the emergence of literary education.* Houndsmill: Macmillan, 1988.

——. "The pastoral bureaucracy: towards a less principled understanding of state schooling". In *Child and Citizen: Genealogies of Schooling and Subjectivity.* Eds. D. Meredyth and D. Tyler. Brisbane: Institute for Cultural Policy Studies, 1993. pp. 237–287.

——. *Rethinking the School: subjectivity, bureaucracy, criticism.* Sydney: Allen and Unwin, 1994.

——. "The rarity of the school". *Southern Review* 28 (1995): 163–71.

——. *Assembling the school.* In *Foucault and Political Reason*, ed. A. Barry. London: UCL Press, 1996.

——. "Uncivil society: liberal government and the deconfessionalisation of politics". In *Governing Australia. Studies in Contemporary Rationalities of Government.* Eds. M. Dean and B. Hindess. Cambridge: Cambridge University Press, 1998. pp. 242–264.

————. *Rival enlightenments. Civil and metaphysical philosophy in early modern Germany*. Oxford University Press, 2001 (forthcoming).

Hunter, I. and D. Meredyth. "Popular education and popular sovereignty". *American Behavioral Scientist* 43.9 (2000): 1462-1486. (Special issue. Eds. D. Meredyth and J. Minson. *Citizenship and Cultural Policy: statecraft, markets and community*).

————. "Competent citizens and limited truths". In *Rethinking Australian Education*. Ed. T. Seddon and L. Angus. Australian Council for Educational Research, Melbourne, 2000 (forthcoming).

Hunter, J.D. *Culture wars: the struggle to define America*. New York: Basic Books, 1991.

Irving, H. "Who were the republicans?". In *Crown or Country: The Traditions of Australian Republicanism*. Eds. D. Headon, J. Warden and B. Gammage. Sydney: Allen and Unwin, 1994. pp. 69–79.

————. *To Constitute a Nation: A Cultural History of Australia's Constitution*. Sydney: Cambridge University Press, 1999.

Irving, T., D. Maunders, and G. Sherington. *Youth in Australia: Policy, administration and politics. A history since World War II*. Melbourne: Macmillan Education Australia Ltd, 1995.

James, S.A. "Australians as global citizens": Curriculum Corporation commissioned paper, 1996.

Jay, G.S. *American literature & the culture wars*. Ithaca, New York: Cornell University Press, 1997

Jensen, R. "The culture wars, 1965–1995: a historian's map". *Journal of social history* 29 (1995): 17–38.

Jones, K. and K. Williamson. "The birth of the schoolroom". *I&C*, 6 (1979): 59–111.

Joppke, C. *Challenge to the Nation-State: immigration in Western Europe and the United States*. Oxford, England; New York: Oxford University Press, 1998.

Jordens, A-M. *Redefining Australians: Immigration, Citizenship and National Identity*. Sydney: Hale and Iremonger, 1995.

Joshee, R. "The Federal government and citizenship education for newcomers". *Education canadienne et internationale* 25.2 (1996): 108–127.

Jupp, J. "Populism in the Land of Oz." *Meanjin* 57.4 (1998): 740–748.

Kaplan, W., ed. *Belonging: the Meaning and Future of Canadian Citizenship*. Montreal: McGill's-Queens University Press, 1993.

Kauffman, P. *Wik, Mining and Aborigines*. Sydney: Allen and Unwin, 1998.

Keane, J. *Civil Society: Old images, New Visions*. Cambridge: Polity Press, 1998.

Kelly, P. *Paradise Divided: The Changes, The Challenges, The Choices for Australia*. Sydney: Allen and Unwin, 2000.

Kemp, D. Discovering Democracy media release: Minister for Schools, Vocational Education and Training, 1997.

———. "Realising the Promise of Democracy". Paper presented at 1997 Curriculum Corporation National Conference. Sydney, 8 May 1997.

Kennedy, K. *Parliamentary Education*. Curriculum Mapping Project: final report: Australian Curriculum Studies Association, Belconnen ACT, 1993.

———. ed. *New Challenges for Civics and Citizenship Education*. ACSA teaching resource no.10. Belconnen ACT: Australian Curriculum Studies Association, 1996.

———. "A tale of ignorance, reality and megatrends". *EQ Australia* 3 (1996): 14–17.

Kercher, B. "Creating Australian law". In *Creating Australia: Changing Australian History*. Eds. W. Hudson and G. Bolton. Sydney: Allen and Unwin, 1997.

Kerr, D. *Citizenship education and the revised national curriculum*. Paper presented to National Foundation for Educational Research annual conference, London, 1998.

———. "Changing the political culture: the Advisory Group on Education for Citizenship and the Teaching of Democracy in Schools". *Oxford Review of Education* 25.1 (1999): 275–284.

Khilnani, S. "Democracy and modern political community: limits and possibilities". *Economy and Society* 20.2 (1991): 196–204.

——. "Individualism and modern democratic culture: recent French conceptions". *Economy and Society* 25.2 (1996): 282–289.

King, N. "The teacher must exist before the pupil: the Newbolt Report on the teaching of English in England, 192". *Literature and History* 3.1 (1987): 14–37.

Kirby, M. "Reflections on Constitutional Monarchy". In *The Republicanism Debate*. Eds. W. Hudson and D. Carter. Sydney: NSW University Press, 1993. pp. 61–76.

Koning, H. "A French mirror (civic solidarity in France)". *The Atlantic Monthly* 276.6 (1995): 95–105.

Kreitzman, L., *The 24 Hour Society*. London: Profile Books, 1999.

Kukathas, C. "Are there any cultural rights?" *Political Theory* 20.1 (1992): 105–140.

——. "Cultural rights again". *Political Theory* 20.4 (1992): 674–681.

——. "The rights of minority cultures". *Political Theory* 20.1 (1992): 140–147.

——. "Liberalism and multiculturalism". *Political Theory* 26.5 (1998): 686–700.

Kwan, E. "Oaths and flags: an ambiguous heritage". *Teaching Young Australians to be Australian Citizens*. Ed. D. Horne. Monash University, Melbourne, National Centre for Australian Studies. 1994. pp. 20–22.

Kymlicka, W. *Liberalism, Community and Culture*. Oxford: Clarendon Press, 1989

——. "Do we need a liberal theory of minority rights? Reply to Carens, Young, Parekh and Forst". *Constellations* 4.1 (1997): 72–87.

Kymlicka, W. and W. Norman. "Return of the citizen: a survey of recent work on citizenship theory". *Ethics* 104 (1994): 257–289.

Laitin, D. D. "Liberal theory and the nation." *Political Theory* 26.2 (1998): 221–237.

Lake, M. *Getting Equal: The history of Australian feminism*. Sydney: Allen and Unwin, 1999.

Land, R. Pedagogies of the political. In *Education for Responsible Citizenship. Classroom Units for Primary and Secondary Teachers*. Ed. R. Land. Adelaide: The Social Education Association of Australia. 1997. pp. 1–18.

Latham, M. *Civilising Global Capital: New Thinking for Australian Labour*. Sydney: Allen & Unwin, 1998.

La Torre, M. "European citizenship: an institutional challenge". *European forum*; 3. Boston: Kluwer Law International, 1998.

Lemke, C. "Citizenship and European integration". *World Affairs* 160.4 (1998): 212–218.

Levinson, M. "Liberalism, Pluralism, and Political Education: paradox or paradigm?" *Oxford Review of Education* 25.1 (1999): 39–58.

Lewis, J. "Designing a cultural policy". *Journal of Arts Management, Law & Society* 24.1 (1994): 41–57.

Limage, L.J. "Education and muslim identity; the case of France". *Comparative Education* 36.1 (2000): 73–94.

Lingard, B., J. Knight and P. Porter, eds. *Schooling Reform in Hard Times*. London: Falmer Press, 1993.

Lingard, R., J. Knight, and P. Porter. Restructuring Australian schooling: changing conceptions of top-down and bottom-up reforms. In *Participative Practices and Policy in Schooling*, Eds. H. Nielsen and B. Limerick. Sydney: Harcourt Brace Jovanovich, 1991.

Lister, I. "Civic education for positive pluralism in Great Britain". In *Education for democratic citizenship: a challenge for multi-ethnic societies*. Ed. R.S Sigel and M.H Hoskin. Hillsdale, New Jersey: Lawrence Erlbaum Associates, 1991. pp. 129–146.

Lohrey, A. *The Pedagogy of Civics and Citizenship Education*. A Review Paper: Curriculum Corporation commissioned paper, 1996.

Macedo, S. *Liberal Virtues: Citizenship, virtue, and community in liberal constitutionalism*. Oxford: Clarendon, 1991.

Macintyre, S. "An expert's confession". *Australian Quarterly*, (Spring 1995): 1–12.

——. The genie and the bottle: Putting history back into the school curriculum. *Australian Journal of Education* 41.2 (1997): 189–199.

——. "Rejoinder to Alan Barcan". *Australian Journal of Education* 41.2 (1997): 213–215.

——. *A Concise History of Australia*. Melbourne: Cambridge University Press, 1999.

Mackey, E. "The cultural politics of populism. Celebrating Canadian national identity". In *Anthropology of Policy. critical perspectives on governance and power*. Eds. C. Shore and S. Wright. London: Routledge, 1997.

Mahant, E. "Are national cultures and identities an optional extra?" *Canadian Review of American Studies* 27.3 (1997): 51–80.

Manne, R. "The Kerr Conundrum". In *The Way We Live Now: Controversies of the Nineties*. Melbourne: Text Publishing, 1998. pp. 141–47.

Mann, R. ed. *The Australian Century: Political Struggle in the Building of a Nation*. Melbourne: Text Publishing, 1999.

Marginson, S. *Education and Public Policy in Australia*. Cambridge: Cambridge University Press, 1993.

———. *Educating Australia. Government, Economy and Citizen since 1960*. Cambridge: Cambridge University Press, 1997.

———. *Markets in Australian Education*. Sydney: Allen and Unwin, 1997.

Marshall, T.H. "Citizenship and social class". In *Class, Citizenship and Social Development*. Chicago: Chicago University Press, 1949.

Matthews, B. *Federation*. Melbourne: Text Publishing, 1999.

Maunders, D. *Keeping them off the streets: a history of voluntary youth organisations in Australia 1850–1980*. Melbourne: Philip Institute of Technology Centre for Youth and Community Studies, 1984.

Matheny, R. "In the wake of the flood: 'like products' and cultural products after the World Trade Organizations' decision in Canada Certain Measures Concerning Periodicals". *University of Pennsylvania Law Review* 147 (1998): 245–270.

McDonagh, K. "Cultural recognition, cosmopolitanism and multicultural education". *Philosophy of Education*, 1995.

McKenna, M. *The Captive Republic: A History of Republicanism in Australia*. Melbourne: Cambridge University Press, 1996.

———. "Republic: a quest to include all". *The Australian*. 6 July 2000, p. 11.

Mellor, S. and M Elliott. *The pedagogy of civics and citizenship education*. Curriculum Corporation commissioned paper, 1996.

——. *School ethos and citizenship*. Curriculum Corporation commissioned paper, 1996.

——. *What's the point? Political attitudes of Victorian Year 11 students*. Melbourne: Australian Council for Educational Research, 1998.

Melleuish, G. and G. Stokes. "Australian political thought". In *Creating Australia: Changing Australian History*. Eds. Wayne Hudson and Geoffrey Bolton. Sydney: Allen and Unwin, 1997.

Melton, van H.J. *Absolutism and the Eighteenth Century Origins of Compulsory Schooling in Prussia and Austria*. Cambridge: Cambridge University Press, 1988.

Meredyth, D. "Invoking Citizenship: education, competence and social rights". *Economy and Society* 19.1 (1997): 1–29.

——. "Corporatising education". In *Governing Australia. Studies in Contemporary Rationalities of Government*. Ed. M. Dean and B. Hindess. Cambridge: Cambridge University Press, 1998. pp. 20–46.

Meredyth, D. and J. Thomas. "Pluralising civics". *Culture and Policy* 2.3 (1996):15–17.

Minson, J. "Aescetics and the demands of participation". *Political Theory Newsletter*, 1998.

Moruzzi, N. C. "A problem with headscarves: contemporary complexities of political and social identity". *Political Theory* 22.4 (1994): 653–673.

Mouffe, C., ed. *Dimensions of Radical Democracy. Pluralism, Citizenship, Community*. London: Verso, 1992.

Mulcahy, D.G. "Social Education in the European Community". *The Social Studies* 85.2 (1994): 83–8.

Murdoch, W.A. *The Australian Citizen. An Elementary Account of Civic Rights and Duties*. Melbourne: Whitcombe and Tombs Ltd, 1912.

National Centre for Australian Studies *How to be Australia*. Melbourne, National Centre for Australian Studies, Monash University, 1994.

National Council for the Centenary of Federation *What's happening. Calendar of events*. National Council for the Centenary of Federation. 2000:

http://www.centenary.gov.au/happen/happen_calendar.htm, 2000.

——. *What's happening. History and education grants*. National Council for the Centenary of Federation. 2000: http://www.centenary.gov.au/happen/happen_grants.html, 2000.

——. *Young Australians to link past, present and future for the Centenary of Federation*. Centenary of Federation. 2000: http://www.centenary.gov.au/media/release/20000406.html, 2000.

Newman, P.C. "Let's not play Pluto to Mickey Mouse". *Maclean's* 109.15 (1996): 44.

Nolan, J.L. *The American culture wars: current contests and future prospects*. Charlottesville: University Press of Virginia, 1996.

Osborne, T. *Aspects of Enlightenment: social theory and the ethics of truth*. London: UCL Press, 1998.

Osler, A. and H. Starkey. "Rights, identities and inclusion: European action programmes as political education [1] ". *Oxford Review of Education* 25.1 (1999): 199–216.

Owen, D. "Dilemmas and opportunities for the young active citizen". *Youth Studies Australia* 15.1 (1996): 20–23.

Parker, W.C. "'Advanced' ideas about democracy: towards a pluralist conception of citizenship education". *Teachers College record* 98.1 (1996): 104–125.

Parry, G. "Constructive and Reconstructive Political Education". *Oxford Review of Education* 25.1 (1999): 23–38.

Parry, L. "Redefining citizenship education: a reappraisal of post-sputnik educational discourse". In *Childhood, Citizenship, Culture* 2. Eds. J. Scott, C. Manathunga, and N. Kyle. Brisbane: Queensland University of Technology, 1996: 473–496.

——.. "Transcending national boundaries; Hilda Taba and the 'new social studies' in Australia, 1969–1981". *Social Studies* (March/April 2000): 69–78.

Peterson, N. and W. Sanders eds. *Citizenship and Indigenous Australians: Changing Conceptions and Possibilities*. Sydney: Cambridge University Press, 1998.

Petit, P. "Liberalism and Republicanism". *Australian Journal of Political Science* 28 (1993): 162–189.

Pratte, R. "The Civic Imperative: examining the need for civic education". In *Advances in Contemporary Educational Thought Series, 3*. Ohio: Teachers' College Press, 1988.

Pridham, G. "Education for responsible citizenship". In *Education for Responsible Citizenship*. Ed. Ray Land. Social Education Association of Australia 1997. Pp. 19–28.

Pring, R. "Political education: relevance of the humanities". *Oxford Review of Education* 25.1 (1999): 71–88.

Print, M. "From civics deficit to critical mass: the new civics education". *Education canadienne et internationale* 25.2 (1996): 184–198.

———. "The new civics education: an integrated approach for Australian schools". *Social Education* 60.7 (1996): 443–7.

———. *Pedagogical strategies for civics and citizenship education*. Curriculum Corporation commissioned paper, 1996.

Prior, W. "Are social education students socially educated? Political literacy and the implications for teachers if social education". *Ethos* (1992): 12–21.

Pritchard, S. ed. *Indigenous peoples, the United Nations and Human Rights*. Sydney: Zed Books/The Federation Press, 1998.

Quigley, C.N. and C.F. Bahmueller. *Civitas: a framework for civic education*. Calabases, California: Centre for Civic Education, 1991.

Read, P. *A Rape of the Soul so Profound: The Return of the Stolen Generations*. Sydney: Allen and Unwin, 1999.

———. *Belonging: Australians, Place and Aboriginal Ownership*. Sydney: Cambridge University Press, 2000.

Reid, A. "Selling civics: the curriculum development process in a national project". *The Social Educator* 15.1 (1996).

Reynolds, H. *This Whispering in our Hearts*. Sydney: Allen and Unwin, 1998.

———. *Why Weren't We Told? A Personal Search for the Truth about our History*. Melbourne: Viking, 1999.

Reynolds, R. "Citizenship and geography education; the role of NSW Geography syllabuses since World War II". *History of Education Review* 28.2 (1999): 60–72.

Rorty, A.O. "The hidden politics of cultural identification". *Political Theory* 22.3 (1994): 152–166.

Rose, N. *Governing the Soul: the shaping of the private self.* London: Routledge, 1990.

——. "Government, authority and expertise in advanced liberalism". *Economy and Society* 22.3 (1993): 283–299.

——. "The death of the social? Refiguring the territory of government". *Economy and Society* 23.3 (1996): 327–356.

——. "Governing 'advanced' liberal democracies". In *Foucault and Political Reason: Liberalism, Neo-Liberalism and Rationalities of Government.* Eds. A. Barry, T. Osborne and N. Rose. London: UCL Press, 1996.

——. *Powers of Freedom: Reframing political thought.* Cambridge: Cambridge University Press, 1999.

Ross, A. "Jobs in Cyberspace". In *Real Love: In Pursuit of Cultural Justice.* New York: New York University Press, 1998. pp 7–34.

Rowse, T. *Australian Liberalism and National Character.* Malmesbury, Vic.: Kibble Books, 1978.

——. *After Mabo Interpreting Indigenous Traditions.* Melbourne: Melbourne University Press, 1993.

——. *White Flour, White Power: From Rations to Citizenship in Central Australia.* Sydney: Cambridge University Press, 1998.

Ryan, D. "Active citizenship and the resources of the Electoral Education Centre". *Ethos* (1992): 45–47.

Ryan, K. and K.E Bohlin. *Building character in schools. Practical ways to bring moral instruction to life.* San Francisco: Jossey-Bass Publishers, 1999.

Saunders, C. "Founding blueprint has faded with time", *The Australian,* 5 July 2000, p. 15.

Saward, M. *The Terms of Democracy.* Cambridge: Polity Press, 1998.

Schudson, M. *The Good Citizen: A History of American Civic Life.* New York: The Free Press, 1998.

——. "Is our civic life really in decline?" *American Heritage* 50.6 (1999): 52–8.

Schmitt, C. *Political Theology. Four Chapters on the Concept of Sovereignty.* Cambridge Massachusetts: MIT Press, 1985.

Seddon, T. "Markets and the English: rethinking educational restructuring as institutional design". *British Journal of Sociology of Education* 18.2 (1997): 165–186.

Sennett, R. *The Corrosion of Character: The personal consequences of work in the new capitalism.* New York: W.W. Norton, 1998.

Shaw, W.H. *Contemporary Ethics: Taking Account of Utilitarianism.* Oxford: Blackwell Publishers, 1998.

Sherington, G. "Education, social change and citizenship in postwar Australia 1945–1995". In *Childhood, Citizenship, Culture 2.* Eds. J. Scott, C. Manathunga and N. Kyle. Brisbane: Queensland University of Technology, 1996: 449–563.

Silvestri, K. "Parent involvement: New Jersey's public policy and public schools program". *Equity and Choice*, (Winter 1991): 22–27.

Simms, M. *Women and citizenship in Australia.* Curriculum Corporation commissioned paper, 1996.

Simons, M. *Fit to Print: Inside the Canberra Press Gallery.* Sydney: UNSW Press, 1999.

Singh, M. G. *Citizenship in Australia's multicultural society.* Curriclum Corporation commissioned paper, 1996.

Singh, B.R. "Liberalism, parental rights, pupils' autonomy and education". *Educational Studies* 24.2 (1998): 165–183.

Smith, B. "Governing Classrooms: privatisation and discipline in Australian schooling". Ph. D. diss, Griffith University, 1991.

Smith, S. "Liberalism, multiculturalism and education: is there a fit?" *Philosophy of Education*, 1995.

Soysal, Y. *Limits of Citizenship: migrants and postnational membership in Europe.* Chicago: University of Chicago, 1994.

Splitter, L. *Values and civics and citizenship education.* Curriculum Corporation commissioned paper, 1996.

Springborg, P. "An Historical Note on Republicanism". In *The Republicanism Debate.* Eds. W. Hudson and D. Carter. Sydney: NSW University Press, 1993. pp. 201–07.

Stanley, W.B. and J.A. Whitson. "Citizenship as practical competence: a response to the new reform movement in social education". *International Journal of Social Education* 7.2 (1992): 57–66.

Stevenson, N. "Globalization, national cultures and cultural citizenship". *Sociological quarterly* 38.1 (1997): 41–67.

Stotsky, S. "The national standards for civics: a backbone for school curricula?" *Journal of Education* 176.3 (1994): 29–39.

Strathern, M. "The nice thing about culture is that everyone has it". In *Shifting contexts: transformations in anthropological knowledge*. Ed. M. Strathern. London; New York: Routledge, 1994. pp. 153–176.

Stratton, J. and I. Ang. "Multicultural imagined communities: cultural difference and national identity in Australia and the USA". *Continuum* 8.2 (1994): 124–158.

Sublet, F. *Education for Industry and Citizenship*. Melbourne: Melbourne University Press, 1936.

Tamir, Y. "Democracy, nationalism and education". *Educational Philosophy and Theory* 24.1 (1992): 17–27.

Tannen, D. *The Argument culture: changing the way we argue*. London: Virago, 1999.

Taylor, C. and A. Gutmann. *Multiculturalism and "The politics of recognition": an essay*. Princeton, N.J.: Princeton University Press, 1992.

——. eds. *Multiculturalism. Examining the politics of recognition*. Princeton, New Jersey: Princeton University Press, 1994.

Thomas, J. "Civics in contemporary Australian higher education" (Appendix 4.3.). In *Whereas the People: civics and citizenship education*. Ed. Civics Expert Group. Canberra: Australian Government Printing Service, 1994. pp. 185–189.

——. "Civics teaching in the past". In *Teaching Young Australians to be Australian Citizens*. Ed. D. Horne. Melbourne: National Centre for Australian Studies, 1994. pp. 23–25.

——. "The history of civics education in Australia" (Appendix 4.1.). In *Whereas the People: civics and citizenship education*. Ed. Civics Expert Group. Canberra: Australian Government Printing Service, 1994.

Thompson, E. "What an American would learn at school about citizenship". *Teaching Young Australians to be Australian Citizens*. Ed. National Centre for Australian Studies. Melbourne: Monash University, 1994.

Tooley, J. "Choice and diversity in education: a defence". *Oxford Review of Education* 23.1 (1997): 103–116.

Touraine, A. *Can We Live Together? Equality and Difference.* Trans. D. Macey. Cambridge: Polity Press, 2000.

Turnbull, M. *Fighting for the Republic: The Ultimate Insider's Account.* Melbourne: Hardie Grant Books, 1999.

Turner, B. "Contemporary problems in the theory of citizenship". In *Citizenship and Social Theory.* Ed. B. Turner. London: Sage, 1993. pp. 1–18.

Turner, B. S., ed. *Citizenship and Social Theory.* London: Sage, 1993.

Uhr, John. *The Australian Republic: The Case for Yes.* Sydney: The Federation Press, 1999.

——. *Deliberative Democracy in Australia: The changing place of parliament.* Melbourne: Cambridge University Press, 1998.

Ungerleider, C.S. "Socialization for democratic citizenship: the development of the Canadian infrastructure". In *Education for democratic citizenship: a challenge for multi-ethnic societies.* Eds. R.S Sigel and M.H Hoskin. Hillsdale, New Jersey: Lawrence Erlbaum Associates, 1991. pp. 149–166.

Vick, M. "Knowledge/culture/citizenship: manuals of teaching method from the 1850s to the 1990s". In *Childhood, Citizenship, Culture 2.* Eds. J. Scott, C. Manathunga and N. Kyle. Brisbane: Queensland University of Technology, 1996: 795–812.

——. "National/ised subjects: constructions of nation and citizen in secondary school history texts". Paper presented at Culture and citizenship conference. Brisbane, July 1996.

Vontz, T.S. *Strict scrutiny: an analysis of national standards on civic education through the perspectives of contemporary theorists: 27.* U.S.; Indiana: ERIC: Clearinghouse: Social Studies/Social Science Education (SO028964), 1997.

Walter, J. "The Failure of Political Imagination." *AQ* Autumn (1993): 546–557.

Walter, J. *Tunnel Vision: The failure of political imagination.* Sydney: Allen and Unwin, 1996.

Walzer, M. "On Involuntary Association". In *Freedom of Association.* Ed A.Gutmann. Princeton: Princeton University Press. pp. 64–74.

Weber, J. "Does Canadian culture need this much protection?" *Business Week,* 6 August 1998, p. 37.

White, P. "Political education in the early years: the place of civic virtues". *Oxford Review of Education* 25.1 (1999): 59–70.

Whitelock, D. *The great tradition: a history of adult education in Australia.* St Lucia: University of Queensland Press, 1974.

Wicks, B. *Understanding the Australian Constitution: The Plain Words.* Sandy Bay: Libra Books, 1997.

Wright, A. ed. *Take power like this old man here.* Alice Springs: Central Land Council, Jukurrpa Books, 1998.

Wyndham, H.S. "Leaves from a professional diary II Vocational guidance and the curricula of the secondary school". *Schooling* XVI.5 (1935).

Yulish, S M. *The search for a civic religion: a history of the Character Education movement in America, 1890–1935.* Washington DC: University Press of America, 1980.

Zemans, Joyce. "Canadian cultural policy in a globalized world". *Canadian review of American studies* 27.3 (1997): 111–117.

Notes

Chapter 1

1   Eamonn Callan, "Beyond sentimental civic education", *American Journal of Education* 102.2 (1994): 190–222.

2   Ian Hunter, *Rethinking the School: subjectivity, bureaucracy, criticism* (Sydney: Allen and Unwin, 1994), pp. 5, 49–51.

3   *Ibid.*, p. 51.

4   William Galston, *Liberal Purposes: goods, virtues and diversity in the liberal state* (Cambridge: Cambridge University Press, 1991).

5   Callan, pp. 199–211.

6   *Ibid.*, pp. 214–15.

7   Bryan Turner, "Contemporary problems in the theory of citizenship", in *Citizenship and Social Theory*, ed. Bryan Turner (London: Sage, 1993), pp.1–18.

8   David Held, "Democracy, the nation-state and the global system", *Economy and Society* 20.2 (1991): 138–72; James Walter, *Tunnel Vision: The failure of political imagination* (Sydney: Allen and Unwin, 1996), pp. 1–14.

9   "Politics brief: Is there a crisis?", *The Economist*, 17 July 1999, pp. 51–52.

10 Amitai Etzioni, *The Spirit of Community: The Reinvention of American Society* (New York: Simon & Schuster, 1993).

11 C. Beem, "Civil is not good enough", *Current* 388 (1996): 22–27.

12 Murray Goot, "Civics, survey research and the republic", *Australian Quarterly* (Spring 1995): 25–39.

13 James Jupp, "Populism in the Land of Oz", *Meanjin* 57.4 (1998): 740–748; Murray Goot, *Two Nations: the causes and effects of the One Nation Party in Australia* (Melbourne: Bookman, 1998).

14 John Hirst, "History and the Republic", *Quadrant* (September 1996): 43.

15 Benedict Anderson, *Imagined Communities: Reflections on the origin and spread of nationalism* (London: Verso, 1991).

16 Hirst, pp. 40–41.

17 Mary Kalantzis, "Citizenship Education after the Monarchy: Five Questions for the Future", *Education Australia* (19–20, 1992–93): 30.

18 Hirst, p.41.

19 Kalantzis, pp. 28, 31.

20 *Ibid.*, p. 29.

21 National Council for the Centenary of Education, *What's happening.* http://www.centenary.gov.au

22 Erebus Consulting Group, *Evaluation of Discovering Democracy Program* (Canberra: DETYA, 1999), p. xviii.

23 Curriculum Corporation website. http://curriculum.edu.au/democracy/connect/classact/fedceleb.html

24 David Kemp, "Realising the Promise of Democracy", Curriculum Corporation National Conference, Sydney, 8 May 1997.

25 Harry C. Boyte and Nan Skelton, "The Legacy of public work: educating for citizenship", *Educational Leadership* 54.5 (1997): 12–18.

26 Terry Irving and D. Maunders et.al. *Youth in Australia: Policy, administration and politics: A History since World War II* (Melbourne: Macmillan, 1995), pp.83–5.

Chapter 2

1   David Kemp, 1997 Ministerial statement, p. 3.
2   John Hirst, cited in Curriculum Corporation "Discovering Democracy project information". Available
    http://www.curriculum.edu.au/democracy/about/projects/project.htm.
3   See the debate between Rob Gilbert and Terry Aulich and contributions from Warren Prior and D. Ryan in Ethos 1992.
4   Civics Expert Group, *Whereas the People: civics and citizenship education* (Canberra: AGPS, 1994) p. 9.
5   David Kemp, *Opening Address*. Celebrating the commencement of the Discovering Democracy School Materials Project, Royal Exhibition Building Melbourne 6 March 1998.
    http://www.curriculum.edu.au/democracy/about/project/kempspch.htm.
6   See discussions within the relevant professional associations: Australian Curriculum Studies Association 1996; Australian Federation of Societies for Studies of Society and Environment 1997.
7   Erebus Consulting Group, *Evaluation of the Discovering Democracy Program* (Canberra: DETYA, 1999).
8   Erebus Consulting Group, p. 39.
9   *Ibid.*, pp. ix–x.
10 *Ibid.*, p. xiii.
11 *Ibid.*, p. 24.
12 *Ibid.*, p. ix.
13 *Ibid.*, p. viii.
14 Marie Brennan, "Schools as public institutions: students and citizenship", *ACE News* (Nov. 1995): 10–11.
15 Reid, p.15; Warren Prior, "Are social education students socially educated? Political literacy and the implications for teachers of social education", *Ethos* (1992): 12–21.
16 Rhonda Craven, "Indigenous Aboriginal Studies: an essential component of citizenship education", *The Social Educator* 14.3 (1995): 32; Rob Gilbert, "Where are the people? Education, Citizenship and the Civics Expert Group Report", *Curriculum Perspectives* 16.1 (1996): 56–61.
17 Kevin Donnelly, "Disneyland and teaching civics", Unpublished paper, 1996; Kevin Donnelly, "The Eureka Stockade or the Boston Tea Party? ", *EQ Australia* 3 (1996): 37–38.
18 Alan Barcan, "History in a pluralist country: Response to Stuart Macintyre", *Australian Journal of Education* 41.2 (1997): 199–212; Alan Barcan, "The curriculum as social studies", *Australian Quarterly* 60.4 (1998): 448–477; Brian Crittenden, "The revival of civics in the school curriculum: Comments on the report of the Civics Expert Group", Curriculum Corporation commissioned paper, 1995, p. 22.
19 Crittenden, p. 26.
20 Stuart Macintyre, "An expert's confession", *Australian Quarterly* 57 (Spring 1995): 1–12.
21 Laurence Splitter, "Values and civics and citizenship education", Curriculum Corporation commissioned paper, 1996, pp. 3–7.

22 Don Alexander and Lloyd Logan, "The informed citizen project: one instance — Two expressions", Connections 97 Conference, Sydney University, July 1997; Yvonne Goudie, "Citizenship and School Ethos", Curriculum Corporation Commissioned Paper, 1996; Kerry Kennedy, ed. *New Challenges for Civics and Citizenship Education*, ACSA Teaching Resource no. 10 (Belconnen, ACT: ACSA, 1996); Suzanne Mellor and M. Elliott, " School ethos and citizenship", Curriculum Corporation Commissioned Paper, 1996.

23 Barcan, pp. 205–6.

24 Stuart Macintyre, "Rejoinder to Alan Barcan", *Australian Journal of Education* 41.2 (1997): 213–15.

25 Stuart Macintyre, "The genie and the bottle: Putting history back into the school curriculum", *Australian Journal of Education* 41.2 (1997): 189–99.

26 Macintyre, "Rejoinder", p. 215.

27 Julian Thomas, "The history of civics education in Australia", in *Whereas the People*, Appendix 4.1; "Civics in contemporary Australian higher education", in *Whereas the People* (Canberra: AGPS, 1994), Appendix 4.3.

28 Walter Murdoch, *The Australian Citizen: An Elementary Account of Civil Rights and Duties* (Melbourne: Whitcombe and Tombs Ltd., 1912).

29 Alice Hoy ed., *Report on the Teaching of History and Civics in Victorian Secondary Schools* (Melbourne: ACER, 1934).

30 See also Terry Irving, David Maunders and G. Sherrington, *Youth in Australia: Policy, Administration and Politics: A History since World War II* (Melbourne: Macmillan, 1995); David Maunders, *Keeping them off the streets: a history of voluntary youth organisations in Australia 1850–1980* (Melbourne: Philip Institute of Technology Centre for Youth and Community Studies, 1984).

31 Hoy, p. 49.

32 John Carter, "New civics", *Parliamentary Patter* 22 (1994): 3; Murray Print, "The new civics education: an integrated approach for Australian schools", *Social Education* 60.7 (1996): 444.

33 Malcolm Vick, "Knowledge/culture/citizenship: manuals of teaching method from the 1850s to the 1990s", in *Childhood, Citizenship, Culture*, eds. Joanne Scott, Catherine Manathunga and Noeline Kyle (Brisbane: Queensland University of Technology, 1996), p. 4.

34 Ruth Reynolds, "Citizenship and geography education: the role of NSW Geography syllabuses since World War II", *History of Education Review* 28.2 (1999): 60–72.

35 Lindsay Parry, "Redefining citizenship education: a reappraisal of post-sputnik educational discourse", in *Childhood, Citizenship Culture*, pp. 512–513.

36 Lindsay Parry, "Transcending national boundaries: Hilda Taba and 'the new social studies' in Australia 1969–1981", *Social Studies* (March/April 2000): 75–76.

37 Carter, p. 4.

38 Print, p. 444.

39 Reynolds, p. 62.

40 Vick, "Knowledge/culture/citizenship", p. 812.

41 Ian Hunter, *Rethinking the School: subjectivity, bureaucracy, criticism* (Sydney: Allen & Unwin, 1994), p. xxi.

42 Julian Thomas, "Civics teaching in the past", in *Teaching Young Australians to be Australian Citizens*, ed. Donald Horne (Melbourne: NCAS, 1994), pp. 23–24.

43 Alastair Davidson, *From Subject to Citizen: Australian Citizenship in the Twentieth Century* (Cambridge: Cambridge University Press, 1997), pp. 51–52.

44 *Ibid.*, pp. 75–6.
45 *Ibid.*, p.80.
46 *Ibid.*, p. 28.
47 *Ibid.*, p. 53.
48 T.H. Marshall, "Citizenship and social class", in *Class, Citizenship and Social Development* (Chicago: Chicago University Press, 1949), p. 37.
49 Davidson, pp. 29–30.
50 *Ibid.*, p. 31.
51 *Ibid.*, p. 29.
52 *Ibid.*, p. 31.
53 *Ibid.*, p. 27.
54 *Ibid.*, p. 21.
55 *Ibid.*, p. 11.
56 *Ibid.*, p. 83.
57 Kemp, 1998, op.cit.
58 These points draw on Ian Hunter's argument in *Rethinking the School*, op.cit.
59 For indicative "critical policy studies" discussions of these issues, see S. Ball *Educational Reform: A Critical and Poststructural Approach* (Buckingham: Open University Press, 1994); Simon Marginson, *Education and Public Policy in Australia* (Cambridge: Cambridge University Press, 1993); *Educating Australia: Government, Economy and Citizen since 1960* (Cambridge: Cambridge University Press, 1997) and *Markets in Australian Education* (Sydney: Allen and Unwin, 1997).
60 R. Lingard, J. Knight and Paige Porter "Restructuring Australian Schooling: changing conceptions of top-down and bottom-up reforms', in *Participative Practices and Policy in Schooling*, eds. H. Nielsen and Brigid Limerick (Sydney: Harcourt Brace Jovanovich, 1991.

Chapter 3

1 Barry Hindess, "Citizens and peoples", *Australian Left Review* 140 (1992): 20–23; Barry Hindess, "Citizenship in the modern West", in *Citizenship and Social Theory*, ed. Bryan Turner (London: Sage, 1993), pp. 19–35.
2 Bryan Turner, ed. *Citizenship and Social Theory* (London: Sage, 1993).
3 M. Featherstone, ed. *Global Culture, Nationalism, Globalisation and Modernity*, (London: Sage, 1990); David Held, "Democracy, the nation-state and the global system", *Economy and Society* 20.2 (1991): 138–172; David Held and Anthony McGrew, "Global transformations", *ReVision* 22.2 (1999): 7–14.
4 Rob Gilbert, "Issues for citizenship in a postmodern world", in *Citizenship, education and the modern state*, ed. Kerry J. Kennedy (London; Washington, D.C.: Falmer Press, 1997), pp. 65–82; Brian Hoepper, "Australians as global citizens": Curriculum Corporation commissioned paper, 1996.
5 Stephen A. James, "Australians as global citizens": Curriculum Corporation commissioned paper, 1996.
6 Civics Expert Group, *Whereas the People: civics and citizenship education*. (Canberra: Australian Government Printing Service, 1994).
7 Curriculum Corporation, "Classroom Activities. This Australian Nation: Who Are We? What Do We Value?"
http://www.curriculum.edu.au/democracy/connect/thisaus.htm

8   Australian Citizenship Council, *Australian Citizens for a New Century*, (Canberra: Commonwealth of Australia, 2000) p. 11. http://www.curriculum.edu.au/democracy/connect/classact/austoday.htm,

9   Brian Crittenden, "The revival of civics in the school curriculum: comments on the report of the Civics Expert Group": Curriculum Corporation commissioned paper, 1995.

10   Philip Hughes, "International best practice in civics education", in *Whereas the People*, 1994), pp. 173–84. cf. Denise Meredyth, and Julian Thomas, "Pluralising civics", *Culture and Policy* 2.3 (1996): 15–17.

11   Hughes, *ibid.*, pp. 173–84.

12   Elizabeth Frazer, "Introduction: the idea of political education", *Oxford Review of Education* 25.1 (1999): 5–22.

13   Will Kymlicka, and Wayne Norman, "Return of the citizen: a survey of recent work on citizenship theory", *Ethics*, 104 (1994): 257–289.

14   L. Albala-Bertrand, "International project; what education for what citizenship?" International Bureau of Education, UNESCO, 1997. Available from http://www.3.itu.int:8002/ibe-citied/the_project.html. See also L. Albala-Bertrand, "First lessons from the research phase: what education for what citizenship?" *Educational Innovation and information*, 90 (1997): 2–8.

15   Barry Hindess, "Divide and rule", Culture and Citizenship Conference, Brisbane, 1996; Barry Hindess, "Governing cultures", *Southern Review* 31.1 (1998): 149–162. Sunil Khilnani, "Democracy and modern political community: limits and possibilities", *Economy and Society* 20.2 (1991): 196–204.

16   Hughes, *ibid.*, pp. 173–84.

17   European Commission, *Accomplishing Europe through education and training*; Report of the study group on education and training (Luxembourg: Office for Official Publications of the European Communities, 1997); European Commission, *Education and active citizenship in the European Union* (Luxembourg: Office for Official Publications of the European Countries, 1998); D.G. Mulcahy, "Social Education in the European Community", *Social Studies* 85.2 (1994): 83–8; Audrey Osler, and Hugh Starkey, "Rights, identities and inclusion: European action programmes as political education [1] ", *Oxford Review of Education* 25.1 (1999): 199–216. See also G. Bell, ed. *Educating European Citizens: citizenship values and the European dimension* (London: David Fulton, 1995); Andy Green, 'Education and state formation in Europe and Asia' in *Citizenship, education and the modern state*, pp. 9–26; Chistiane Lemke, "Citizenship and European integration", *World Affairs* 160.4 (1998): 212–18.

18   Osler and Starkey, *ibid.*, pp. 199–216.

19   Carol Hahn, "Citizenship education: an empirical study of policy, practices and outcomes", *Oxford Review of Education* 25.1 (1999): 231–250. Cf. Christian Joppke, *Challenge to the Nation-State: Immigration in Western Europe and the United States,* (Oxford and New York: Oxford University Press, 1998); Massimo La Torre, "European citizenship: an institutional challenge", *European Forum* 3 (Boston: Kluwer Law International, 1998).

20   Ian Lister, "Civic education for positive pluralism in Great Britain", in *Education for democratic citizenship: a challenge for multi-ethnic societies*, ed. Robert S. Sigel and Marilyn H Hoskin (Hillsdale, New Jersey: Lawrence Erlbaum Associates, 1991), pp. 129–146. See also R. Baubock, ed. *From Aliens to Citizens: redefining the status of immigrants in Europe* (Aldershot: Avebury, 1994); Aysegul Baykan, "Issues of difference and citizenship for 'new identities':

a theoretical view", *Innovation: the European journal of social sciences* 10.1 (1997): 61–67; John Grahl, and Paul Teague, "Is the European social model fragmenting? " *New Political Economy* 2.3 (1997): 405–427; Osler and Starkey, *ibid.*; Y. Soysal, *Limits of Citizenship: migrants and postnational membership in Europe* (Chicago: University of Chicago, 1994).

21 R. Brubaker, *Citizenship and Nationhood in France and Germany,* Cambridge Mass: Harvard University Press, 1992); Hughes, *ibid.*

22 Leslie J. Limage, "Education and muslim identity; the case of France", *Comparative education* 36.1 (2000): 73–94. See also Sunil Khilnani, "Individualism and modern democratic culture: recent French conceptions", *Economy and Society* 25.2 (1996): 282–289.

23 Anna Elisabetta Galeotti, "Citizenship and equality: the place for toleration", *Political Theory* 21.4 (1993): 585–596; Anna Elisabetta Galeotti, "A problem with theory; a rejoinder to Moruzzi", *Political Theory* 22.4 (1994): 673–8; Amy Gutmann, "Challenges of multiculturalism in democratic education", *Philosophy of Education* (1995); Norma Claire Moruzzi, "A problem with headscarves: contemporary complexities of political and social identity", *Political Theory* 22.4 (1994): 653–673.

24 Bernard Crick "Education for citizenship and the teaching of democracy in schools"; Final report of the advisory group on citizenship (London: Qualifications and Curriculum Authority Department for Education and Employment, on behalf of the Citizenship Advisory group, 1998); David Kerr, "Citizenship education and the revised national curriculum", in National Foundation for Educational Research annual conference, London, 1998; David Kerr, "Changing the political culture: the Advisory Group on Education for Citizenship and the Teaching of Democracy in Schools", *Oxford Review of Education* 25.1 (1999): 275–284.

25 Crick, *ibid.*

26 Michel Foucault, "Omnes et singulatum: towards a critique of political reason" in *The Tanner Lectures on Human Values*, ed. S. McMurrin (University of Utah Press, 1981); Michel Foucault, "Governmentality", in *The Foucault Effect: Studies in Governmentality*, ed. G. Burchell, C. Gordon, and P. Miller (London: Harvester and Wheatsheaf, 1991), pp. 87–104; Barry Hindess, "Citizenship in the modern West", in *Citizenship and Social Theory*, ed. Bryan Turner (London: Sage, 1993), pp. 19–35; Paul Hirst, "The international origins of national sovereignty", unpublished working paper, 1996; Ian Hunter, "Uncivil society: liberal government and the deconfessionalisation of politics", in *Governing Australia: Studies in Contemporary Rationalities of Government*, ed. Mitchell Dean and Barry Hindess (Cambridge: Cambridge University Press, 1998), pp. 242–264; Thomas Osborne, *Aspects of Enlightenment: social theory and the ethics of truth* (London: UCL Press, 1998); Carl Schmitt, *Political Theology. Four Chapters on the Concept of Sovereignty* (Cambridge Massachusetts: MIT Press, 1985).

27 Horn J. van Melton, *Absolutism and the Eighteenth Century Origins of Compulsory Schooling in Prussia and Austria* (Cambridge: Cambridge University Press, 1988). cf. Andy Green, *Education and state formation: the rise of education systems in England, France and the USA* (London: Macmillan, 1990).

28 Ian Hunter, *Rethinking the School: subjectivity, bureaucracy, criticism* (Sydney: Allen and Unwin, 1994).

29   Geraint Parry, "Constructive and Reconstructive Political Education", *Oxford Review of Education* 25.1 (1999): 23–38.; Frazer, *ibid.*

30   Limage, *ibid.*

31   Ian Hunter, *Culture and Government: the emergence of literary education* (Houndsmill: Macmillan, 1988).

32   K. Jones, and K. Williamson, "The birth of the schoolroom", *I&C* , 6 (1979): 59–111; Hunter, *Culture and Government;* Hunter, *Rethinking the School.*

33   Cf. Michel Foucault, *Discipline and Punish: the birth of the prison* (Harmondswoth: Penguin, 1977); Bruce Smith, "Governing Classrooms: privatisation and discipline in Australian schooling", diss, Griffith University, 1991.

34   Ian Hunter, "The pastoral bureaucracy: towards a less principled understanding of state schooling", in *Child and Citizen: Genealogies of Schooling and Subjectivity*, ed. Denise Meredyth and Deborah Tyler: (Brisbane: Institute for Cultural Policy Studies, 1993), pp. 237–287; Denise Meredyth, "Invoking Citizenship: education, competence and social rights", *Economy and Society* 19.1 (1997): 1–29; Denise Meredyth, "Corporatising education", in *Governing Australia* , pp. 20–46.

35   Crick, *ibid.*

36   Wilfred Carr and Anthony Hartnett, "Civic education, democracy and the English political tradition", in *Beyond Communitarianism: Citizenship, Politics and Education*, ed. Jack Demaine and Harold Entwhistle (London: St. Martin's Press, 1996), pp. 64–82. Cf. Ian Davies, "What has happened in the teaching of politics in schools in England in the last three decades, and why?" *Oxford Review of Education* 25.1 (1999): 125–140; Ken Fogelman, "Education for citizenship and the National Curriculum", in *Beyond Communitarianism: Citizenship, Politics and Education*, pp. 83–91; Ken Fogelman, "Citizenship education in England", in *Citizenship, education and the modern state*, ed. Kerry J. Kennedy (London ; Washington, D.C.: Falmer Press, 1997), pp. 85–95. C. Harber, *Political Education in Britain* (London: Falmer Press, 1987).

37   Crick. *ibid.*

38   Ian Lister, "Civic education for positive pluralism in Great Britain", in *Education for democratic citizenship: a challenge for multi-ethnic societies*, ed. Robert S Sigel and Marilyn H Hoskin (Hillsdale, New Jersey: Lawrence Erlbaum Associates, 1991), pp. 129–146.
     Richard Pring, "Political education: relevance of the humanities", *Oxford Review of Education* 25.1 (1999): 71–88.

39   Rob Gilbert, "Identity, culture and environment: education for citizenship for the 21st century", in *Beyond Communitarianism*, pp. 42–63.

40   Crick, *ibid.*

41   Mike Cole and David Hill, "'New labour', old policies: Tony Blair's 'vision' for education in Britain", *Education Australia,* 1998.
     http://www.edoz.com.au/edoz/archive/issues/blair.html

42   Cf. Seamus Dunn and Valerie Morgan, "'A fraught path' — education as a basis for developing improved community relations in Northern Ireland", *Oxford Review of Education* 25.1 (1999): 141–154; Terri Seddon, "Markets and the English: rethinking educational restructuring as institutional design", *British Journal of Sociology of Education* 18.2 (1997): 165–186; James Tooley, "Choice and diversity in education: a defence", *Oxford Review of Education* 23.1 (1997): 103–116; T. Englund, "Education as a citizenship right — a concept in

transition: Sweden related to other Western democracies and political philosophy", *Journal of Curriculum Studies* 26.4 (1994): 389–399.

43 Nikolas Rose, "The death of the social? Refiguring the territory of government", *Economy and Society* 23.3 (1996a): 327–356; Nikolas Rose, "Governing 'advanced' liberal democracies", in *Foucault and Political Reason: Liberalism, Neo-Liberalism and Rationalities of Government*, eds. A. Barry, T. Osborne, and N. Rose (London: UCL Press. 1996).

44 Patrick Brindle and Madeleine Arnot, "'England expects every man to do his duty': the gendering of the citizenship textbook. 1940–1966". *Oxford Review of Education* 25.1 (1999): 103–124; Ian Davies, "What has happened in the teaching of politics in schools in England in the last three decades, and why? ", *Oxford Review of Education* 25.1 (1999): 125–140.

45 Jack Demaine, "Beyond communitarianism: Citizenship, politics and education", in *Beyond Communitarianism*, pp. 6–29.

46 Parry, *ibid*.

47 Frazer, *ibid*., pp. 5–22.

48 Rob Gilbert, "Identity, culture and environment", pp. 42–63.

49 Chantal Mouffe, ed. *Dimensions of Radical Democracy. Pluralism, Citizenship, Community*. (London: Verso. 1992).

50 Meira Levinson, "Liberalism, Pluralism, and Political Education: paradox or paradigm?", *Oxford Review of Education* 25.1 (1999): 39–58.

51 Stephen Macedo, *Liberal Virtues: Citizenship, virtue, and community in liberal constitutionalism* (Oxford: Clarendon, 1991); William Galston, *Liberal Purposes: goods, virtues and diversity in the liberal state* (Cambridge: Cambridge University Press, 1991).

52 Kymlicka, and Norman, *ibid*., pp. 257–289. Cf. Jeffrey Minson, "Aescetics and the demands of participation", *Political Theory Newsletter* 1998.

53 See commentary on this in Patricia White, "Political Education in the Early Years: the place of civic virtues", *Oxford Review of Education* 25.1 (1999): 59–70.

54 Stephen Holmes cited in White, *ibid*., pp. 59–70.

55 White, *ibid*., pp. 59–70.

56 Levinson, *ibid*., pp. 39–58.

Chapter 4

1 Center for Civic Education, *National Standards for Civics and Government*. (Calabasas, California, 1994); Congress, United States of America. *Goals 2000: Educate America Act*, 1994. See also Sandra Stotsky. "The national standards for civics: a backbone for school curricula?" *Journal of Education* 176.3 (1994): 29–39; Thomas S. Vontz, *Strict scrutiny: an analysis of national standards on civic education through the perspectives of contemporary theorists; 27*. (U.S.; Indiana: ERIC: Clearinghouse: Social Studies/Social Science Education (SO028964), 1997).

2 Citizenship Education Research Network, *Towards a research agenda for citizenship education in Canada* (Alberta: Canadian Society for the Study of Education, 1998).

3 Brian Elliott and David MacLennan, "Education, modernity and neo-conservative school reform in Canada, Britain and the US", *British Journal of Sociology of Education* 15.2 (1994): 165–185.

4   Jody Berland, "Politics after nationalism. culture after 'culture'", *Canadian Review of American Studies* 27.3 (1997): 35–52; Jerome H Black, "Government as a source of assistance for newly-arrived immigrants in Canada: some initial observations", in *Education for democratic citizenship: a challenge for multiethnic societies*, ed. Robert S Sigel and Marilyn H Hoskin (Hillsdale, New Jersey: Lawrence Erlbaum Associates, 1991), pp. 167–192; Reva Joshee, "The Federal government and citizenship education for newcomers", *Education canadienne et internationale* 25.2 (1996): 108–127; W. Kaplan, ed. *Belonging: the Meaning and Future of Canadian Citizenship*. (Montreal: McGill's -Queens University Press, 1993); Charles S Ungerleider, "Socialization for democratic citizenship: the development of the Canadian infrastructure", in *Education for democratic citizenship*, pp. 149–166.

5   Linda Cameron and Manju Varma, "Citizens for a new century", *Canadian Ethnic Studies* 29.2 (1997): 121–136; Vicki A. Green, "The globalization of citizenship education: a Canadian perspective", in Connections 97 Conference, University of Sydney, 1997.

6   Peter C. Newman, "Let's not play Pluto to Mickey Mouse", *Maclean's* 109.15 (1996): 44.

7   Alexander Crawley, "Canadian cultural policy — bridging the gaps: Or the cultural activist — a laboratory specimen", *Canadian Review of American Studies* 27.3 (1997): 99–110; Eva Mackey, "The cultural politics of populism: Celebrating Canadian national identity", in *Anthropology of Policy: critical perspectives on governance and power*, ed. Chris Shore and Susan Wright (London: Routledge, 1997); Edelgard Mahant, "Are national cultures and identities an optional extra?" *Canadian Review of American Studies* 27.3 (1997): 51–80; Richard Matheny III, "In the wake of the flood: 'like products' and cultural products after the World Trade Organizations' decision in Canada Certain Measures Concerning Periodicals", *University of Pennsylvania Law Review* 147.1 (1998): 245–270; Joseph Weber, "Does Canadian culture need this much protection?" *Business Week*, 6 August 1998, 37; Joyce Zemans, "Canadian cultural policy in a globalized world", *Canadian Review of American Studies* 27.3 (1997): 111–117.

8   Citizenship Education Research Network, *Towards a research agenda for citizenship education in Canada*, (Alberta: Canadian Society for the Study of Education, 1998); Amelie Oksenberg Rorty, "The hidden politics of cultural identification", *Political Theory* 22.3 (1994): 152–166.

9   Charles Taylor and Amy Gutmann, 1992, *Multiculturalism and "The politics of recognition": an essay* (Princeton, N.J.: Princeton University Press, 1992); Charles Taylor and Amy Gutmann, eds. *Multiculturalism: Examining the politics of recognition* (Princeton, New Jersey: Princeton University Press, 1994).

10   Veit Bader, "The cultural conditions of transnational citizenship", *Political Theory* 25.6 (1997): 771–814; Javier Perez de Cuellar, "Our creative diversity", *Report of the World Commission on Culture and Development* (Paris: UNESCO, 1995); Chandran Kukathas, "Are there any cultural rights?" *Political Theory* 20.1 (1992): 105–140; Chandran Kukathas, "Cultural rights again", *Political Theory* 20.4 (1992): 674–681; Chandran Kukathas, "The rights of minority cultures", *Political Theory* 20.1 (1992): 140–147; Nick Stevenson, "Globalization, national cultures and cultural citizenship", *Sociological quarterly* 38.1 (1997): 41–67.

11   Tony Bennett and Colin Mercer. "Improving research and international co-operation for cultural policy", in *Intergovernmental Conference on Cultural*

Policies for Development (Stockholm, Sweden, 1998); Anthony Everitt, "Designer global culture", *New Statesman and Society* 9.388 (1996): 31–3; Yves Evrard, "Democratizing culture or cultural democracy? (State intervention in culture)", *Journal of Arts, Management, Law and Society* 27.3 (1997): 167–175; Justin Lewis, "Designing a cultural policy", *Journal of Arts Management, Law & Society* 24.1 (1994): 41–57.

12 Yvonne Hebert, "Citizenship education: towards a pedagogy of social participation and identity formation", *Canadian Ethnic Studies* 29.2 (1997): 82–97.

13 Chandran Kukathas, "Cultural rights again"; Will Kymlicka, "Do we need a liberal theory of minority rights? Reply to Carens, Young, Parekh and Forst", *Constellations* 4.1 (1997): 72–87; Kevin McDonagh, "Cultural recognition, cosmopolitanism and multicultural education", *Philosophy of Education*, 1995; Amelie Oksenberg Rorty, "The hidden politics of cultural identification", *Political Theory* 22.3 (1994): 152–166; Marilyn Strathern, "The nice thing about culture is that everyone has it", in *Shifting contexts: transformations in anthropological knowledge*, ed. Marilyn Strathern (London ; New York: Routledge, 1994), pp. 153-176.

14 Chandran Kukathas, "Liberalism and multiculturalism", *Political Theory* 26.5 (1998): 686–700; Will Kymlicka, *Liberalism, Community and Culture* (Oxford: Clarendon Press, 1989); Amelie Oksenberg Rorty, "The hidden politics of cultural identification", *Political Theory* 22.3 (1994): 152–166; Stacey Smith, "Liberalism, multiculturalism and education: is there a fit?" *Philosophy of Education*, 1995.

15 Will Kymlicka and Wayne Norman, "Return of the citizen: a survey of recent work on citizenship theory", *Ethics* 104 (1994): 257–289.

16 Richard Jensen, "The culture wars, 1965–1995: a historian's map", *Journal of social history* 29, (1995): 17–38.

17 Allan Bloom, *The closing of the American mind* (New York: Simon and Schuster, 1987); E D Hirsch, *The schools we need. And why we don't have them* (New York: Doubleday, 1996).

18 Mary Ann Glendon and David Blankenhorn, *Seedbeds of virtue: sources of competence, character, and citizenship in American society* (Lanham, Md.: Madison Books, 1995); Michael Schudson, "Is our civic life really in decline?" *American Heritage* 50.6 (1999): 52–8.

19 Chip Berlet, *Eyes right!: challenging the right wing backlash* (Boston, Mass.: South End Press, 1995); Henry Louis Gates, Jr. *Loose Canons: notes on the culture wars* (New York: Oxford University Press, 1992); Todd Gitlin, *The twilight of common dreams: why America is wracked by culture wars* (New York: Metropolitan Books, 1995); James Davison Hunter, *Culture wars : the struggle to define America* (New York: Basic Books, 1991); Gregory S. Jay, *American literature & the culture wars* (Ithaca, N.Y.: Cornell University Press, 1997); James L. Nolan, *The American culture wars: current contests and future prospects* (Charlottesville: University Press of Virginia, 1996).

20 R. Freeman Butts, *The Morality of Democratic Citizenship: Goals for Civic Education in the Republic's Third Century* (Calabasas, California: Center for Civic Education, 1988); R.F. Butts, D.H. Peckenpaugh, and H. Kirschenbaum, eds. *The School's Role as Moral Authority* (Washington: Association for Supervision and Curriculum Development. 1977).

21 Benjamin Barber, *An Aristocracy of Everyone: the Politics of Education and the Future of America* (New York: Ballantine, 1992).

22 Kevin Ryan and Karen E Bohlin, *Building character in schools: Practical ways to bring moral instruction to life* (San Francisco: Jossey-Bass Publishers, 1999). See also Character Education Institute *Character Education Curriculum* (San Antonio, Texas: Character Education Institute, 1996); Glendon and Blankenhorn, *ibid.;* S M. Yulish, *The search for a civic religion: a history of the Character Education movement in America, 1890–1935* (Washington DC: University Press of America, 1980).

23 R. Freeman Butts, "The time is now: to frame the civic foundations of teacher education", *Journal of Teacher Education* 44.5 (1993): 325–335.

24 Robert N. Bellah *Habits of the Heart: Individualism and Commitment in American Life* (Berkley: University of California Press, 1985); R. Pratte, "The Civic Imperative: examining the need for civic education", in *Advances in Contemporary Educational Thought Series,* 3 (Ohio: Teachers' College Press, 1988); C.N. Quigley and C.F. Bahmueller *Civitas: a framework for civic education* (Calabasas, California: Centre for Civic Education. 1991); W.B. Stanley and J.A. Whitson, "Citizenship as practical competence: a response to the new reform movement in social education", *International Journal of Social Education* 7.2 (1992): 57–66.

25 Michael Apple, "Power, meaning and identity: critical sociology of education in the United States", *British Journal of Sociology of Education* 17.2 (1996): 125–144; Stephen Ball, *Education Reform: A Critical and Poststructural Approach* (Buckingham: Open University Press, 1994); R.W. Connell, D.J. Ashenden, S. Kessler, and G. Dowsett, *Making the Difference: schools, families and social divisions,* (Sydney: Allen & Unwin, 1983); H.A. Giroux, *Schooling for Democracy: critical pedagogy in the modern age* (London: Routledge. 1988).

26 Angie Cannon, "Civics or religion?" *US News & World Report* 2 August 2000 36; John A. Coleman, "Under the cross and the flag: reflections on discipleship and citizenship in America", *America*, May 11, 1996, pp. 6–15; Glendon and Blankenhorn, *ibid.*; Richard C. Harwood, "Originating civic faith: Self-trust in America", in *Vital Speeches of the Day*. Address to the Health Resources and Services Administration and Bureau of Primary Care at a symposium in Bethesda Maryland, 1999.

27 Peter Bailey, *Bringing Human Rights to Life,* (Sydney: Federation Press, 1993); Tony Edwards and Geoff Whitty, "Parental choice and educational reform in Britain and the United States", *British Journal of Educational Studies* 40.2 (1992): 101–117; K. Silvestri, "Parent involvement: New Jersey's public policy and public schools program", *Equity and Choice*, Winter (1991): 22–27; Basil R. Singh, "Liberalism, parental rights, pupils' autonomy and education", *Educational Studies* 24.2 (1998): 165–183.

28 Amy Gutmann, *Democratic Education.* (Cambridge MA: Princeton, 1987); Kymlicka and Norman, *ibid*.

29 Christopher Beem, "Civil is Not Good Enough", *Current* 388 (1996): 22–27. See also Bob Edwards and Michael J Foley, "Editors' introduction: escape from politics? Social theory and the social capital debate", *American Behavioral Scientist* 40.5 (1997): 550–561; Michael W Foley and Bob Edwards, "Escape from politics? Social theory and the social capital debate", *American Behavioral Scientist* 40.5 (1997): 550–562; and Andrew Greeley, "Coleman Revisited: Religious Structures as a Source of Social Capital", *American Behavioral Scientist* 40.5 (1997): 562–574.

30 Center for Civic Education, "About the Center for Civic Education", March 1995. Available from http://ericr.syr.edu/Civnet/partners/Center/excsum.html.

31 Quigley and Bahmueller.

32 Margaret Branson, "The education of citizens in a market economy and its relation to a free society", in *International Conference on Western Democracy and Eastern Europe: Political, Economic and Social Changes* (East Berlin: Center for Civic Education, 1991); Margaret Branson, "Rights: An international perspective", in *First Plenary Session of the Annual Leadership conference of the Center for Civic Education* (Marina del Rey, California, 21 June 1991); Margaret Branson, "What does research on political attitudes and behaviour tell use about the need for improving education for democracy?", in *The International Conference on Education for Democracy* (Serra Retreat, Malibu, California, 3 October 1994).

33 Jeffrey Minson and Colin Mercer pointed out some of these elements to us.

34 Walter C. Parker, "'Advanced' ideas about democracy: towards a pluralist conception of citizenship education", *Teachers College Record* 98.1 (1996): 104–125.

35 Sandra Stotsky, "The national standards for civics: a backbone for school curricula?", *Journal of Education* 176.3 (1994): 29–39.

36 Amy Gutmann, "Challenges of multiculturalism in democratic education". Accessed. 1995. Available from http://www.ed.iuc.edu/COE/EPS/PES-Yearbook/95_docs/gutmann.html.

37 For an extended commentary, see Ian Hunter and Denise Meredyth, *American Behavioral Scientist*, 43, 2000.

38 Ian Hunter, "The rarity of the school", *Southern Review* 28 (1995): 163–71. Noel King, "The teacher must exist before the pupil: the Newbolt Report on the teaching of English in England, 1992", *Literature and History* 3.1 (1987): 14–37.

39 Stuart Macintyre, "An expert's confession", *Australian Quarterly*, Spring 1995: 1–12.

40 Warren Prior, cited in Suzanne Mellor, *What's the point? Political attitudes of Victorian Year 11 students.* (Melbourne: Australian Council for Educational Research, 1998).

41 ANOP Research Services, *Young People's Attitudes to Postcompulsory Education* (Canberra: Australian Government Printing Service, 1994).

42 Minson, *ibid.*

43 Meira Levinson, "Liberalism, Pluralism, and Political Education: paradox or paradigm?", *Oxford Review of Education* 25.1 (1999): 39–58.

44 Colin A. Hughes, "The good citizen: past and futures for citizenship education", *Australian Journal of Politics and History* 42.1 (1996): 1–9.

45 H.K. Colebatch, "Political knowledge and political education", *Australian Quarterly*, Spring (1995): 13–23.

46 Suzanne Mellor, *What's the point? Political attitudes of Victorian Year 11 students* (Melbourne: Australian Council for Educational Research, 1998).

47 Carol Hahn, "Citizenship education: an empirical study of policy, practices and outcomes", *Oxford Review of Education* 25.1 (1999): 231–250)

48 David Owen, "Dilemmas and opportunities for the young active citizen", *Youth Studies Australia* 15.1 (1996): 20–23.

49 e.g. Rob Gilbert, "Where are the people? Education, citizenship and the Civics Expert Group Report", *Curriculum Perspectives* 16.1 (1996): 56–61; Rob Gilbert, Issues for citizenship in a postmodern world", in *Citizenship, education and the modern state*, ed. Kerry J. Kennedy (London; Washington, D.C.: Falmer Press, 1997), pp. 65–82.

50 Macintyre, *ibid.*

51   John Dunn, "How democracies succeed", *Economy and Society* 25.4 (1996): 511–528; Barry Hindess, "The Greeks had a word for it": the polis as political metaphor", *Thesis Eleven*, 40 (1995): 119–32; and Barry Hindess, "Democracy and disenchantment", *Australian Journal of Political Science* 32.1 (1997): 79–92.

52   Levinson, *ibid.*

Chapter 5

1   Thanks to Wayne Hudson for drawing my attention to this point. See also Bill Brugger, *Republican Theory in Political Thought: Virtuous or Virtual?* (Basingstoke: Macmillan, 1999).

2   Helen Irving, *To Constitute a Nation: A Cultural History of Australia's Constitution,* (Sydney: Cambridge University Press, 1999), p. 214.

3   Robert Murray, "The Split", in *The Australian Century: Political Struggle in the Building of a Nation,* ed. Robert Manne (Melbourne: Text Publishing, 1999), p. 157–58.

4   Bain Attwood and Andrew Markus, *The 1997 Referendum, Or when Aborigines didn't get the vote,* in collaboration with Dale Edwards and Kath Schilling, (Australian Institute of Aboriginal and Torres Strait Islander Studies, 1997).

5   Michael Kirby, "Reflections on Constitutional Monarchy", in *The Republicanism Debate*, eds. Wayne Hudson and David Carter (Sydney: NSW University Press, 1993), p. 67.

6   John Hirst, "Can subjects be citizens?", in *Crown or Country: The Traditions of Australian Republicanism*, eds. David Headon, James Warden and Bill Gammage (Sydney: Allen and Unwin 1994), p. 120.

7   Hirst, *ibid.*, p. 118.

8   Andrew Fraser, "Strong Republicanism and a Citizen's Constitution" in *The Republicanism Debate*, pp. 36–60.

9   Brian de Garis, "Federation" in *The Australian Century*, p. 11.

10   Irving, *ibid.,* p. 209.

11   John Hirst, "Towards the Republic", in *The Australian Century*, p. 299.

12   Bertram Wicks, *Understanding the Australian Constitution: The Plain Words* (Sandy Bay: Libra Books, 1997), p. 15.

13   de Garis, *ibid.*, pp. 34–36.

14   Hirst 1994, p 118.

15   Attwood and Markus, *ibid.*, p. 14.

16   Gregory Melleuish and Geoff Stokes, "Australian Political Thought" in *Creating Australia: Changing Australian History*, eds. Wayne Hudson and Geoffrey Bolton (Sydney: Allen and Unwin, 1997), pp. 115–117.

17   Bruce Kercher, "Creating Australian law" in *Creating Australia*, pp. 106–110.

18   Michael Saward, *The Terms of Democracy*, (Cambridge: Polity Press, 1998), p. 60.

19   Marilyn Lake, *Getting Equal: The history of Australian feminism,* (Sydney: Allen and Unwin, 1999), pp. 49–71.

20   Peter Beilharz, "Republicanism and citizenship" in *The Republicanism Debate*, p. 144.

21   Phillip Petit, "Liberalism and Republicanism", *Australian Journal of Political Science* 28 (1993): 164.

22   Hirst 1994 *ibid.*, p. 119.

23 Hirst, *ibid.*, p. 120.

24 Stephen Holmes, *Passions and Constraint: On the theory of liberal democracy,* (Chicago: University of Chicago Press, 1995), p. 5.

25 Holmes, *ibid.*, p. 6.

26 Holmes, *ibid.*, p. 6.

27 The unanimous finding of the court, in Frank Brennan, *Legislating Liberty: A Bill of Rights for Australia?*, (St Lucia University of Queensland Press, 1998), p. 171.

28 Brennan, *ibid.*, p. 173.

29 Brennan, *ibid.*, p. 175.

30 Brennan, *ibid.*, p. 175.

31 Tony Stephens, "Fraser gives his party a crash course in Aboriginal rights" *Sydney Morning Herald*, 26–27 August 2000, p. 1.

32 Helen Irving, "Who were the republicans?" in *Crown or Country,* p. 69.

33 Irving, *ibid.*, p. 74.

34. Irving, *ibid.*, p.74.

35. Holmes, *ibid.*, p. 5.

36 Michael Schudson, *The Good Citizen: A History of American Civic Life*, (New York: The Free Press, 1998), p. 188.

37 Patricia Springborg, "An Historical Note on Republicanism" in *The Republicanism Debate*, p. 204.

38 Schudson, *ibid.*, p. 16.

39 Alain Touraine, *Can We live Together? Equality and Difference,* trans. David Macey, (Cambridge: Polity Press, 2000).

40 Alastair Davidson, "*Res publica* and citizen" in *Crown or Country*, pp. 161–174.

41 Cheryl Saunders, "Founding blueprint has faded with time", *The Australian* 5 July 2000, p. 15.

42 Robert Manne, "The Kerr Conundrum", in *The Way We Live Now: Controversies of the Nineties*, (Melbourne: Text Publishing, 1998), p. 147.

43 Manne, *ibid.*, p.146.

44 Manne, *ibid.*, p. 147.

45 Steve Vizard, *Two Weeks in Lilliput: Bear-baiting and backbiting at the Constitutional Convention,* (Ringwood : Penguin Books , 1998).

46 Attwood and Markus, *ibid.*, p. ix.

47 Mark McKenna, "Republic: a quest to include all", *The Australian*, 6 July 2000, p. 11.

48 McKenna, *ibid.*, p. 11.

Chapter 6

1 Benedict Anderson, *Imagined Communities,* (London: Verso, 1983).

2 Richard White, *Inventing Australia: Images and Identity 1688—1980* (Sydney: Allen and Unwin, 1981); "*Inventing Australia* revisited" in *Creating Australia: Changing Australian History*, eds. Wayne Hudson and Geoffrey Bolton (Sydney: Allen and Unwin, 1997), pp. 12–22.

3 Garran cited in Paul Kelly, "The forgotten centenary" in *Paradise Divided: The changes, The Challenges, The Choices for Australia,* (Sydney: Allen and Unwin, 2000), p. 32.

4 Peter Berkowitz, *Virtue and the Making of Modern Liberalism*, (Princeton: Princeton University Press,1999), p. 126.

5   Peter Berkowitz, *ibid,* p. 124.

6   James Walter, *Tunnel Vision: The failure of political imagination,* (Sydney: Allen and Unwin, 1996), p. x.

7   *Ibid.*, p. x.

8   Judith Shklar, *Ordinary Vices* (Cambridge: Harvard University Press, 1984), pp. 232–33.

9   Bill Brugger, *Republican Theory in Political Thought: Virtuous or Virtual?* (Basingstoke: Macmillan, 1999), p. 1.

10 Heather Goodall, *Invasion to Embassy: Land in Aboriginal Politics in New South Wales,* (Sydney: Allen and Unwin, 1996), p. 180–81.

11 Patricia Grimshaw, Marilyn Lake and Ann McGrath, *Creating a Nation*, (Melbourne: McPhee Gribble, 1994), pp. 284–85.

12 Ann-Mari Jordens, *Redefining Australians: Immigration, Citizenship and National Identity,* (Sydney: Hale and Iremonger, 1995), pp. 25–42.

13 *Ibid.*, pp. 200–201.

14 Lynette Finch, *The Classing Gaze: Sexuality, Class and Surveillance.* (Sydney: Allen and Unwin, 1993), pp. 106–24.

15 Judith Brett, *Robert Menzies' Forgotten People* (Melbourne: Macmillan, 1992), pp. 5–14.

16 Michael Keating and Deborah Mitchell, "Security and equity in a changing society: social policy", *The Future of Governance: Policy Choices,* eds. Glyn Davis and Michael Keating (Sydney: Allen and Unwin, 2000), p. 133.

17 Richard Sennett, *The Corrosion of Character: The Personal Consequences of Work in the New Capitalism,* (New York : W.W. Norton,1998), pp. 15–16.

18 James Walter, "The failure of political imagination", *Australian Quarterly* (Autumn 1993): 555–56. See also Eva Cox, *A Truly Civil Society* (Sydney: ABC Books, 1995) and Mark Latham, *Civilising Global Capital: New thinking for Australian labour* (Sydney: Allen & Unwin, 1998)

19 Paul Kelly, *The End of Certainty: The Story of the 1980s* (Sydney: Allen and Unwin, 1992).

20 Patrick Weller, "In search of governance", in *The Future of Governance:*, p. 3.

21 Michael Pusey, *Economic Rationalism in Canberra: A Nation-building State Changes Its Mind,* (Sydney: Cambridge University Press, 1991).

22 Asa Wahlquist, "Great Dividing Rage", *The Australian* 26–27 September, 1998, pp. 23–24.

23 Weller, *ibid.*, p. 2.

24 Robert D. Putnam, "Bowling Alone", *Journal of Democracy*, 6 (1995): 65–78.

25 Leon Kreitzman, *The 24 hour Society,* (London: Profile Books, 1999).

26 Schudson, p. 310.

27 Sennett, *ibid.*, p. 137.

28 Kreitzman, *ibid* p. 34.

29 Sohail Inayatullah, "Consuming fashions", *Sydney Morning Herald,* Spectrum, 24 September, 2000.

30 Andrew Ross, "Jobs in cyberspace" in *Real Love: In Pursuit of Cultural Justice,* (New York: New York University Press, 1998), pp. 7–34.

31 Cited in Schudson, *ibid.*, p. 98.

32 Michael Walzer, "On Involuntary Association" in *Freedom of Association,* ed Amy Gutmann (Princeton: Princeton University Press, 1998), pp. 64–74.

33 Sam Fleischacker, "Insignificant Communities", in *Freedom of Association,* pp. 273–313.

34 Win Fahey, *'There's more to music than music': Folk music, folk festivals and cultural difference*, MA Dissertation, School of Humanities, Griffith University, 1999.

Chapter 7

1   See for example, David Walker, *Anxious Nation: Australia and the Rise of Asia 1850-1939* (St Lucia: University of Queensland Press, 1999); and *Queensland Review*, 6.2 (1999), Special issue: "Asians in Australian History".
2   Inga Clendennin, *True Stories: Boyer Lectures 1999* (Sydney: ABC Books, 1999), p. 8.
3   Wayne Hudson, "Citizenship and Multiple Identities", *Southern Review* 31.1 (1998): .54–63.
4   Robert Manne ed. *The Australian Century: Political Struggle in the Building of a Nation* (Melbourne: Text Publishing, 1999).
5   Garth Nettheim, "The UN Charter-based human rights system: an overview", in *Indigenous Peoples, the United Nations and Human Rights*, ed. Sarah Pritchard (Sydney: The Federation Press, 1998), p. 33.
6   Frank Brennan, "Land Rights — The Religious Factor", in *Religious Business: Essays on Australian Aboriginal Spirituality*, ed. Max Charlesworth (Cambridge: Cambridge University Press, 1998), p. 165.
7   R.H. Tawney, *Equality* 1931, cited in Scott Bennett, *White Politics and Black Australians*, (Sydney: Allen and Unwin, 1999), p. 2.
8   Michael Schudson, *The Good Citizen: A History of American Civic Life*, (New York: The Free Press, 1998), p. 242.
9   Sarah Pritchard, "The significance of international law" in Pritchard 1998, p. 4.
10 Pritchard, *ibid.,* p. 6.
11 Michael Dodson, "Comment", in Pritchard 1998, pp 63–64.
12 Bain Attwood and Andrew Markus, *The Struggle for Aboriginal Rights: A Documentary History* (Sydney: Allen and Unwin, 1999) p. 79–80.
13 Bain Attwood and Andrew Markus with Dale Edwards and Kath Schilling, *The 1967 Referendum, or When Aborigines Didn't get the Vote* (Canberra: Aboriginal Studies Press, 1997).
14 G.Gray, "A.P.Elkin and Aboriginal Advancement" in *Citizenship and Indigenous Australians: Changing Conceptions and Possibilities*, eds. Nicholas Peterson and Will Sanders (Sydney: Cambridge University Press, 1998), p. 57. It is Elkin's opinion that the proposal would have succeeded.
15 Attwood and Markus, "The 1967 Referendum and Citizenship", in eds. Peterson and Sanders *ibid.*, p. 123.
16 Attwood and Markus, 1997, pp. 115, 117.
17 Attwood and Markus, 1999, pp. 9–11.
18 Marilyn Lake, *Getting Equal: The history of Australian feminism*, (Sydney: Allen and Unwin, 1999), pp. 110–35.
19 Attwood and Markus, 1997, p. 17.
20 Lake, *ibid.*, pp. 124–26.
21 Attwood and Markus, 1999, pp. 160–61.
22 Gray, *ibid.*, p. 55
23 Gray, *ibid*, p. 69.
24 Attwood and Markus, 1999, pp. 68–69.

25   Heather Goodall, *Invasion to Embassy: Land in Aboriginal Politics in New South Wales, 177–1972* (Sydney: Allen and Unwin, 1996).

26   Patrick Dodson, "Lingiari: Until the Chains are Broken" in *Essays on Australian Reconciliation*, ed. Michelle Grattan (Melbourne: Back Inc, 2000), p. 266.

27   Mr. Inverway, " Take Power like this old man here" in *Take Power like this old man here*, ed. Alexis Wright (Alice Springs: Jukurrpa Books, 1998), p. 2.

28   Brennan in Charlesworth 1998, p. 151.

29   Tim Rowse, "Nugget Coombs and the contradictions of self-determination", in Wright 1998, p. 30.

30   Brennan *ibid.*, p. 155.

31   Bennett 1999, p. 155.

32   Peter Butt and Robert Eagleson, *Mabo, Wik and Native Title* (Sydney: The Federation Press, 1998), pp. 97–98.

33   Butt and Eagleson, *ibid.*, p. 101.

34   cited in Butt and Eagleson, *ibid.*, p. 105.

35   Frank Brennan, *Legislating Liberty: A Bill of Rights for Australia?* (St. Lucia: University of Queensland Press, 1998), p. 148.

36   Frank Brennan, *One Land, One Nation. Mabo — towards 2001.* (St. Lucia: University of Queensland Press, 1995), p. 126.

37   Bennett, *ibid.*, p. 201.

38   Tim Rowse, *White Flour, White Power: From Rations to Citizenship in Central Australia,* (Sydney: Cambridge University Press, 1998), p. 204.

39   Dodson, *ibid.*, p. 266.

40   Gustav Nossal, "Symbolism and Substance in the Surge Towards Reconciliation", in Grattan 2000, p. 300.

41   Rowse, *ibid.*, p. 205.

42   Henry Reynolds, "Sovereignty", in Peterson and Sanders, 1998, p. 213.

43   Brennan in Charlesworth 1998, p. 164.

44   Mark Finnane, "'Payback', customary law and the criminal law in colonised Australia", unpublished paper delivered at IAHCCJ Colloquium, Bad Homburg, Stuttgart, Germany, 24–26 June, 1999. See also Australian Law Reform Commission, *The Recognition of Aboriginal Customary Laws* (Canberra: Australian Government Publishing Service, 1986).

45   Butt and Eagleson, *ibid.*, pp. 39–40.

46   Butt and Eagleson, *ibid.*, p. 104.

47   Brennan, *Legislating Liberty,* p. 151.

48   Marilyn Lake, "Nation gazing", *The Australian's Review of Books*, (October 1999): 10–12, 26.

49   Henry Reynolds, *Why Weren't We Told?: A Personal Search for the Truth about our History* (Ringwood: Viking, 1999), p. 245.

50   Clendennin, *ibid.*, p. 5.

Chapter 8

1   Susan Wolf, "Moral Saints", *Journal of Philosophy,* 79.8 (1982): 419–39.

2   Deborah Tannen, *The Argument Culture: Changing the way we argue,* (London: Virago, 1999).

3   Robert Hughes, *Culture of Complaint: The Fraying of America* (New York: Oxford University Press, 1993).

4   Judith Brett, "The politics of grievance", *The Australian Review of Books*, 2.4 (1997): 12–13, 26.

5   Inga Clendennin, *True Stories,* (Sydney: ABC Books, 1999), p. 6.

6   Peter Berkowitz, *Virtue and the Making of Modern Liberalism*, (Princeton: Princeton University Press, 1999), p. 9.

7   Berkowitz. *ibid.*, p.10.

8   Will Kymlicka, "Ethnic Associations and Democratic Citizenship", in *Freedom of Association,* ed. Amy Gutmann (Princeton: Princeton University Press, 1998), pp. 187–90.

9   Berkowitz, *ibid.*, p. 11.

10   Cited in Bill Brugger, *Republican Theory in Political Thought: Virtuous or Virtual?* (Basingstoke: Macmillan, 1999), p. 3.

11   Kymlicka, *ibid.*, p. 181.

12   Stuart Rintoul, "Silence as songs are lost for words", *The Australian Higher Education Supplement*, 20 September 2000, pp. 41, 38–39.

13   Joy Damousi, *The Labour of Loss: Mourning, Memory and Wartime Bereavement in Australia*, (Melbourne: Cambridge University Press, 1999); Kate Darian-Smith, *On the Homefront: Melbourne in Wartime, 1939–45* (Melbourne:Oxford University Press, 1990).

14   John Howard, "Anzac flame is ours to keep alive", *The Australian,* 26 April 2000, p. 11.

15   "Carve their names with pride", *Australian Story*, ABC TV 4 November 1999.

16   Deborah Hope, "Bangarra aims for the real thing", in *The Australian*, 16–17 September 2000, p. 24.

17   Gough Whitlam, *Take Power like this old man here*, ed. Alexis Wright for the Central Land Council (Alice Springs: Jukurrpa Books, 1998) p. 321.

18   Jennifer Hewitt, "Inside the picket fence", *Sydney Morning Herald*, 16 September 2000, Spectrum pp. 1, 6–7.

19   Judith Brett, "The politics of grievance", *The Australian Review of Books*, 2.4 (1997): 12–13, 26.

20   Henry Louis Gates Jr, "Critical Race Theory and Freedom of Speech", in *The Future of Academic Freedom,* ed. Louis Menand (Chicago: University of Chicago Press, 1996), pp. 119–59.

21   Tannen *ibid.*, p. 265.

22   William Galston, *Liberal Purposes: Goods, Virtues and Diversity in the Liberal State* (Cambridge: Cambridge University Press, 1991), p. 221–24.

23   Newspoll, Saulwick and Muller and Hugh Mackay, "Public Opinion on Reconciliation: Snap Shot, Close Focus, Long Lens", in *Reconciliation:Essays on Australian Reconciliation*, ed. Michelle Grattan (Melbourne: Black Inc, 2000), p. 35.

24   Robert Manne, "Why I have resigned", in *The Way We Live Now: Controversies of the Nineties* (Melbourne: Text Publishing, 1998), pp. 279–80.

25   Jeffrey Wallen, *Closed Encounters: Literary Politics and Public Culture,* (Minneapolis: University of Minnesota Press, 1998), pp. 160–65.

26   Mark Davis, *Gangland: Cultural elites and the new generationalism* (Sydney: Allen and Unwin, 1997).

27   Wallen, *ibid.*, p. 162.

28   Jamie Mackie, "Reconciliation, racial prejudice and 'soft Hansonism' in Australia's future", *Dissent* 3, Spring (2000): 12.

29   Cited in Raymond Gaita, *A Common Humanity: Thinking about Love, Truth and Justice,* (Melbourne: Text Publishing, 1999) pp. 88–90.

30 Cass Sunstein and Stephen Holmes, *The Cost of Rights: Why Liberty Depends on Taxes* (New York: W.W. Norton, 1999).

Index